CONTENTS

PREFACE

As I read the manuscripts submitted for my previous anthology, *Non-Native Educators in English Language Teaching* (1999), I was moved by the personal narratives of some authors, reflecting on their struggles and triumphs as nonnative English-speaking teachers. I therefore contemplated a follow-up book consisting of autobiographies of these teachers from around the world.

The temptation to focus on autobiographies was strong; the lives of these teachers, the distinct English teaching contexts of their countries, and the ways in which they made sense of their careers as nonnative speakers of English would make for interesting reading. The voices of nonnative English speaking teachers, especially those who live in what is termed the *periphery*—outside the United States, the United Kingdom, and other English speaking countries (usually termed the *center*), are not often heard within the center. These voices belong to English teachers, they are the voices of our colleagues, and they deserve to be heard.

As I mulled over this project, an even better idea came to mind. What if these teachers, living, teaching, and conducting research in their countries, were asked to describe the history of English language teaching (ELT) and the English language curriculum of their own countries and place their autobiographies alongside the histories and curricula? After all, these teachers would have the best access to historical sources and would be the most familiar with the ways in which English is taught in their countries. This book was born on that premise.

My expectations have been more than fulfilled. The chapters in this volume were written by teachers who were born or reside in the countries they represent, who speak one or more of the languages of their country of residence, and who are all nonnative speakers of English. The authors have risen to the challenge and describe and reflect in their personal and often delightful ways. These authors, their writing styles, and the contents of their chapters are evidence of the diversity and multiple ownership of English.

These accounts reflect the growth of these writers as teacher-scholars, recalling their professional journeys, reflecting on their challenges and successes, and providing insights into their teaching philosophies. These are voices that must be listened to if the Teachers of English to Speakers of Other Languages (TESOL) profession is to grow and develop.

THE AUDIENCE

Teaching English to the World: History, Curriculum, and Practice is meant for a mainly Western audience. According to one study that examined 173 TESOL graduate programs in North America, 40% of the students training to be English teachers in TESOL and Applied Linguistics Programs were nonnative speakers (Liu, 1999). At some U.S. institutions, the percentage of nonnative speaker students is as high as 70% (Kamhi-Stein, 1999). Because programs that train ESL teachers in North America enroll large numbers of nonnative speakers of English, most of them from abroad, this volume could become required reading as it presents case studies of ELT around the world, as well as of successful nonnative speaker English teachers.

Partly as a result of the establishment of the Nonnative English Speakers' Caucus in the TESOL organization in 1999, and my previous volume on the topic, *Non-Native Educators in English language Teaching* (Braine, 1999), there has been a surge of interest in, and empowerment of, nonnative speaker English teachers. At the TESOL 2003 conference in Baltimore, for instance, more than 20 presentations included the acronym NNS (nonnative speaker) in their titles, and most of these presentations were made by nonnative speakers themselves. The present volume will be a sequel to *Non-Native Educators in English language Teaching,* which mainly featured teachers based in the United States. *Teaching English to the World: History, Curriculum, and Practice* will extend the empowerment to teachers around the world, adding powerful new voices to the cause of nonnative speaker English teachers. It will be welcomed by members of the NNS caucus as well as by English teachers in other areas, especially in ELT powerhouses such as China, Japan, and the Middle East.

OVERVIEW

Teaching English to the World: History, Curriculum, and Practice includes chapters from Brazil, China, Germany, Hong Kong, Hungary, India, Indonesia, Israel, Japan, Lebanon, Poland, Saudi Arabia, Singapore, Sri Lanka, and Turkey. All the chapters follow a consistent pattern, first describing the history of English language teaching in a particular country, then the current ELT curriculum, followed by the biography or the autobiography of an English teacher of that country. This consistency in the structuring of chapters will enable readers to assimilate the information easily while also comparing and contrasting the context of ELT in each country.

The history of ELT and descriptions of the curricula are no doubt informative, but the most interesting section of each chapter is the biography or autobiography of a local teacher, because it brings the author to life, allowing the readers to share the author's triumphs and struggles on their way to professional growth Whatever their place of origin, these teachers are alike in their aspirations, training, and commitment to English language teaching. But the similarities end there. We see He An E in China, learning English while bicycling to work. We meet Péter Medgyes' English tutors—Aunt Franciska, Aunt Ila, and Dr. Koncz—and see Péter turning Hungarian somersaults instead of practicing English grammar. We watch as Kassim Shaaban, in Lebanon, memorizes a Shakespearean sonnet without knowing what it means. We hear the patter of Malay, Cantonese, Hokkien, and English around Antonia Chandrasegaran as she grows up in Singapore. And, in Turkey, we observe admiringly as Bahtişen Yavuz grows professionally from a teacher of general English to a teacher trainer. These are our colleagues, and their distinct and interesting stories deserve to be heard.

Readers might wonder why some chapters have two authors while others have only one. A second author was needed for the autobiographical section when the principal author was not born in the country that the chapter represented, or lacked sufficient local experience to reflect upon professional growth in one's homeland.

One noticeable gap in the book is the lack of a chapter from Africa. This is not for lack of trying. I attempted to find authors through the U.S. Information Agencies, British Councils, and Ministries of Education in a number of African countries, and through personal contacts. I didn't succeed, and I believe my failure to some extent reflects the trauma of the African continent, devastated by civil wars, the AIDS epidemic, and economic and political crises. According to my information, English language teaching (in fact, education as a whole) is in a perilous state in some African countries. But I hope the publication of the book will inspire African authors and that their contributions could be included in a future volume. South America is only represented by Brazil (the author from Argentina dropped out), and I hope more South American countries could be included in a future volume.

ACKNOWLEDGMENTS

These authors are not only representatives of diverse countries, languages, and cultures, but also scholars at various stages of professional growth. Some names here are easily recognizable through their numerous publications; others are only now making a name for themselves. Two, Péter Medgyes and Masaki Oda, authored chapters in *Non-Native Educators in English Language Teaching*. I was acquainted with He An E, Icy Lee, Junaidi Mistar, and Antonia Chandrasegaran through the *Asian Journal of English Language Teaching,* which I co-edit. Joanna Radwanska-Williams was my colleague in Hong Kong. Hence, editing this book has given me the opportunity to continue my links with other TESOL professionals worldwide. I thank all the authors for their contributions, patience, and trust. I also thank Diane Belcher, Jun Liu, and Brock Brady for their steadfast support. A big Thank You, as always, to Naomi Silverman of Lawrence Erlbaum Associates for quickly seeing the significance of yet another book edited by me, and to Erica Kica and Providence Rao, also of Lawrence Erlbaum Associates for their editorial support. Thanks also to Luo Shaoqian and Liu Meihua for help with the indexes. Finally, I am deeply grateful to Fawzia for carefully checking and correcting the entire manuscript and the indexes.

—George Braine

REFERENCES

Braine, G. (1999). *Non-native educators in English language teaching.* Mahwah, NJ: Lawrence Erlbaum Associates, Inc.

Kamhi-Stein, L. D. (1999). Preparing non-native professionals in TESOL: Implications for teacher education programs. In G. Braine (Ed.), Non-native educators in English language teaching (pp. 145–158). Mahwah, NJ: Lawrence Erlbaum Associates, Inc.

Liu, D. (1999). Training non-native TESOL students: Challenges for TESOL teacher education in the West. In G. Braine (Ed.), Non-native educators in English language teaching (pp. 145–158). Mahwah, NJ: Lawrence Erlbaum Associates, Inc.

INTRODUCTION

George Braine

Historical evidence suggests that English was being taught as a second or foreign language as far back as the 15th century. William Caxton, who introduced the printing press to England, may have been the first to produce "course material" for learners of English. His 1483 manual, subtitled *Right good lernyng for to lerne shortly frenssh and englyss,* is highly pragmatic in aim and content. The manual consists of a set of typical greetings, useful words for household items, servants, short dialogues, and a detailed dialogue on the buying and selling of various kinds of textiles. The second half of the manual consists mainly of vignettes of trades people such as "Agnes our maid," "George the book sellar," and "Martin the grocer." (cited in Howatt, 1984). Surprisingly, little appears to have changed in how such manuals are prepared even today, despite the centuries of experience in teaching English in all corners of the world and the multitude of research that has been conducted to determine which types of texts and which teaching methods are most effective.

During the 16th century, the rise of England as a maritime power and the expansion of the British Empire led to the recognition of English as an important language alongside French, Italian, and Latin, and to a growing interest in learning English. According to Howatt (1984), Gabriel Meurier, a Frenchman who lived in Antwerp, could be the first teacher of English as a foreign language that we know by name. *A Treatise for to Learn to Speak French and English* authored by Meurier was published in 1553.

In the latter half of the 16th century, about 360,000 refugees from Flanders, France, Italy, and Spain settled in England. Many of these settlers were skilled craftsmen and needed to know English in order to work in their adopted homeland. Ironically, some who taught English to these settlers were themselves refugees or immigrants, and therefore nonnative teachers of English. The best known among them, Jaques Bellot, taught English to the French community in the London area, and authored two books: *The English Schoolmaster* (1580), and *Familiar Dialogues* (1586). Two other well-known immigrant language teachers of this period were Claudius Holyband, a Frenchman, and John Florio, an Italian (see Howatt, 1984, for detailed accounts of their work). With this tangible evidence of English being taught in England by nonnative speakers of the language, we may safely assume that the rapid spread of English from the 16th century may have spawned a parallel growth in English language teaching, and enterprising nonnative speakers may have been quick to assume the role of teachers.

No reliable statistics are available on the current number of English teachers worldwide, but there is little doubt that the majority of them are nonnative speakers (NNS). According to the British Council,[1] English is spoken as the first language by around 375 million speakers, as the second language by another 375 million speakers, as a foreign language by about 750 million speakers, and has official or special status in at least 75 countries with a total population of over 2 billion. Such staggering numbers of second- and foreign-language users could only be taught by indigenous nonnative speaker English teachers.

Nevertheless, little is known about these English teachers outside their own countries. There are a number of reasons for this. The field of English language teaching—in terms of textbook publishers, journals, teacher-training programs, and teacher organizations—is dominated by British and American interests. The two dominant teacher organizations in the world are the International Association of Teachers of English as a Foreign Language (IATEFL), based in Britain, and Teachers of English to Speakers of Other languages (TESOL), based in the United States. Although both IATEFL and TESOL boast of members worldwide, the overall membership is dominated by local (British and American) members. For instance, the breakdown for TESOL shows this imbalance clearly: over 11,000 of its members are from the United States, whereas China, India, and Indonesia—three of the most populous countries in the world, and countries that have hundreds of thousands of indigenous English teachers—have less than 130 members combined.

This dominance of the ELT profession by British and American interests affects indigenous English teachers in other ways too. What most English teachers in the West take for granted—membership in international organizations, attendance at international conferences, subscriptions to academic journals, and easy access to computers and the Internet—are not within the means of many English teachers from less-privileged countries. This isolates them from mainstream ELT. As a result, only a handful of such teachers and scholars have come to the attention of their colleagues in the West.

Barriers to academic publication are further obstacles to indigenous teachers. As already noted, the leading academic journals are published in the West, and as Altbach (1997, 1998) pointed out, their editors and reviewers generally focus on their own national audiences and may not be interested in non-Western based re-

---

[1] See www.britishcouncil.org/english/engfaqs.htm

search. Teachers and scholars from other parts of the world would therefore find it extremely difficult to gain acceptance in major scholarly publications. Thus, for the most part, the accomplishments of these indigenous teachers remain unknown, their research remains unpublished, and their stories remain untold.

As stated in the Preface, the aim of *Teaching English to the World: History, Curriculum, and Practice* is to bring these teachers and the countries they represent to a mainstream Western audience. The authors are "insiders"—they were born in or are residents of the countries they represent, and speak the local language or languages as well. They, unlike expatriate authors, are better able to provide localized perspectives on ELT as well as the challenges facing local English teachers. The authors have learned English as a second or foreign language in their own countries, often from local teachers. Most of them have obtained advanced degrees, some in their own countries, and many have remained or returned to their countries to teach English. In terms of ELT, these authors are also the ultimate success stories.

A number of themes run through the 15 chapters. The history of ELT and the ELT curricula are the most obvious themes. Nevertheless, the limitations imposed by the structure of this volume, such as chapter length and the designated topics to be covered, have restricted the coverage of other topics such as the reasons for the global spread of English, the rise of English at the expense of another colonial/European language, and the challenges faced by (nonnative) English teachers in countries with only a recent history of English language teaching.

In exploring these topics in the rest of the Introduction, the 15 countries have been loosely organized into four groups in relation to the English language.[2] They are former colonies of Britain (India, Hong Kong, Singapore, and Sri Lanka), European countries (Germany, Hungary, and Poland), former colonies of other nations (Brazil, Indonesia, Lebanon), and countries that have no colonial past, whether British or otherwise, and that belong to what Kachru (1985) termed the expanding circle as far as the use of English is concerned (China, Israel, Japan, Saudi Arabia, and Turkey).

THE GROWTH OF ENGLISH IN INDIA

The spread of English to countries where a large number of native speakers of English have settled—Australia, Canada, New Zealand, South Africa, and the United States—which has been described in detail elsewhere (e.g., see Baugh & Cable, 1993; Bryson, 1990; McCrum, Cran, & MacNeil, 1992), is not the concern of this volume. On the other hand, the spread of English to other contexts, either as a second or a foreign language, does not appear to have received much coverage. The reasons are obvious: The topic itself is so vast (with more than 200 countries to be

---

[2]Although the countries fall into these four broad groupings, the chapters are presented chronologically by country.

covered) and the research so daunting (with evidence not always easily accessible), that it would require an army of writers and a volume of encyclopedic length. Hence, the following discussion centers on India, considering it representative of former British colonies.

Hong Kong, India, Singapore, and Sri Lanka are distinct in that English has had a foothold within them lasting more than a century. In these countries, English is part and parcel of everyday life. Except perhaps in Hong Kong, which saw the British leave as recently as 1997, this lengthy association with English followed by a half century of independence may have resulted in the distinctly local varieties of English—Indian English, Singlish, and Lankan English—in India, Singapore, and Sri Lanka, respectively. The history of ELT in these countries also reflects early attempts to transplant the British system of education with the aim of producing lower-end civil servants to ensure the smooth running of the empire.

Among these countries, India is a colossus in more than one sense. It has the second highest population in the world, the most number of official languages (18) and "major" languages (350) found within one country, and probably the largest number of nonnative speakers of English (see Crystal, 1999). The history of English in India dates back to 1600, when a group of London merchants who formed the British East India Company were granted a trading monopoly by Queen Elizabeth I (Crystal, 1999). The Company's activities, which began in 1612, gradually extended to the major cities such as Bombay, Calcutta, and Madras. Later, as a colony of Britain from 1765 to 1947, English became the language of administration and of education throughout British India. Indeed, according to Howatt (1984), the first ELT textbook written for Indian students appeared in 1797.[3]

When the historian Thomas Macaulay, during his service on the Supreme Council of India, presented his oft-quoted Minutes in 1835, advocating the teaching of English to Indians so that the latter could be turned into interpreters between the British administrators and millions of Indians they governed, he also made the controversial statement that "a single shelf of a good European library was worth the whole native literature of India and Arabia" (McCrum et al., 1992). According to Krishnaswamy & Burd (1998), British teachers of English who subsequently came to colonial India may have held a similar view of local knowledge. In fact, Pennycook (1989) claimed that the *New Method* textbooks written by Michael West for use in India were meant to provide sufficient English language skills "to produce clerks to run the colonial system" (p. 593).

Nevertheless, like the English game of cricket, the English language has found a ready home in India. By 1978, there were about 3,000 English newspapers in India, second in number only to Hindi newspapers, in a country with at least five indigenous languages with over 50 million speakers for each of the five languages (McCrum et al., 1992). English is now an "associate" official language in India and

---

[3]The complete title was *The Tutor or a New English & Bengalee Work well adapted to teach The Natives English.*

continues to be used within the legal, administrative, educational, and business sectors. Although exact estimates of English speakers are difficult to come by, most linguists (Crystal, 1999) agree that about 4% of the Indian population—37 million by current figures—speaks English. However, a survey commissioned in 1997 by the local magazine, *India Today,* indicated that almost one third of Indians claimed to understand English, although only 20% of the populations claimed to speak it confidently (cited in Graddol, 1999).

ENGLISH IN EUROPE

While the former British colonies form one group within the 15 countries represented in this volume, Germany, Hungary, and Poland, as representatives of European countries, form another distinct group. The spread of English into Germany goes back to the Middle Ages, but the rapid growth of English in former Soviet bloc countries such as Hungary and Poland appears to be more recent.

Hungary, for instance, is truly a multilingual country. Although less than 5% of the population claim an ability to communicate in a second language, English, German, French, Russian, Italian, and Spanish are being studied there, while national minorities in border areas speak Slovak, Romanian, Serbo-Croation, and Ukrainian (Fodor & Peluau, 2003). According to statistics provided by the Hungarian Ministry of Education, the four main foreign languages studied in Hungarian high schools and vocational high schools are English, German, French, and Russian. What is remarkable about these statistics is that, between the academic years of 1989–1990 and 1996–1997, the number of students learning English rose from 93.385 (34.2%) to 223,142 (61.8%), while the number for Russian declined rapidly from 222,373 (81.3%) to a mere 13,352 (3.7%).[4] Seven years ago, Graddol (1997) claimed that English was already the *lingua franca* of Hungary.

The situation in Poland is similar to that of Hungary. Learning of one foreign language is mandatory at primary level, increasing to two languages at secondary level. Although most students in primary and secondary schools were taking Russian as a compulsory subject during the 1989–1990 school year and English was taken by less than 9% of the students, the numbers taking English had risen to 65% by 1994–1995 (cited in Fodor & Peluau, 2003). Initially, a shortage of qualified teachers slowed the growth of English teaching in schools, but Pawelec (2000) claimed that 19,000 qualified English teachers had been provided to secondary schools by 1999. No doubt, more recent statistics should show a rapid rise in the teaching of English similar to that seen in Hungary.

In contrast to Hungary and Poland, English has had a foothold in Germany for centuries. Gnutzmann (see chap. 3, this volume) points out that, at the end of the 16th century, merchants in cities such as Hamburg were learning English for trading purposes and that English was first taught at a German university as far back as

---

[4]All statistics cited in Fodor & Peluau (2003).

1669. Howatt (1984) dated the spread of English to Germany to the 17th century, and states that an abiding interest in English literature, especially in the works of Shakespeare, prevailed towards the end of the century. Henry Offelen's *Double-Grammar for Germans to learn English and for Englishmen to learn the German tongue,* published in 1687, was the earliest work for the teaching of English as a foreign language published in Germany.

Turning to modern times, the formation of the European Union (EU) has seen English begin to dominate Europe. One language that is most likely to pay the price of this domination is German. Itself a major world language with about 100 million native speakers, German also has the highest number of native speakers among official EU languages, and the highest economic strength within the EU in terms of the gross national product (GNP) of its speakers (see Ammon, 2003). Nevertheless, German only ranks third as a working language within EU institutions (Ammon, 2003).

REPLACING OTHER COLONIAL LANGUAGES

Brazil, Indonesia, and Lebanon could be grouped together because of a common historical feature: at one time in history, they were colonies of Portugal, the Netherlands, and France, imperial powers that brought their respective languages to the colonies. As the relevant chapters in this volume attest, English is challenging these colonial languages for dominance in Indonesia and Lebanon, whereas it has already superseded French as the foreign language of choice in Brazil.

Of the three countries, Brazil offers an interesting study in the global expansion of English. With a population of about 170 million people, Brazil has the most number of Portuguese speakers in the world. Despite the fact that Spanish has more prestige internationally, and that Brazil is the only Portuguese- speaking country in South America in the midst of about 20 Spanish-speaking neighbors, the economic and technological strength of Brazil has ensured that Portuguese is recognized as one of the official languages of Mercosur, the South American Common Market[5] (Hamel, 2003).

Among the countries considered for this volume, Brazil is unusual in that Portuguese, a nonindigenous language, has become the official language of the country. Although nearly 200 indigenous languages survive, they are spoken by less than 1% of the population. Instead, repeated immigration from Europe, the forcible importation of African slaves over 3 centuries, and the immigration of a significant Japanese population have all contributed to the language mix in Brazil. When Brazil began to trade with Europe at the beginning of the 19th century, French was the foreign language of choice in the school curriculum because of its prestige. Later, in order to accommodate the large numbers of European immigrants, French, English, and Spanish were made official foreign languages in the school curriculum, with German and Italian considered optional languages. However, af-

---

[5]The other official language is Spanish.

ter World War II, following the establishment of closer links with the United States, Brazil abandoned this multilingual policy in favor of English. Since the 1960s, English has been the only compulsory foreign language in public schools (Graddol, McArthur, Flack, & Amey, 1999; Hamel, 2003).

By all accounts, the teaching of English is thriving in Brazil. Rajagopalan (2002) said that an "astonishing" number of English schools are springing-up all over Brazil, as fast as McDonald's outlets. This, naturally, has led to a conflict between British and American models of English. Because the United States is the most powerful trading partner and Brazilians need American English for business communication, the American model is prevailing now. According to Graddol et al. (1999), there is a "marginal" preference for British English because it is seen as culturally neutral.

As far as Brazilian Portuguese is concerned, the global dominance of English is mainly seen in the inroads of English into Portuguese, especially in the lexicon. Although the younger generation of Brazilians may not be concerned by this invasion of English, others are alarmed at the prospect of "Portuguese losing its identity through relentless Anglicization, massive borrowings and indiscriminate use of English" Rajagopalan (2002, p. 5). Responding to these concerns, a federal deputy tabled a bill in the lower house of Brazil's legislature to "promote, protect and defend the Portuguese language."

CHINA: THE NEW ELT POWERHOUSE

China, Israel, Japan, Saudi Arabia, and Turkey could belong to one group because English has a more recent history in these countries, and considered to be part of the outermost "expanding circle" by Kachru (1985). Although not colonized by Britain, English plays a prominent and ever-expanding role in these countries. At a glance, it could be said that the English in these countries could have been more influenced by the American model than the British one.

Among these countries, China is probably the most interesting to explore, because, without doubt, it is a powerhouse in terms of English language teaching. Data gathered in the late 1980s (see McConnell, 2003) indicated that about 40 million students were learning English in secondary schools in China.[6] China's open-door policy, which began in the late 1970s, China's more recent entry to the World Trade Organization (WTO), and preparations for the Beijing Olympics scheduled for 2008, have all created a dramatic impact on the growth of English in China. Huang (1999), for instance, described global, regional, and local forces that have created a great demand for business English in China. This demand has also led to an increase in English proficiency and the integration of English proficiency with business expertise.

---

[6]In contrast, only about 43 million were studying in state schools in India, which had been a colony of Britain and had experienced more than a century of English language teaching.

Already, in a significant move towards bilingualism, China has made the teaching of English compulsory from grade 3 onwards (Zhang & Luan, 2002). According to China's Ministry of Education, more than 239 million students were enrolled in primary, junior, secondary, and tertiary level in 2003 ("Ministry of Education"), and all of them are required to study English. Such massive numbers of students would obviously require millions of English teachers. However, evidence suggests that the quality of teaching needs much improvement.

In order to investigate how English teachers at tertiary level provided practice opportunities for their students, He (2001) observed 35 teachers who taught the College English Syllabus to non-English majors at 11 institutions in China. Seven of the teachers had taught for more than 25 years, and most teachers had more than 5 years of experience. All had bachelor's or master's degrees. Question and answer was the classroom activity used most often by the teachers, resulting in fewer opportunities for language processing and less room for comprehension, manipulation, and production of language by students. When textbooks were used, a mismatch was observed between the stated aim of the lesson and the teaching method used. Because no pair or group work was used, there were no opportunities to enhance interaction among students. He (2001) attributed the teachers' behavior to traditional Chinese views of teaching and learning, the teachers' own learning experiences, the existing teacher training system, and sociocultural constraints

Another area that merits attention is academic publications by Chinese English teachers, mainly those teaching at tertiary level. The "publish or perish" culture of Western academia is now spreading to China, where scholarly publications in international journals are now rewarded with not only academic advancement but also financial incentives. As noted earlier in this Introduction, editors and reviewers of international (that is, Western) journals generally focus on their own national audiences and may not be interested in non-Western based research (Altbach, 1997, 1998). Teachers and scholars from China would therefore find it extremely difficult to gain acceptance in major scholarly publications.

Evidence of this was uncovered by Shi (2002), who examined the writing of Chinese professors of English who had returned home after graduate studies in Anglo-American universities. In all, Shi interviewed 14 English professors in Chinese universities, six of them with Ph.D.s. All had trained at an Anglo-American university as a graduate student or a visiting scholar. They had authored a total of 38 academic papers in English and 262 papers in Chinese. At the time of the study, only two professors had published a total of three papers in international journals.

Publication in English was constrained because most local journals were in Chinese, and the only applied-linguistics journal that occasionally published an article in English, *Foreign Languages,* was not refereed. According to another professor, only authors well known in the field or whose papers the editors liked could hope to get published in this journal (Shi, 2002). Of the three most prestigious applied-linguistics journals in China—*Foreign Languages, Foreign Lan-*

guage Teaching and Research, and *Applied Linguistics*—only *Applied Linguistics* is refereed (Shi, 2003).

Shi (2003) also interviewed nine professors of TESOL who had returned from the West and were teaching at key universities in China. Being biliterate and bicultural, these scholars felt that the conventions of academic writing in English were influencing their writing in Chinese, especially in the structuring and development of logical arguments. In fact, some professors felt that they were more competent in writing academic papers in English than in Chinese. Nevertheless, of the professors' 273 publications, only 85 were in English, and these publications were mostly textbooks, dictionaries, and translations of Chinese literary works.

In the years to come, China will have to enhance its English teaching methods as well as its place in terms of research publications in English language teaching. With China's rapid economic growth, the prosperity that is observed in the fields of business, science, and technology will spread into areas such as language education. This is already observable in the large numbers of Chinese English teachers returning with foreign qualifications and training, who will no doubt infuse new ideas into the curriculum and contribute to a healthy growth in terms of academic publications.

CONCLUSION

The descriptions of English language curricula in the chapters reveal a clear pattern of planning and implementation. For the most part, the design and management of the curriculum is seen to be top–down, with a government ministry or department of education in control. What this implies, however, is that the teaching of English is now an indigenous activity, planned and conducted by local experts with a sound knowledge of local students and conditions. This augurs well for the future of ELT worldwide, although a shortage of qualified English teachers appears to be a problem common to many of the countries included in this volume.

REFERENCES

Altbach, P. (1997). Straitjacket scholars. *South China Morning Post,* January 10, p. 11.

Altbach, P. (1998). *Comparative higher education: Knowledge, the University, and development.* Hong Kong: Comparative Education Research Centre.

Ammon, U. (2003). The international standing of the German language. In J. Maurais & M. Morris (Eds.), *Languages in a globalising world* (pp. 231–249). Cambridge, England: Cambridge University Press.

Baugh, A., & Cable, T. (1993). *A history of the English language* (4th ed.). Englewood Cliffs, NJ: Prentice-Hall.

Bryson, B. (1990). *The mother tongue.* New York: William Morrow.

Crystal, D. (1999). The Cambridge Encyclopedia of the English language. Cambridge, England: Cambridge University Press.

Fodor, F., & Peluau, S. (2003). Language geostrategy in Eastern and Central Europe: Assessment and perspectives. In J. Maurais & M. Morris (Eds.), *Languages in a globalising world* (pp. 85–98). Cambridge, England: Cambridge University Press.

Graddol, D. (1997). *The future of English?* London: The British Council.

Graddol, D. (1999). The decline of the native speaker. In D. Graddol & U. Meinhof (Eds), *English in a changing world* (pp. 57–68). Association Internationale de Linguistic Appliqueé, Milton Keynes, UK.

Graddol, D., McArthur, T., Flack, D., & Amey, J. (1999). English around the world. In D. Graddol & U. Meinhof (Eds), *English in a changing world* (pp. 3–18). Association Internationale de Linguistic Appliqueé, Milton Keynes, UK.

Hamel, R. (2003). Regional blocs as a barrier against English hegemony? The Language policy of Mercosur in South America. In J. Maurais & M. Morris (Eds.), *Languages in a globalising world* (pp. 111–142). Cambridge, England: Cambridge University Press.

He, A. E. (2001). An observational study of practice opportunities in Chinese tertiary English classrooms. *Asian Journal of English Language Teaching, 11,* 87–112.

Howatt, A. (1984). *A history of English language teaching.* Oxford: Oxford University Press.

Huang, Z. (1999). The impact of globalisation on English in Chinese universities. In D. Graddol & U. Meinhof (Eds). *English in a changing world* (pp. 79–88).Association Internationale de Linguistic Appliqueé, Milton Keynes, UK.

Kachru, B. (1985). Standards, codification and sociolinguistic realism: The English language in the outer circle. In R. Quirk & H. Widdowson (Eds.), *English in the world* (pp. 11–30). Cambridge, England: Cambridge University Press.

Krishnaswamy, N., & Burd, A. S. (1998). *The politics of Indian's English: Linguistic colonialism and the expanding English empire.* Delhi, India: Oxford University Press.

McConnell, G. (2003). Towards a scientific geostrategy for English. In J. Maurais & M. Morris (Eds.), *Languages in a globalising world* (pp. 298–312). Cambridge, England: Cambridge University Press.

McCrum, R., Cran, W., & MacNeil, R. (1992). *The story of English.* New York: Penguin.

Ministry of Education. China Education Development Statistics Report (2003). Web site. Retrieved on November 4, 2004, from http://www.edu.cn/HomePage/english/index/shtml

Pawelec, D. (2000). *Teaching English to young learners in Poland.* Retrieved June 26, 2004, from http://www.britishcouncil.org/English/eyl/article03.htm

Pennycook, A. (1989). The concept of method, interested knowledge and the politics of English teaching. *TESOL Quarterly, 23,* 589–618.

Rajagopalan, K. (2002). National languages as flags of allegiance; or the linguistics that failed us: A close look at emerging linguistic chauvinism in Brazil. *Journal of Language and Politics, 1,* 115–147.

Shi, L. (2002). How Western trained Chinese TESOL professionals publish in their home environment. *TESOL Quarterly, 36,* 625–634.

Shi, L. (2003). Writing in two cultures: Chinese professors return from the West. *The Canadian Modern Language Review, 59,* 369–391.

Zhang, H., & F. Luan (2002). A survey on EFL teaching in different countries of the world. Retrieved on June 12, 2004, from http://www.cbe21.com/subject/english/html/050203/2002_11/20021105_1977.html

1

THE ENGLISH LANGUAGE IN BRAZIL— A BOON OR A BANE?

Kanavillil Rajagopalan
State University at Campinas, Brazil

Cristina Rajagopalan
Sociedade Brasileira de Cultura Inglesa-São Paulo, Brazil

Brazil is the largest country in South America and boasts the eighth largest economy in the world. Its gigantic territorial dimensions—proudly remembered and fondly sung in the country's national anthem—and plentiful natural resources make it a major player in the geopolitics of the continent. The 8,511,965 square kilometers of its territory make Brazil the fifth largest country in the world, with a population density of barely 18 persons per square kilometer—one of the sparsest in the world. If that is not impressive enough, consider the following comparative statistics: Brazil's population, currently estimated at approximately 170 million, inhabits an area that is more than twice the size of western Europe, and has borders with all but two of the twelve other countries that, together with it, make up the continent of South America (Instituto Brasiliero, 2003; Sistema Estadual, 1999; United Nations, 2000).[1]

Like its neighbors in the South American continent, Brazil belongs to what Kachru (1988) called the "expanding circle" of countries with respect to the use and status of English. In the last 20 years, the language has become increasingly prominent in the daily lives of Brazil's citizens. Judging by the number of schools offer-

---

[1]The statistics cited in this chapter have been taken from the following sources: Brazilian Institute of Geography and Statistics at http://www.ibge.gov.br/english/default.php; *Statistical Yearbook for Latin America and the Caribbean 1999,* edition UN (2000); *Anuário Estatístico de Estade de São Paulo* (Statistical Yearbook of the State of São Paulo), 1998, SEADE, Government of São Paulo (1999).

ing courses in English, whose numbers and enrollment figures rise exponentially every year, it seems safe to say that this trend is here to stay.

HISTORY OF ELT IN BRAZIL

The rise of English to the status of Brazil's number one foreign language is a fairly recent phenomenon in the country's history, which began with the discovery of the land in 1498 by the Portuguese seafarer, Pedro Alvares Cabral. Traditionally, that status belonged to French, which was avidly sought after by the nobility during the days of the monarchy. At that time, a knowledge of French meant social status, and those who could afford to had their children educated in France, while those who were less well off at least made sure that their children had private tutoring in the language (Souza Campos, 1940).

The unequaled prestige of France as the nation's favorite role model, and of French as the repository of cultural finesse and sophistication, is evidenced by the fact that when Dom João VI, the reigning monarch, instituted by ordinance the teaching of French and English in public schools on June 22, 1809, steps were initially taken to introduce the teaching of French, on the grounds that, as the universal language, it should be an integral part of education. And when, in 1889, the radical wing of the Republican Party pressed for a popular uprising to topple the monarchy, its charismatic leader, Antônio da Silva Jardim, invoked the memory of that exceptional year in French history, 1789, that had heralded the era of popularly elected governments all over the world. Until fairly recently, the Brazilian elite has continued to look to France as the center of intellectual stimulation and cultural refinement (Pinto, 1986).

In his diagnostic study of higher education in Brazil, Souza Campos (1940) observed that "the French language was one of the first foreign languages, if not the very first, to be taught [as part of the normal curriculum] in the country. For this reason, practically all of Brazilian intellectuals speak the language" (p. 161). Even today, one does not have to look very carefully to find traces of French influence in Brazil's cultural life. A sizeable part of the intelligentsia, most notably academics, writers, senior civil servants, and jurists, have had some grounding in French in their formative years. When Itamarati, Brazil's foreign office, decided a few years ago no longer to require its trainee diplomats to become proficient in French, and instead made a working command of Spanish a prerequisite for overseas assignments, there was a general hue and cry, not only from the French government but also from the local elite.

To complicate matters, the language issue is intertwined with the geopolitics of the region, as indeed it is in many other parts of the world. English is typically associated with the hegemonic power of the United States and with what many in South America view as a takeover of their continent by their mighty neighbor in the northern hemisphere. This growing resentment often takes the form of complaints, voiced in the popular press, that the sort of culture being disseminated together with the spread of English—Hollywood blockbusters and American pop art and music, for example—is pastiche and blasé and aimed at mass consumption and quick profit. The implication is that it pales before the high culture that Brazil used to receive from continental Europe, and is therefore a clear sign of a cultural degradation underway worldwide.

Records from the national archives show that early interest in the teaching of English was largely due to growing ties between Portugal and Great Britain. These ties meant that, from January 1808 onwards, Brazilian ports were open for trade with Britain, with the blessings of Lisbon. As a result of Napoleonic expansionism, the Portuguese imperial family courted the friendship of France's enemy, Britain. The British responded positively, with an eye on the enormous commercial prospects such a friendship would present. In 1807, France invaded Portugal, forcing King João VI to flee to Brazil with a British naval escort. In 1810, the king signed new treaties with Great Britain, giving it trade preferences and "privileges of extraterritoriality." In 1831, the new statutes of the *Academias de Ciências Jurídicas do Império* [Imperial Academies of Juridical Sciences] incorporated English into the school curriculum and stipulated basic knowledge of the language as a prerequisite for admission to its courses (de Oliveira, 1999; Souza Campos, 1940).

Since that time, the importance of English has grown by leaps and bounds in Brazil, but ambivalence about it has grown as well. The cold war between the United States and the Union of Soviet Socialist Republics that followed the end of World War II meant increased concern on the part of successive U.S. governments over political developments in South America. Having lost Cuba to the communists, the United States was determined to keep the rest of the hemisphere from being taken over by leftist governments. Many members of Brazil's intelligentsia are vociferously skeptical and suspicious of U.S. pretensions vis-à-vis Latin America, and openly critical of Brazil's programmed entry into the U.S.-dominated, free-trade zone. "The entire continent [of South America]," writes sociologist Emir Sader (2001), "is under the threat of becoming a free trade zone for North-American corporations" (p. A3).

It is not surprising, therefore, that the English language has become an ambiguous symbol in the mind of the average Brazilian. On one hand, it is part and parcel of daily-lived reality, appearing on billboards and neon signs, in shop windows and newspaper and magazine ads, and in more restricted discursive spheres, such as information technology and electronic commerce. Most middle- and upper-class Brazilians know that their children must acquire an adequate command of English or they run the risk of missing out on opportunities for the better paid jobs offered by multinational corporations.

On the other hand, many in Brazil are understandably concerned about the possible negative consequences of the unbridled advance of English into the country's cultural scenario (Rajagopalan, 2000, 2001). Massive borrowings from English into Portuguese, the country's official language—there are, in addition, some 180 or so indigenous languages (Rodrigues, 1993)—has understandably fomented worries in some sectors of the intelligentsia about the capacity of the vernacular to withstand what is perceived by many as a systematic onslaught on its integrity and long-term survival. Increased use of English words, even where Portuguese equivalents are readily available or vernacular substitutes with a local flavor could easily be coined, continues to disturb those who have resisted learning English for whatever reason (Segismundo, 2000).

This atmosphere of distrust and dismay is, as we have seen, further aggravated by the widespread perception of the advance of English as the most visible sign of the growing influence of the United States in South America. Newspaper columnists are given to adding fuel to the fire by constantly reminding their readers of the big-stick diplomacy that successive U.S. governments have been perceived to have practiced in their 'backyard.'

THE ELT CURRICULUM

English is taught in Brazil as part of the regular curriculum at primary and secondary levels, but its fortunes have remained at the mercy of the whims and fancies of the bureaucrats and politicians who make the policy decisions at the federal and local levels of public administration. *The Guidelines and Basic Principles Act* of 1971 (da Costa, 1986) highlighted the importance of "not overlooking the 'deprovincializing' role of foreign languages in the context of a life style becoming genuinely international against the backdrop of a world rapidly shrinking in response to the impact of technology and means of mass communication" (p. 42). But such enthusiastic proclamations of the advantages of introducing the teaching of foreign languages at the school level have seldom been followed up by concrete measures designed to raise standards, such as investment in teacher training and materials production.

At the level of the states, the disparity is even more striking. A closer look at what happened in some of the more advanced states in the south and southeast gives a rough idea of the none-too-encouraging state of affairs insofar as ELT (English Language Teaching) in state schools is concerned. In the State of São Paulo, for instance, a June 1980 resolution made English and French optional subjects in the primary-school curriculum. It was up to the students (and their parents) to decide whether they wanted to have lessons in a foreign language (da Costa, 1986).

However, this did not guarantee that those who wished to learn either of these languages were able to do so. The methods used by mostly unprepared, grossly underpaid, and understandably unmotivated teachers showed little influence from the advances made in applied linguistics and teaching methodology. In the last 2 years of primary schooling, the students were exposed to an average of three classes per week, of 50 minutes duration each, administered mostly through old-fashioned methods such as grammar translation. As the students moved to middle and higher secondary levels, they had 2 hours of English lessons per week. A survey undertaken by da

Costa in the early 1980s revealed that most teaching was either text- or teacher-centered, with the pupils' active participation limited to parrotlike repetition of chunks of text from set books read out aloud by the teacher (da Costa, 1986). A similar survey conducted in 1988 in the north-eastern state of Paraíba revealed the following breakdown of classroom activities: grammar 32%, translation 30%, reading 17%, writing 12% and speaking 9%. (Victor & Melo, 1988). And, ironically, in the same country where the education specialist Freire (1970) had made an international reputation for his ground-breaking research into the failure of mass education in many developing nations, teaching in general still followed what he had condemned as the "banking approach": teachers mechanically going about their jobs, attempting to fill the heads of their pupils with knowledge in the apparent hope that it would grow over the years like a bank deposit.

But the worst was yet to come. A 1984 resolution concerning foreign languages transformed their status from 'disciplines' to 'activities'. The ensuing confusion as to what the change in nomenclature really meant was resolved a year later, when a second resolution stipulated that the teaching of foreign languages was to be considered a mere activity from then on. Among other things, this meant that student progress was to be evaluated, not on the basis of conventional examinations, but by taking into consideration the interest evinced by students in class as well as their perseverance. Evaluation of any kind was to be undertaken solely for the sake of better monitoring of overall results and planning future courses of remedial action (Viola, 1996).

Interestingly however, the opportunity to study English as an elective subject was extended to even those remote rural areas of the state where conditions had traditionally been even more precarious. This suited the interests of the bureaucrats at the top, who could celebrate steady statistical progress in their annual reports. But, if anything, those numbers only helped to camouflage the actual appalling conditions of teaching in those schools, and the growing disenchantment among students and teachers alike. As Viola (1996) observed:

> The much-vaunted democratization of education appears, therefore, to attend to the insistent demands from traditionally marginalized sectors of the population for equal opportunities merely by providing them with the material conditions, given that the kind of teaching offered to the socially underprivileged classes still leaves much to be desired and is all too frequently downright discriminatory. (pp. 112–113)

Viola's (1996) words confirm a somber diagnosis of the educational scenario made by Celani (1984), one of Brazil's leading applied linguists and a pioneering figure in ELT:

> The (recent) educational reform, after having identified the democratization of education as its main objective, paradoxically created an extremely elitist state of affairs when it rendered the possibility of learning foreign languages, with reasonable chances of success, unavailable to all but a handful. (p. 32)

English is also offered as an elective subject at the universities in Brazil, the earliest of which, such as the prestigious University of São Paulo, date back to the 1920s (Maza, 1999). These courses are primarily geared towards forming future language teachers. In the 1970s, several postgraduate courses began to be offered, with the Catholic University of São Paulo announcing the country's first M.A. (and, later, Ph.D.) program in Applied Linguistics. In subsequent years, a handful of other universities opened M.A. and Ph.D. programs in English, with an emphasis either on applied linguistics or on literature. (As is often the case elsewhere in the world, there is frequently a standoff between the two as well.)

However, it is not at all clear that these concerted efforts at improving standards have produced the desired results. Thus, we find scholars like Machado (1989) complained "despite all the innovations, the teaching of English is going through a difficult phase" (p. 69). Speaking specifically about her home state, Rio Grande do Norte, the author notes "College students do not seem to be interested in L2 courses as much as they did in the past" (p. 65). She also presents statistics showing "a significant decrease in the number of students graduating in English" (p. 67).

In view of the utter precariousness of ELT nationwide, and the urgent need to help university students gain access to the cutting edge scientific and technological information available in journals and elsewhere, an ambitious English for special purposes project was launched in the late 1970s with the active collaboration of the British Council. The project set out "to improve the use of English by Brazilian researchers, science teachers, and technicians, especially with regard to reading specialist and technical publications" (Celani, 1988, p. 234).

For effective English language instruction, most middle- and upper-class Brazilians turn to privately run language schools. Such schools are located all over the country, and offer reasonably good regular and intensive courses in English and other languages, although at a price beyond the reach of the vast majority of the population. Many of these schools employ native speakers of English—mostly from the United States and Britain—though not many of them have any credentials for teaching English beyond the fact of being fully at home with the language.

One of the most traditional and prestigious private language schools offering courses in English is the *Cultura Inglesa*. Founded in 1935, a year after the British Council came into existence, the *Cultura Inglesa of São Paulo* alone has a total of 53,000 students enrolled in its 15 branches in the metropolitan area as well as some adjacent cities (Cultura Inglesa, 2003). If one considers that it is just one among scores of similar large enterprises in São Paulo offering EFL courses at different levels, albeit perhaps the oldest and the biggest of its kind, and, furthermore, that the same is true in almost every other major city in the country, one begins to realize the extent to which English has become a marketable commodity in Brazil. The growing lure of English, principally among Brazil's adolescent population, is attested to by the fact that, for some years now, Brazil has been second only to Greece in the number of candidates annually taking Cambridge examinations in EFL (English as a foreign language).

BECOMING AN ENGLISH TEACHER

Born into a family of Spanish immigrants to Brazil, Cristina Rajagopalan (née Serrano), was brought up speaking Spanish (to her parents and, especially, her grandparents) and Portuguese. Her grandfather worked for a multinational corporation, and had moved to South America in the early 1920s, initially to Monte Video, Uruguay, and subsequently to Rio de Janeiro, Brazil. Internationally known for its scenic beauty, sunny beaches, tasty tropical cuisine, lilting music, and colorful annual festivals, Rio de Janeiro is also an important center of Brazilian culture and point of convergence for poets, artists, and singers from all over the country and abroad. The city also impresses the visitor with its mosaic of races and creeds. The blend of cultures—the original Portuguese settlers, successive waves of European immigrants, Africans originally brought as slaves, and indigenous people—can be seen readily in the cuisine, the music, and other manifestations of popular culture, with *feijoada,* the national dish, and *samba,* the musical rhythm for which the country is known everywhere in the world, being the stereotypical highlights.

As a child, Cristina went to *Sacré Coeur de Marie,* a convent school in Rio de Janeiro run by French nuns. French was thus her first foreign language. Besides learning French as part of her normal school curriculum, she also studied the language for 13 years at *Alliance Française,* a privately run organization with the express mission of promoting French language and culture. Recognizing the rising importance of English, her parents also made sure that she had some exposure to that language early on. This meant reinforcing her regular school lessons with private lessons in English.

Things went on smoothly until her father's sudden transfer to the city of São Paulo—Brazil's industrial and financial hub—which meant having to start all over again at the age of 17, at least as far as daily habits and circle of friends were concerned. With mounting feelings of despair and revolt, Cristina toyed with the idea of not going to college, but eventually changed her mind and received her Bachelor of Arts in Philosophy at the Catholic University of São Paulo. However, she remained committed to the study of languages, a passion that continues today.

She continued her study of English at *Cultura Inglesa,* the language school referred to in the previous section, where she received her Cambridge Proficiency Certificate and was subsequently offered a teaching position. Since then, she has developed a professional career in ELT, constantly keeping herself up to date with the latest in language teaching methods by signing up for in-service courses such as the Diploma for Overseas Teachers of English—Cambridge University and the ARELS (Association of Recognized English Language Services) Diploma. In addition to teaching in the classroom for several years, she has served as listening center supervisor and academic coordinator for levels ranging from basic through upper intermediate. Thanks to a scholarship from the *Cultura Inglesa,* she also did postgraduate studies in Britain and obtained a Diploma in Applied Linguistics from the University of Edinburgh. Currently she holds the post of Examinations Officer at the *Cultura Inglesa,* where she is responsible for administering and supervising Cambridge examinations in EFL. She is also involved, off and on, in teacher training and refresher courses, as well as in-service recycling and assessment of teachers at different levels.

Cristina's interest in the English language has not eclipsed her passion for French, nor obscured her native command of Spanish. Most of her contact with these languages today is thanks to cable television. Her interest in foreign cultures and languages led her to take evening lessons in modern Greek, which she now speaks with reasonable fluency. She also has a mostly passive command of Italian, in which she can get by should every other language in her communicative repertoire fail to produce the desired results.

In addition to her experience as a graduate student in Scotland, Cristina had direct contact with an English-speaking environment when she spent a year in California, accompanying her husband on a postdoctoral visit to the University of California at Berkeley. Being married to a person (the co-author of this chapter) who was born and brought up in India means that Cristina often finds herself code-switching between Portuguese and English, both at home and at work. English is thus very much a part of her daily life.

CONCLUSION

In the context of Brazil's heterogeneous and complex cultural reality, the English language is today best described as being strategically located at a crossroads. Its presence in the country's social, cultural, and economic life is undeniable and is growing rapidly. Every year, more and more people, especially from the younger age groups, acquire proficiency in the language, which guarantees them better opportunities in a job market that is steadily becoming more demanding and competitive. The negative side is that English is also fast becoming a divider between the urban rich and the rural poor, thus reinforcing an economic and cultural chasm that has long been a major source of embarrassment for the country's statesmen and elected representatives. The English language itself is probably not to blame for what it has come to represent.

What is perhaps most worrying of all is that the recent wave of antiEnglish sentiment sweeping the country may find an analogue in one of the outbursts of linguistic chauvinism that have been known to occur in other parts of the world. A case in point is the drive to make English the only legally admissible language of use in the United States.

Fortunately, in Brazil the current sentiment against English has a different sort of breeding ground, and is unlikely to assume such dangerous proportions, because a lot of it is simply misguided and based on erroneous beliefs about the role of English in the emerging world order (Rajagopalan, 1999).

REFERENCES

Celani, M. A. A. (1984). Uma abordagem centrada no aluno para os cursos de letras [A student-centered approach to language courses]. In M. A. A. Celani (Ed.) *Ensino de Línguas* [Language Teaching] (pp. 32–39). São Paulo: Educ.

Celani, M. A. A. (1988). A retrospective view of an ESP teacher education programme. *The ESPecialist, 19,* 233–244.

Cultura Inglesa. (2003). Web site. Retrieved July 24, 2003, from http://www. culturaing lesasp.com.br/

Da Costa, D. (1986). *A Língua Estrangeira na Escola de 1 grau: o Aspecto Formativo* [Foreign language in primary school: the formative aspect]. Unpublished master's thesis, Catholic University of São Paulo, Brazil.

de Oliveira, L. E. M. (1999). *A Historiografia Brasileira da Literatura Inglesa: Uma História do Ensino de Inglês no Brasil (1809-1951)* [The Brazilian historiography of the English language: A history of English language teaching in Brazil (1809-1951)]. Unpublished master's thesis, State University at Campinas, Brazil.

Freire, P. (1970). *Pedagogy of the oppressed.* New York: Herder.

Instituto Brasiliero de Geogragia e Statística [Brazilian Institute of Geography and Statistics]. Web site. Retrieved July 8, 2003, from *http://www.ibge.gov.br/english/default.php*

Kachru, B. (1988). *ERIC/CLL News Bulletin 12, 1.*

Machado, M. C. (1989). 'What is the matter with our ESL programs at the university?' *Trabalhos em Lingüística Aplicada [Papers in Applied Linguistics], 13,* 65–69.

Maza, F. T. (1999). Pesquisa em Formação de Educadores: o Professor de Inglês e o Ensino Superior [Research on teacher education: The teacher of English and higher education]. Unpublished master's thesis, Catholic University of São Paulo, Brazil.

Pinto, V. (1986). Comunicação e Cultura Brasileira [Communication and Brazilian culture]. São Paulo: Editora Ática.

Rajagopalan, K (1999). Of EFL teachers, conscience, and cowardice. *ELT Journal, 53,* 200–206.

Rajagopalan, K. (2000). Critical pedagogy and linguistic imperialism in the EFL context. *TESOL Journal, 9,* 5–6.

Rajagopalan, K. (2001). ELT classroom as an arena for Identity clashes. In M. Grigoletto & A. M. G. Carmagnani (Eds.), *English as a Foreign Language: Identity, Practices, and Textuality* (pp. 79–90). São Paulo: Humanitas.

Rodrigues, A. D. (1993). Línguas indígenas: 500 anos de descobertas e perdas [Indigenous languages: 500 years of discoveries and losses]. *D.E.L.T.A. 9, 1,* 83–103.

Sader, E. (2001, April 3). O Brasil fora da Alca [Brazil out of the NAFATA]. *Folha de São Paulo,* A3.

Segismundo, F. (2000). A preservação do Português nos meios de comunicação [The preservation of Portuguese in the mass media]. Available at http://www.cnol.com.br/cnol/ not/cam/00/11/07/12.shtml

Sistema Estraudual de Análise de Dados [State System for the Analysis of Data]. (1999). *Anuário estatístico de estado de São Paulo, 1998* [Statistical yearbook of the state of São Paulo, 1998]. São Paulo, Brazil: Author.

Souza Campos, E. (1940). *Educação Superior no Brasil* [Higher Education In Brazil]. Rio de Janeiro: Ministério da Educação [Ministry of Education].

United Nations (2000). *Statistical yearbook for Latin America and the Caribbean, 1999.* New York: Author.

Victor, D. R., & Melo, R. S. (1988). An experiment in teacher training. *The ESPecialist, 9,* 321–328.

Viola, M. C. (1996). O ensino de língua inglesa no contexto de zona rural: Uma perpectiva social entre linguagem e escola [The teaching of English in the rural context: A social perspective between language and school]. Unpublished master's thesis, Catholic University of São Paulo, Brazil.

2

LEARNING AND TEACHING ENGLISH
IN THE PEOPLE'S REPUBLIC OF CHINA

An E He
The Hong Kong Institute of Education, Hong Kong

China is the most populous country in the world with 1.3 billion people residing in a land of 9,600,000 square kilometres in Asia. Since 221 *B.C.*, China has been governed by 11 different dynasties, mostly as a unified and centrally controlled nation. In 1911, the Republic of China came into being, indicating an end of about 2,000 years of feudalism. In 1949, the People's Republic of China (PRC) was established. The country then experienced isolation from the outside world for about 30 years. Since the late 1970s, China has adopted an open-door policy and progressed at a fast pace towards modernization. In 2001, China joined the World Trade Organization (WTO), a landmark for the country's further development in the 21st century.

China is a multiethnic country. There are altogether 56 ethnic groups, but the Han nationality accounts for about 92% of the total population. The Han speak Chinese, a group of languages (or dialects as traditionally called) belonging to the Sino–Tibetan language family. As a logographic system, the Chinese characters, especially the ancient ones from which the modern writing system is derived, resemble the real entities they represent. Pu Tong Hua, or the common speech, which has been developed on the basis of northern dialects, is the official language of the country. Pin Yin, the invented Romanising system, provides phonetic spellings to its writing system. Some of the minority nationalities such as Tibetan, Mongol, and NaXi have their own languages (spoken and/or written) for daily communication and education.

English language teaching (ELT) first entered the Chinese school curriculum at the beginning of the last century. Since then, ELT has been through some dramatic ups and downs because of the overall sociopolitical changes in the country (Boyle,

11

2000). A historical review of ELT, a description of its curriculum, and a personal account of the making of an ELT teacher now given serve as an illustration of the events China has seen in the last century.

THE HISTORY OF ELT IN CHINA

Before the New China (1902–1949)

The English language came into China together with Western technology in the late 19th century. Under the influence of the philosophy of "Chinese learning as the essence, Western learning for its usefulness" (Hayhoe, 1999, pp. 37–38), foreign subjects known as 'Yang Wu' were introduced to the university examination system. Young people were sent overseas to learn about science and technology. Important texts of English such as *On the Origin of Species,* by Charles Darwin (1859/1999) were translated into Chinese by Chinese scholars. At the same time, trade with foreigners became more and more popular in the coastal cities such as Guangzhou and Fu Jian. Also an increasing number of British and American missionaries came to China to preach Christianity, helping spread English in the country, especially to those of lower social classes. This interest in Western technology and more frequent contact with English speakers in daily life paved the ground for ELT in China.

The English language first entered the secondary school curriculum together with German and Japanese in 1902. After about 10 years, it became part of the primary curriculum. Nine years later, English was recommended as the major foreign language for secondary schools. From then on until 1948, a total of 12 English syllabi were issued, aiming to cultivate learners' interest in the learning of another language and culture, and to enable learners to use English as a tool for other subjects (Institute of Curriculum Studies, 2001). These aims revealed the function and role that the English language played in the first half century of ELT history in China.

The Early Years of the PRC (1949–1966)

After the establishment of PRC in 1949, ELT swung to the other end of the pendulum. In 1953, seven out of eight English language departments in normal universities were closed down (Hu, 2001). In 1954, the teaching of foreign languages in junior secondary schools was abolished, and the Russian language became the major foreign language for senior secondary schools (Hu, 2001). These changes came as a direct result of the overall sociopolitical climate in the country. The relationship between China and the Western world was bitter, and the former Union of Soviet Socialist Republics (USSR) was then the major ally of China. A few years later, however, some ideological differences arose between the Chinese government and the USSR, leading to a complete withdrawal of Russian expertise from the country. This served as a warning to the Chinese leaders that a sole reliance on one country was not only undesirable but also impossible. As a result of such a political change, ELT came back gradually to the school curriculum. In 1956, ELT reappeared in junior secondary schools and in 1959, two thirds of the A-Band secondary schools in metropolitan areas started teaching English (Institute of Curriculum Development, 2001). Despite this shift in the mid 1950s, the number of Russian teachers in secondary schools continued to increase until 1965. At the same time, graduates majoring in English were in short supply by almost 50% (D. C. He, 1993). Such a shortage continued to haunt ELT even in the late 1970s to early 1980s, when former graduates of Russian had to teach English under a new socioeconomic climate (A. E. He, 1998).

As revealed in all the syllabi before 1949, English was once regarded as a tool for learning other subjects in the curriculum. This, however, was no longer the case by the 1950s and early 1960s. No functional use was required, and literature appreciation and development of basic language skills became the focus both in the syllabi (Institute of Curriculum Development, 2001) and practice. Such a phenomenon was partly a result of the strong influence of the Russian teaching methodology popular in the 1950s, but above all, a reflection of the social reality of the times. During China's long isolation from the outside world, there was simply no opportunity and, consequently, no requirement for students to use foreign languages functionally in their study and work.

During the Cultural Revolution[1] (1966–1976)

ELT was hit badly during the Cultural Revolution. Schools were virtually shut down from 1966 to 1968 and universities remained closed until 1971. Everything foreign (books, films, music, etc.) was regarded bourgeois and therefore forbidden. In some schools, students were still taking English lessons, not for the purpose of economic advancement, but to prepare for possible wars against the former Soviet Union and China's long-standing enemies in the Western world. Hence, ELT focused almost exclusively on the themes of political propaganda. When a number of universities finally reopened, English majors did not learn much English, but spent half of the 3 years learning how to work in factories or on farms. No ELT syllabus was issued during the Cultural Revolution. The English language did not disappear completely only because it was regarded as a 'weapon' for political struggle.

Under the Open-Door Policy (1976–Present)

In the late 1970s, China finally opened its door to the West after 30 years of isolation. This came as a direct result of its urgent need for economic advancement. The

---

[1]The Cultural Revolution was on of the worst disasters in the history of the PRC. It was initiated in 1966 by Chairman Mao to eliminate the influence of capitalist ideology in China. Hundreds and thousands of innocent people lost their lives during 10 years of catastrophe and the whole country was paralyzed in all possible aspects of its growth by the end of 1976.

Chinese government set up a grand plan targeting four areas for modernisation: agriculture, industry, national defence, and science and technology. The open-door policy has brought about important changes in ELT in China. First, because modernization involves consistent updating of databases, and this is mainly done through English, the English language has established its dominant position among other foreign languages in the curriculum. Second, with China's entry into the World Trade Organization (WTO), English is no longer simply a subject in the school curriculum, but an instrument for work and daily communication. The fast-growing country means a large market for ELT. It was estimated that there would be about 196 million learners of English in the education sector by 2001 (Liu & Gong, 2001, cited in Hu, 2001). This figure is expected to increase continuously in the years to come.

THE ELT CURRICULUM

In response to the needs of the national economic reform agenda, new aims for education were formulated with an orientation towards modernisation, the outside world, and the future. ELT has received much more attention in such a context. A series of ELT syllabi and guidelines were issued for primary,[2] secondary, and tertiary institutions (see Institute of Curriculum Studies, 2001). This has not only revealed the government's willingness to promote ELT, but also manifested an open attitude towards some concepts of language development that originated in the West.

Curriculum for Primary Schools

Although ELT at the primary level was promoted in a number of policy documents in the past, the actual implementation was confined only to those key schools in metropolitan areas due to difficulties in staffing and resources. In early 2001, the central government launched a new campaign whereby primary schools across the country would offer English programs to pupils from Year 3 and above by September 2001 (Ministry of Education, 2001). The ultimate aim of the program is to develop pupils' interest and confidence in English, and nurture their positive attitudes towards learning the language. The syllabus divides the program into two stages. Stage One for Year 3 and Year 4 focuses on development of oral/aural skills; Stage Two for Year 5 and Year 6 adds reading skills into the objectives. Pupils are required to take four English lessons per week (single lesson for Stage One and double lessons for Stage Two). Interactive activities such as games, role-plays, songs, and so forth, are recommended, especially for

---

[2]The Chinese education system is divided into three levels: primary, secondary, and tertiary. Primary education is compulsory and designated for 6 years. It is followed by another 6 years of secondary education, the first 3 of which are compulsory. Tertiary level programs are about 4 years, leading in most cases to a bachelor's degree.

Stage One. Formative assessment is done at school level with classroom observation and interaction with pupils recommended as the major means of achieving this end. To support the implementation of the new curriculum, textbooks were published and training courses were offered to key personnel at primary schools (Ministry of Education, 2001).

Curriculum for Secondary Schools

Two new syllabi for secondary level were issued in 2000 (Institute of Curriculum Development, 2001); one for junior schools, and the other for senior schools. The new syllabi see a child's development as a continuum and attempt to establish a link between the learning of English at primary and secondary levels. The new syllabi aim to develop students' competence in five domains: namely skills, knowledge, affective, strategies, and culture. ELT thus is no longer confined to the development of language skills but taken as a matter of developing a whole person.

The English language is also taken in the new syllabi as a means of communication in oral and written form. To materialize such a concept, a list of functions/notions such as invitations and responses, apologies and responses, and so forth, is provided together with those of pronunciation, vocabulary and grammar (Institute of Curriculum Development, 2001). Learners are considered the centre of classroom instruction, and the teacher, instead of being the key person controlling the classroom, is expected to function as facilitator, providing appropriate methodology to accommodate students' needs in cognitive and psychological development.

Junior secondary students are required to take four English lessons per week and seniors, 12 per week (Institute of Curriculum Development, 2001). English is prescribed as the medium of instruction in the classroom. The use of information technology such as computers, the Internet, and software for learning–teaching is also considered an integral part of ELT (Institute of Curriculum Development, 2001).

Both formative and summative assessments are recommended in the syllabi. Individual schools are responsible for their own assessment at junior secondary level, and a district/region organises examinations for seniors. The Ministry of Education is planning to establish a national band system, in which students are expected to pass Band 3 upon graduation from junior secondary, and Band 6 upon graduation from senior secondary (Hao, 2000). Outstanding students can take Band 8 examination voluntarily.

Curriculum for Tertiary Institutions

Although the new syllabus for primary level aims to nurture young children's interest in learning English, and that of the secondary is to develop a whole person, the syllabi at tertiary level, named the *College English Syllabus*,[3] have

---

[3]The *College English Syllabus* was issued in 1985 for students of science and engineering and 1 year later, another one with the same name cane out for students of humanities and social sciences. The two syllabi share the same principles of design with only a slight difference in the vocabulary lists.

focused attention on the development students' communicative competence in using English language functionally for study and work. Reading is no longer the only objective; listening, speaking, and writing become part of teaching objectives for non-English majors. Linguistic knowledge and usage are not the sole concern; use of information at discourse level has its place in the objectives. In order to tailor the course to cater for individual needs, a six-level band system is adopted and students are encouraged to skip bands if they can manage to pass the examination at a higher level. A national examination is held annually and certificates indicating satisfactory performance in Band 4 are required before a bachelor's degree can be conferred.

It is commonly acknowledged that generalization of any findings about China is impossible (Boyle, 2000; Cortazzi & Jin, 1996) "since China is not one place geographically, but many" (Maley, 1995, p. 7). This large diversity has been a serious problem for policy making and implementation, and a centrally controlled practice of curriculum development has made things worse. In the past, the State Education Commission was responsible for the development of syllabi. Schools and tertiary institutions across the country, whether top ones in metropolitan areas or those in remote rural villages, were expected to implement the syllabus with the same vigour. However, this did not actually happen in reality. In recent years, the government has made an effort to deal with this problem by introducing a minimum curriculum at primary and secondary level. Under this policy, local governments are allowed to make decisions on learning objectives, teaching hours, and textbooks according to the needs and resources of the region (Hao, 2000). In light of this policy, big cities like Beijing, Shanghai, and Guangzhou have designed their own syllabi with higher exit standards and tougher criteria than those of the national curriculum. They are also producing (or have already produced) their own teaching materials through cooperation with publishing companies overseas such as Oxford University Press and Longman. This indicates that the government policy to hand over the central control to local governments might benefit only those areas with power and economic strength. The long-term effect of this decentralized policy on ELT is yet to be seen.

BECOMING AN ENGLISH TEACHER

I first started learning English at secondary school in the mid 1960s. That was the time when English and Russian co-existed in the school curriculum. We had about 40 students in the class, sitting in rows. Lessons were conducted mainly in Chinese and drilling was the major means of presentation. Students were asked to memorize the spelling and meaning of words through translation. By the end of the first year, we learned some basic lexical items such as 'pencil', 'ink', 'chicken' and 'this/that is', 'these/those are'. There was little genuine interaction in English in the class and games and activities were simply beyond our imagination. Despite this, however, English was one of my favourite subjects probably because it sounded exotic.

Because of the Cultural Revolution, our school was shut down for about 2 years. In mid-1968, we resumed our studies. We sat with the same group of students, with the same teacher, and used the same teaching method. The difference was in the content. Basic linguistic items from daily life disappeared. Instead, we were learning slogans such as 'Long live Chairman Mao', and 'Down with imperialism'! An incident that occurred at that time illustrates the general atmosphere of our classrooms. One day, a girl in our class challenged the teacher with the word order of a slogan. She insisted that instead of "Long live Chairman Mao", we should write "Chairman Mao long live" because we ought to show our respects to the great leader by placing his name at the beginning of the sentence. The teacher tried to explain to her about English word order but the girl was not convinced. She simply went to the blackboard and changed the sentence on her own! Like the rest of the class, the teacher was astounded and speechless.

Such lessons did not last long. In January 1969, I, together with eight other students of my age, went to a small village on the Yellow Plateau to be reeducated by local peasants. We worked from dawn to dusk in the parched land with a severe shortage of water, and often went hungry because of insufficient food. Two years later, local factories held their recruitment in our county and I became a worker in a small tractor factory, putting parts in the gearbox on an assembly line. The job was hard during the day, but I had plenty of time to kill after work. Then in 1971, the provincial broadcast station began to offer an English course. I followed the program 30 minutes each day by listening to the sentence patterns and reading the structures after the teachers. In a year and a half, I managed to learn more words and sentence structures than I had done in secondary school. Although English did not seem to be of any practical use then, the act of learning enriched my life in a culturally scarce time.

The Cultural Revolution finally ended and everything in the country gradually came back to normal. In 1977, tertiary institutions started a large-scale recruitment, the first since the outbreak of the Cultural Revolution 10 years before. As a favourable policy, the "educated youth", those who had graduated between 1966 to 1968 but worked in factories or in the countryside, were allowed to take the national entrance examination together with new graduates from the secondary schools. I took advantage of this policy and prepared myself for the examination in the summer of 1978. Taking English as a major was a natural choice as I had developed a liking for the subject, and learning English seemed to be an opportunity to know more about the world, something everyone might want after a long time of isolation. For about 8 months, I spent almost all my spare time on preparation. My normal day started at 5:00 a.m., reading for about an hour before leaving for work, coming back home at about 6:00 p.m. and studying after dinner until one or two o'clock in the morning. To make the best use of time, I wrote English words on small cards and placed them on the front of my bicycle, trying to memorize them while cycling to work. I also studied in the workshop during the day when it was less busy.

My reading of English finally caught the eye of a colleague, who recommended me to do substitute teaching of English in the secondary school affiliated with the factory. After a written examination and microteaching, I was given the job. This was the first teaching post I had ever had, and I was learning English myself at the same time I was teaching it to others. I tried to imitate what my teacher did in the secondary school, using drills and translation to present and practice vocabulary and sentence patterns. I consolidated what I knew through teaching in the classroom, and I furthered my knowledge of English by taking free tutorials on grammar and pronunciation from friends.

My formal learning of the language began in 1978 when I passed the very competitive national entrance examination and became an English major in a key university. This was a 4-year course. We had about 15 periods of English lessons each week, including intensive and extensive reading, listening, speaking, translating, English literature, English poetry, the study of Shakespeare, the history and geography of the United Kingdom and the United States, and teaching methodology. However, our exposure to authentic English was limited. There were no English TV programs in the late 1970s and English radio programs were not broadcasting news but teaching the language. Very few English publications were available in our library. To compensate for these, I spent hours and hours on grammar, doing exercises on tense, word formation, sentence conversion; sitting in the language lab, trying to 'detect' the smallest morphemes attached to the end of a sound in the listening materials of Linguaphone. The limited resources basically prescribed the way that I learned the language.

I wished to become a teacher from the third year of my study. Having taught in a secondary school before was certainly one of the reasons behind the decision. I took teaching methodology as my elective and read almost all the journals and books on language teaching available in the university library. For the graduate thesis, my research was teaching related, and it won me the second prize for *The Excellent Graduates' Thesis of 1982* at the university.

Upon graduation, I was given a lecturing job in the department of foreign languages in a key university. But my first assignment was on *secondment,* teaching a Form One class in the newly established secondary school affiliated to the university. The students were hard working and very well behaved. However, my teaching was not as good as I anticipated. All the theories I had read before seemed to have disappeared, and once again, I found myself imitating what my first teacher had done in her class—grammar translation and drilling. I was puzzled about this until I observed a few lessons given by a native-speaking teacher of English. This was the first time that I witnessed a learner-centred classroom and I was impressed and adopted some of the activities in my own class. However, I was not consciously aware why I did so, nor its relation to language development on the part of students; imitation was the main feature of my learning to teach at that time.

Because of such a lack of awareness, I gave up using the activities after the secondment. The focus of the courses in the department was reading ability. But instead of encouraging students to read, teachers and students paid attention to grammatical rules and lexical items exclusively. Trying hard to adjust myself to the new situation, I followed the examples of colleagues, researching every rule of a particular word/phrase in dictionaries and grammar books so as to provide students with as detailed information as possible. Tertiary ELT to me then was about grammatical rules and I did my best to deliver the rules to my students.

As a student majoring in English language and literature, I learned how to teach through trial and error, and such learning seemed to be piecemeal. In 1984, I enrolled in a postgraduate diploma course, hoping to develop a more systematic understanding of teaching. The lecturers in charge were two American MATESOL (Master of Arts in Teaching of English to Speakers of Other Languages) graduates, who tried to teach methodology by involving us in activities. We were asked to stand in circles and interview each other with a frequent change of partners. We also sang songs and played games. Students, however, showed more interest in theory-based subjects, and did not want to 'waste' time on those activities, which did not constitute any 'serious learning' in a Chinese sense. The lecturers were confused and did not understand why we had strong objections to activities. This fundamental difference between the Chinese culture and Western culture regarding learning and teaching was, unfortunately, not addressed, and the philosophy and underlying principles of ELT were not made explicit. As a result, the relationship between the lecturers and the class turned sour and both parties seemed to be dissatisfied about what was going on. However, unconvinced as we were, these activities exposed us to some new concepts of ELT, and 'forced' us to interact with each other in the classroom. The influence of the course was not immediate, but it had, as I felt a few years later, some long-term effects on my study and teaching.

Having passed a series of examinations, I got the opportunity to earn a master's degree in an Australian university in 1988. Studying in the Faculty of Education instead of in the Department of Linguistics came as a surprise because language teaching in China had been traditionally related to the study of language rather than education. Cultural shocks like this followed one after another in the new environment. Learning in this case was not only about a particular subject matter, but a whole new culture! The lectures, seminars, large amount of reading, and self-initiated activities during that period provided me with initial but systematic understanding of the principles and methodology of ELT. The activities I witnessed and experienced with the American teachers in China began to make sense.

My studies in Australia continued for 7½ years, much longer than I first expected. After the master's degree, I decided in 1991 to do a Ph.D. to enrich myself with the experience of research. My Chinese background prescribed the topic of my research: "Teaching English as a Foreign Language in China: Policy, Practice and Future Prospects." I used an ethnographic approach for the study, aiming to identify patterns and problems in ELT teaching, searching for possible solutions to the problems, and ultimately bringing about an improvement of ELT in China. The next 5 years were the most unforgettable in my life. When I had seen my intentions turned into action, when I was convinced by the results of study that classroom-based research could benefit language development, and that teachers play an important role in creating optimal learning environment, all the frustrations, stress, and uncertainties became a worthwhile price to pay.

I took a lecturing position in Hong Kong in 1995, training primary English teachers. At first, I thought I had the credentials for the job. I held a Ph.D. with five years' experience in classroom research and I had taught at the secondary and tertiary level before; but, I was proved wrong. My previous training and teaching experience did not seem to be sufficient in the new context, and my lack of first-hand experience in primary schools and lack of knowledge of the local education system and sociocultural environment bothered me. At the beginning, I relied mostly on my declarative knowledge of language teaching and learning. As time passed by, I was able to highlight issues in language development with first-hand information and evidence obtained from school visits and classroom observations.

In 1998, I participated in a lecturer attachment scheme[4] and taught as an English teacher in a local primary school. This gave me an opportunity to go back to school and become a learner again through the school experience. This also gave me a chance to carry out a self-study on my own beliefs and assumptions on ELT and teacher education. Following the principles of reflective practice (Schon, 1987), I began my attachment with a problem in mind: to identify components of the knowledge base involved in primary English classroom teaching. I kept a journal during the attachment, reflecting on my own actions in and outside the classroom, and analysing the occurrences in light of the specific context attached. On the basis of my new experiences at the school, I reframed my assumptions and beliefs of ELT, and applied and tested them in my own practice (A. E. He, 2001). This series of actions coincided with the process of an experiential learning cycle, namely, concrete experience, observation and analysis, abstract reconceptualisation, and active experimentation (Osterman & Kottkamp, 1993). Reflecting on my limited but valuable experience, I realised that the significance of the experience did not lie in the fact that I had been to the classroom, but in that I became consciously aware of the importance of teaching experience as the inspiration for ELT and teacher education.

CONCLUSION

I have witnessed and lived through some of the most tumultuous periods in the history of China, and the long way I have walked through from an ELT learner to an ELT educator has been closely related to the ups and downs in the country. I con-

---

[4]The Scheme began in late 1997. Staff members are required to teach in a local primary school for at least 2 weeks in order to update their local school teaching experience and understanding of the local teaching and learning environment.

sider myself a fortunate survivor and I am glad to see China is now making great progress towards modernization, and hundreds and thousands of young learners of English nowadays do not have to experience what I, and my generation, have been through. Looking back, I realise that there has always been something keeping me there, that is, a love of learning. This love is best represented on the coat of arms of one of the universities I have attended, which says ANCORA IMPARO, meaning "Ever Learning". This is and will be my motto for life.

REFERENCES

Boyle, J. (2000). A brief history of English language teaching in China. *IATELT, 155,* 14–15.

Cortazzi, M., & Jin, L. (1996). English teaching and learning in China. *Language Teaching, 29,* 61–80.

Darwin, C. (1999). *On the origin of species.* New York: Bantam. (Original work published 1859)

Hao, J. P. (2000). *Features of English curriculum.* Retrieved on July 8, 2001, from http://www.pep.com.cn/yingyu/forum/hao-kc.htm

Hayhoe, R. (1999). *China's universities 1895–1995: A century of cultural conflict.* Hong Kong: The University of Hong Kong.

He, A. E. (1998). The Chinese experience with implementing the College English Syllabus. *International Journal of Educational Reform, 7*(4), 319–329.

He, A. E. (2001). The battle starts when the bell rings. *Reflective Practice, 2*(1), 81–98.

He, D. C. (Ed.). (1993). *Collection of important education documents in People's Republic of China: 1949–1997.* Beijing, China: Higher Education Press.

Hu, W. Z. (2001). Foreign language planning in China: Gains and losses. *Foreign Language Teaching and Research, 33*(4), 245–251.

Institute of Curriculum Studies (2001). *A Collection of twentieth century curriculums and syllabi for secondary and primary schools in China: English.* Beijing, China: People's Education Press.

Maley, A. (1995). *The English 2000 landmark review of the use, teaching and learning of English in the People's Republic of China.* Manchester, England: The British Council.

Ministry of Education (2001). Guidelines of ELT courses in primary schools. Web site. Retrieved December 10, 2001, from http://www.pep.com.cn/yingyu/syllabus/instruction.htm

Osterman, K. F., & Kottkamp, R. B. (1993). *Reflective practice for educators: Improving schooling through professional development.* Thousand Oaks, CA: Sage.

Schon, D. A. (1987). *Educating the reflective practitioner.* San Francisco, CA: Jossey- Bass.

3

ENGLISH LANGUAGE TEACHING IN GERMANY: A REFLECTION OF THE NATIONAL AND UNIVERSAL IMPORTANCE OF ENGLISH[1]

Claus Gnutzmann
Technical University of Braunschweig, Germany

The scientific study of English language and culture(s), as well as the teaching and learning of English in schools and other contexts, have been salient features of the history of the humanities and of education in Germany. Over the course of history, the methods, contents and aims of teaching English have undergone many changes, which can be encapsulated in the following four dichotomies:

- Knowledge about language versus linguistic skills;
- The cultural dimension of English versus the language dimension;
- Deliberate use of the mother tongue versus dogmatic avoidance of the mother tongue;
- Foreign language teaching only for very gifted pupils versus foreign language teaching for all pupils.

Germany today is a country with about 82 million inhabitants and an area of 356,854 square miles. The country consists of 16 federal states reaching from the North Sea and Baltic Sea to the Alps. The official language is German, which exists as standard German and as a large number of regional and local accents and dia-

[1] I would like to thank Nadja Lother (Braunschweig) for the preparatory research she did for this paper and Elizabeth White (York, England) for checking and improving my English.

lects. Furthermore, there is a Danish minority in Schleswig-Holstein, the federal state next to Denmark, and a Sorb minority in the federal states of Brandenburg and Saxony. Another language spoken in parts of the federal states of Lower Saxony and Schleswig-Holstein is "Friesisch" (sometimes also referred to as a variety of "Plattdeutsch"). Due to considerable processes of migration and immigration to Germany over the past 40 years, the number of non-German inhabitants has risen to 7,297,000. These demographic changes have had a considerable impact and contributed to a hitherto unknown linguistic and cultural variation in Germany.

Until the 1960s, English was taught as a foreign language in schools mainly for educational purposes, and to a far lesser extent, to enable pupils to communicate with native speakers of the language. However, due to its growing use as a global language, English is employed more and more as a means of communication among nonnative speakers of English. Furthermore, several scientific journals brought out in Germany are published entirely in English (e.g. *Clinical Chemistry and Laboratory Medicine, Foreign Language Studies,* and *Psychological Research/Psychologische Forschung*).

History of English Language Teaching (ELT) in Germany

The history of ELT in German-speaking areas[2] goes back to the 17th century. However, verifiable beginnings of learning English in noninstitutional settings dates back to the Middle Ages, when, for instance, the language was learnt by people from cities that belonged to the Hanseatic League (e.g. Bremen, Hamburg, and Lübeck), in order to trade with merchants from England. By the end of the 16th century, French, Spanish and Italian were established at German universities whereas English played only a minor role; it was first taught at the University of Greifswald, in the state of Mecklenburg-West Pomerania, near the Baltic Sea, in 1669. Just 1 year later, lessons were introduced at the "Ritterakademie" (academy for knights) in Wolfenbüttel, in the state of Lower Saxony. The aim of such teaching was utilitarian, and the *Sprachmeister* (language teachers), who often also taught dancing and fencing, worked without textbooks and grammar books. Instead, in their teaching, they used model phrases and sentences that the students had to repeat, assuming that by applying such practice the students would automatically develop the rules of the foreign language. As French had been the European *lingua franca* of the 17th and 18th centuries, it was mostly taught in schools, along with Latin, Greek, Spanish, Italian, and, only occasionally, English. The first private lessons in English at school date back to 1669, when it was taught at the grammar school in Corbach (modern Korbach), in the state of Hesse (Sauer, 1979).

With reference to the universities in the German-speaking area, it was above all the University of Göttingen, in the state of Lower Saxony, that, in the 18th century, took a strong interest in the study of English language and culture, and also in edu-

---

[2]This article focuses on those German-speaking areas that belong to Germany today.

cating teachers of English. This development occurred mainly as a result of the union between the kingdoms of Hanover[3] and England, which was initiated in 1714. Around 1860, chairs, including chairs in French and English, were established at the universities. "Anglistik" (English philology) became an autonomous subject with separate chairs in 1872. The discipline of "Anglistik" grew very quickly, and the needs of schools were taken into account by placing greater emphasis on practical language training. One should bear in mind, however, that it was above all Latin and Greek that dominated the German grammar schools, which were also called humanistic schools. In 1859, English became the third language in Prussia[4] after Latin and French in the modern secondary schools ("Real-und höhere Bürgerschulen"), and in 1870 a law was passed in the city of Hamburg to introduce the language as a school subject in all public schools. Throughout the 19th century, however, French remained the dominant modern language at school.

Until the end of the 18th century, English was mainly taught by native English-speaking teachers, who focused on the mastery of oral and written skills. Later on in the 19th century, great importance was attached to grammar, translation, and classical English literature lessons. In this period, it was above all the high regard for Shakespeare and the translations of his works into German that contributed to the growing esteem of English.

From 1900 onwards, English could be chosen as a third obligatory language instead of French at the humanistic (grammar) school, following Latin and Greek. In the early 1920s, English even became the main compulsory modern language in Bavaria, Brunswick[5] and Hamburg with some other parts of Germany following later. In the course of the 1920s, Spanish became a serious competitor to French, which added to the confusion about language preference. As a result, in 1931, Prussia decided to reinstate French as the first language in the modern secondary schools; other parts of Germany followed. Owing to the alleged common Germanic origin and because of the great historical achievements attributed to the British Empire, the National Socialists determined a positive picture of England in the school curricula and made English the main foreign language in 1937, thus displacing French again (Mugdan & Paprotté, 1983).

The objectives for teaching and learning foreign languages, as well as the order in which they were taught and the actual teaching methods, were strongly influenced by World War I and World War II and the debates about methods before World War I. As a consequence, in the 1920s, the teaching of English and French focused on mediating the cultures ("Kulturkundebewegung") of the respective countries. Initially, the main aim of such cultural studies was to find out more about the foreign country and gain a better understanding of it. Subsequently, the insights into the foreign culture were used to provide a framework

---

[3]George I was a Hanoverian king; today Hanover is the capital of the federal state of Lower Saxony.
[4]The state of Prussia was abolished in 1946.
[5]Brunswick (Braunschweig), a former duchy, is today a city in Lower Saxony and home of the oldest technical university in Germany, founded in 1745.

for the analysis and better understanding of one's own culture. Ultimately, after the National Socialists had seized power in Germany, the comparison between foreign and German culture was misused in order to demonstrate the supposed superiority of the German culture.

After World War II, in order to communicate with members of the occupying powers, mastery of foreign languages assumed a very important if not existential role in Germany, which had been divided into four zones: American, British, French and Russian. Depending on the zone, English, French, or Russian was the language most used. Because reeducation of German society was a common aim of the occupying powers, the study of modern languages was encouraged to proceed without prejudice against the cultures associated with them. The first foreign language to be taught was usually the language spoken by one of the four occupying powers. When it emerged that there would be two German states, one with strong ties to the West and one with strong ties to the Soviet Union, it became obvious that this was to have an impact on the status and the study of English. Although English was displaced by Russian as the first foreign language in the German Democratic Republic (East Germany), it was generally taught as the first foreign language in the Federal Republic of Germany (West Germany). In 1957, English became an optional second foreign language alongside French in East Germany. On the whole, English could only be taught and learned there under relatively unfavorable conditions, and students of English in East Germany had practically no opportunity to visit the countries of their target language (Christ & Hüllen, 1995). However, after the reunification of Germany in 1990, a phase of political change began in the eastern part, and, very soon, English became the first foreign language and displaced Russian.

The western part of Germany was strongly affected by the federal system, but the most important regulations applying to all the states of West Germany were stated in two conventions and in the resolutions of the Standing Conference of the *Kultusministerkonferenz* (Standing Conference of the Ministers of Education) for all federal states. At the Convention of Düsseldorf in 1955, it was agreed that, as a rule, English should be the first foreign language taught in the upper grades of grammar schools. Following the Convention of Hamburg in 1964, English became the main obligatory foreign language in all types of secondary schools.

In the 1960s and early 1970s, textbooks, which were very much influenced by the ideas and ideology of the language laboratory, followed audiolingual and audiovisual approaches. During this period, however, strong criticism was leveled against foreign language classes that were dominated by teachers and media. As a consequence, the learners' individuality and needs came into focus, and the acquisition of communicative and social skills was propagated and implemented. In foreign language teaching, this led to the application of the concept of *communicative competence* and to the introduction of the *communicative approach* (see the seminal book by Piepho, 1974). Due to the rapid increase in intercultural encounters, which arose largely from migration and political changes in Eastern Europe, the concept of intercultural communicative competence has been further developed. It emphasizes how different cultural backgrounds can be a source of misunderstandings and communication breakdowns, and aims to prepare learners accordingly.

According to a well-known scheme that distinguishes among English as a native, a second, and a foreign language (see, e.g., Kachru, 1992), English used in Germany has generally been classified as a foreign language. However, the widespread and rapidly increasing use of English in Germany indicates that, as in Scandinavia and the Netherlands, the language is on its way to becoming a second language. The development of English as a second language in Germany is especially noticeable in recent innovations such as introducing English into primary schools, and using English in secondary schools as a medium of communication in nonlanguage subjects such as history and politics, and the sciences.

THE ELT CURRICULUM

English is undoubtedly the main foreign language taught in primary and secondary schools today. Very few schools start out with another foreign language, and all pupils are obliged to learn English at some stage in their school education. Fundamental points of the curricula are similar at all teaching levels because they have been developed and scheduled by the Standing Conference of the Ministers of Education and Cultural Affairs for the federal German states. The following sections summarize the curricula for the different school types on primary and secondary levels and give an overview of the tertiary sector.

For several years, English has been growing more and more popular in primary education. This development is very much a result of the European integration process and the need for a European *lingua franca*.[6] English is even taught in some nursery schools, but does not usually begin until primary school. Until now, it has not been compulsory, and there is no federal state in which every primary school has English as a subject. However, great efforts are being made to offer English in all primary schools, particularly because other countries in the European Union (Luxembourg, Norway, Austria, etc.) have already introduced an obligatory foreign language into the primary curriculum (Eurydice, 2001).

Because the Standing Conference of Ministers of Education has agreed that English should become a compulsory subject, all federal states have now started to develop English as a Foreign Language (EFL) curricula for primary schools. However, the number of English lessons taught per week varies among the individual federal states and the primary schools in them. The main emphasis is placed on listening and speaking, and the raising of linguistic and cultural awareness is also part of the curriculum, especially when the pupils are of multilingual and multicultural backgrounds.

---

[6]According to European language policy and language legislation, there exists no official *lingua franca* in Europe. In practice, however, English fulfills this function. For cultural and political reasons, the Council of Europe has adopted a policy in favor of *pluralingualism,* which means that European pupils and citizens should be enabled to communicate in at least two foreign languages.

Overall, English in primary schools can be characterized by the following features: playful approach, integrated and holistic learning, learning with all senses, and no graded assessment of performance.

With regard to EFL in secondary schools, English can be taught up to 5 hours a week. On the whole, the common objective of EFL, especially in the upper- secondary schools, is to give pupils the opportunity to increase and intensify their communicative skills. English is, above all, seen as an instrument for international and intercultural communication.

Being able to communicate in situations in everyday life can be listed as the major objective of English teaching in the *Hauptschule* (school for pupils with lower abilities). Main situations and topics include school, eating out, shopping, family, friends, leisure activities, jobs, and traveling. Specific information about English-speaking countries, culture, and people is only dealt with to a very limited extent.

The aims of teaching English in the *Gymnasium* (grammar or humanistic schools) are more complex. The ability to communicate in everyday situations is certainly very important, but emphasis is also placed on studying literary and nonliterary texts and on developing the pupils' ability to explain themselves in oral and written discourse. The upper-secondary school level (grades 11 through 13) is part of the academic structure of grammar schools, certain comprehensive schools, and certain technical secondary schools specializing in technology, commerce, and business studies. Depending on the type of course students take, English can be learned in basic courses ("Grundkurs"), which consist of about 3 school hours per week, and extension courses ("Leistungskurs") of 5 hours per week. If English is taken as an extension course, it is a written and oral part of the school graduation examination. In grades 11 through 13, authentic texts of various literary sources are read, and the history, geography, and economy of English-speaking countries are studied in some detail.

The *Realschule* is another type of secondary school, in which pupils stay for 4 or 6 years depending on the federal state. When pupils leave the *Realschule* at age 16, they can start a 3-year apprenticeship with a company, or they can move on to upper-secondary education if their achievements and results are appropriate. Therefore, the objectives of the English curriculum focus on communication skills, but pupils should also gain some knowledge of English-speaking countries, and develop a positive attitude to work, so that they will be able to go to a vocational school or continue their studies at an upper-secondary school. The *Gesamtschule* (comprehensive school) includes the school types Hauptschule, Realschule and Gymnasium, and in it the English curriculum has to somehow find a compromise with respect to the objectives of the three school types. If an upper secondary level is added, the objectives of the grammar schools' upper level (years 11 to 13) are valid. The *Sonderschule* (special school for pupils with disabilities), which has its own English curriculum, includes both the primary and the secondary level. The objectives in the ELT at these schools are defined with regard to the pupils' abilities.

ELT in the tertiary sector takes place in vocational schools, universities, adult-education classes, further training in general and on-the-job training. A binding curriculum for English developed by the Ministry of Education for particular federal states exists only for the vocational schools. A common objective of all tertiary-level English teaching and learning is the ability to communicate fairly fluently in English. Students also gather information on cultural, economic, geographical, or social topics to support the linguistic and communicative objectives.

The university sector can be subdivided into a number of fields: the study of "Anglistik" to become a teacher, translator, or lecturer; English in language centers as supplementary, very often nonvocational language training; and English for special purposes, such as engineering, technology, or business studies. Furthermore, there are English-speaking study courses in the natural sciences, economics, engineering, and other subjects designed to attract foreign students to German universities. These courses, which have only been in existence for a very short time, can lead to a B.A., B.S., M.A., or a M.S. degree. Also of note are the recently founded international universities in Germany, where English is the overall campus language.

In university language centers, English is a language with a great range of different courses. With respect to their abilities and interests, students can choose from courses in different levels of English and courses with a special focus on speaking, writing, or technical or business English. Often, subjects such as engineering and business studies require language for special purposes classes in at least one language; in the majority of cases, that language is English. For those who want to study abroad, courses are offered to prepare for the Test of English as a Foreign Language (TOEFL) or the Cambridge Certificate of Proficiency.

Further training of English in companies is quite common and big companies often have their own language center or provide language software and appropriate computers for their employees. English courses can be divided into two forms: they can take place as long-term programs that meet once or twice a week at a certain time, or as intensive courses that last for 1 or 2 weeks with several lessons per day.

Language teachers are educated in university degree programs and admission requirement to such programs is based on certification that one has passed the upper secondary school leaving examination ("*Abitur*"). Teacher education and teacher training can be split into two stages: the first stage, which includes a fair amount of theoretical knowledge relating to the study of English philology as well as to psychology and to pedagogy, focuses on teacher education, and ends with a state-administered examination that is the prerequisite to the *Vorbereitungsdienst* (preparatory service, teaching practice). The second stage of training takes place in so-called *Studienseminare,* teacher-training centers set up by the Ministries of Education and detached from universities. This training period lasts between 18 and 24 months, depending on the school type one wants to teach in and on the federal state. During this time, the trainee teachers stay in one or more schools and have to teach the subjects that they have studied.[7] The number of lessons taught is between 10 to 14 per week. Once or twice a week the teacher trainees have to attend seminars in their chosen subjects. Seminars on the teaching of English are devoted to foreign-language pedagogy, methodology, and the practical use of media and technology in language teaching.

In primary schools, every teacher is allowed to teach English, even those who have not studied the language. If a generalist teacher lacks English language skills because (s)he has not studied the language, a teacher from lower- or upper- secondary level can be called in to teach English at the primary level (Eurydice, 2001). Although future primary-level English teachers focus on pedagogic studies in addition to language studies, future English teachers in lower- and especially upper-secondary education pursue more content-oriented language studies. Both kinds of study include teaching practice, which is part of teacher training in every federal state.

In-service training can be used to brush up on the English language and get to know new technologies and new English teaching methods. Courses are offered by regional or local authorities, by universities, and often by publishing companies that deal especially with schoolbooks and literary and nonliterary texts adapted for teaching purposes.

The proportion of native English-speaking teachers in the national school sector is not very high, probably because of the civil-servant status that teachers have in Germany. More people from abroad teach in universities, private schools, or institutes like the *Volkshochschule,* because these are less complicated to get into than the state school sector.

Employing a language assistant is another way in which schools can engage a native English speaker in their teaching. These assistants, who have often studied German in their home countries, work in one or more schools for approximately 9 months. Most English language assistants are employed in secondary schools, especially the "Gymnasium".

BECOMING AN ENGLISH TEACHER

Born in 1946, I grew up in a small village in the north of Germany, where I attended the local school for 4 years. The school consisted of one large room, in which one very skillful and caring teacher taught about 40 pupils of nine different ages and abilities simultaneously. When I was at the school, there were certainly no English classes for the very young pupils like myself. Anyway, in the early 1950s, particularly in the rural parts of Germany, hardly anybody, parents or pupils, could imagine themselves in a position in which they could benefit from competence in or knowledge about English. Obviously, this state of affairs had an impact on most pupils' attitude toward the subject and on their motivation to learn the language.

From the age of 10 onwards, I attended a grammar school in Kiel, and English immediately became my favorite subject. To a large extent, this was due to my Eng-

---

[7]Future teachers have to study at least two, sometimes three subjects.

lish teacher, who—as I found out later on—had spent a fair amount of time in Britain and had an excellent command of the language. In addition, he was also very much interested in the emotional and physical well-being of his pupils and how this might affect their learning.

At the age of 16, I took part in an exchange programme between the cities of Kiel and Coventry, England, which were both heavily destroyed during the war, and which became twin towns in the late 1950s. This was my first visit to an English-speaking country, and the beginning of my lasting interest in and fascination with Britain, the English language, and its culture(s).

Because of this history, it was natural for me to want to become a teacher of English, and, consequently, I embarked on the study of English (and German) philology at the University of Kiel in 1966. From 1968 through 1969, I was able to participate in an exchange programme between the University of Kiel and the City University of New York, in the United States. I spent a year at Queens College, also in the United States, where I took part in postgraduate courses in English language and literature, and where I also worked as a German instructor, teaching introductory German courses to undergraduates. I had had no previous training in the teaching of German as a foreign language, but I think I got on all right, especially because the students were about the same age as I was and the teaching—in spite of the marking and grading—took place in a very friendly atmosphere. However, looking back at this experience, and from the perspective of a native German-speaking teacher, I feel that I probably quite often underestimated the learning problems of my students. I was a lot more aware of these problems when teaching English to native German-speaking learners later on.

Although I was invited to stay another year in the United States, I decided to return to Germany and then to get to know another English-speaking university environment. After my return from New York, I spent one highly interesting year at the English department of the University of Stuttgart, which was a new department with lots of possibilities and scope for the students to develop their own ideas. In 1970, I applied to the British Council for a scholarship and I was privileged to be awarded one that enabled me to attend the M.A. course in Modern English Language at University College, London. In 1975, I completed my Ph.D. thesis on aspects of connected speech at the University of Kiel. After a 2-year research contract for a phonetics project at Kiel University, I was appointed lecturer in the English Department of the University of Hanover. Because most of our students wanted to become teachers of English, it was quite natural for me to take this into consideration in the planning of my lectures and seminars.

In 1978, my growing interest in making language and linguistics applicable to teacher education made me take up a post in English language and applied linguistics at the Hanover Institute of Education, in Germany. My teaching load included courses in applied linguistics, language teaching methodology, and practical language classes, and all these courses had to be made meaningful to my students, who were prospective teachers of English. In addition to holding classes and doing research, a fair amount of my work in this job was devoted to the supervision of students' teaching. This took place during term time 1 day per week or during the college vacation, when it is, of course, much easier for the students to get a more concentrated and realistic taste for their future jobs. For me, this meant being able to spend a lot of time in schools, working together with teachers of English and with my students. This kind of cooperation has always been very beneficial to me because it has continually made me adjust my own teaching to bring it more in line with the demands of the school context.

In 1991, I was appointed chair of English linguistics and applied linguistics at the University of Paderborn. This post was similar to my previous one, but also involved my being in charge of the university language centre and being responsible for the integration of English for specific purposes and other language classes into degree courses in engineering and business studies. In 1996, I was offered the post of chair of English language and applied linguistics at the Technical University of Braunschweig. This post gives me the opportunity to concentrate fully on English teacher education at the primary and secondary school levels. Because my present job allows me to cooperate with colleagues from the English Department and the School of Education as well as with English teachers from neighbouring schools, I have become more and more convinced of the desirability of a teacher education programme in which representatives of language, linguistics, literature, cultural studies, as well as practicing teachers and representatives of education, psychology, and sociology, all have their proper say.

CONCLUSION

After a long period of confusion about language priorities during the 19th and the first half of the 20th century, English has become the foreign language to be taught in most schools in Germany. The development of English teaching started fairly slowly and seemed to be stagnating at some points after World War II. However, it is growing rapidly now and it is one of the most important subjects at secondary schools and is becoming more and more an obligatory subject at the primary level, too. A wide range of English courses is offered at the tertiary level and teacher education seems to be slowly modifying and adapting to the new developments.

To sum up, one can say that the status of English is still changing in Germany, especially with respect to its use as a lingua franca. Different and complementary priorities have to be set in teaching and in English teacher education in order to better fit the linguistic and intercultural requirements of globalization (see Gnutzmann, 1999). On the other hand, owing to the bilateral relationships between Germany and the United Kingdom, the United States, and other countries in which English is spoken as a native language, it is also important to consider the function of English as a foreign language. With regard to teacher education and the teaching of English in schools, this means that a sustainable balance will have to be found between culture-detached uses of the language (i.e., in its use as a lingua franca), and its culture-embedded use as a foreign language (i.e., its use as a means of communication with native speakers of English).

REFERENCES

Christ, H., & Hüllen, W. (1995). *Geschichte des Fremdsprachenunterrichts seit 1945* [The history of foreign language teaching since 1945]. In K. R. Bausch, H. Christ, & H. J. Krumm (Eds.), *Handbuch Fremdsprachenunterricht* [Handbook for the teaching of foreign languages] (pp. 565–572). Tübingen, Basel: Francke.

Eurydice [The Information Network on Education in Europe]. (2001). *Foreign language teaching in schools in Europe.* Brussels: Les Éditions Européennes.

Gnutzmann, C. (1999). English as a global language. Perspectives for English language teaching and for teacher education in Germany. In C. Gnutzmann (Ed.), *Teaching and learning English as a global language: Native and non-native perspectives* (pp.157–169). Tubingen, Germany: Stauffenburg.

Kachru, B. (1992). World Englishes: Approaches, issues and resources. *Language Teaching,* *25*(1), 1–14.

Mugdan, J., & Paprotté, W. (1983). *Zur Geschichte des Faches Englisch als Exempel für eine moderne Fremdsprache* [The history of the school subject English as an example of a foreign language]. In A. Mannzmann (Ed.), *Geschichte der Unterrichtsfacher I. Deutsch, Englisch, Franzosisch, Russisch, Latein, Griechisch, Musik, Kunst* [The history of school subjects I. German, English, French, Russian, Latin, Greek, Music, Art.] (pp. 65–93). Munich, Germany: Kosel.

Piepho, H. E. (1974). *Kommunikative Kompetenz als übergeordnetes Lernziel im Englischunterricht* [Communicative competence: Superordinate learning target in the teaching of English]. Dornburg-Frickhofen: Frankonius.

Sauer, H. (1979). *Englisch als Schulfach in erziehungswissenschaftlicher, historischer und internationaler Perspektive* [English as a school subject: Pedagogical, historical and international perspectives]. In H. Hunfeld, & K. Schroder (Eds.), *Grundkurs Didaktik Englisch* [Introduction to the teaching of English as a foreign language] (pp. 27–39). Konigstein, Germany: Scriptor.

4

ENGLISH LANGUAGE TEACHING IN HONG KONG SPECIAL ADMINISTRATIVE REGION (HKSAR): A CONTINUOUS CHALLENGE

Icy Lee
Hong Kong Baptist University, Hong Kong

Hong Kong has a good reputation internationally as a successful commercial and financial center. Amazingly, for a tiny region of 1,092 square kilometers situated on the southeastern coastline of China, Hong Kong has a massive population of 6.6 million people. About 98% of the population is ethnic Chinese and the rest are a variety of nationalities such as American, British and Indian. The territory was first administered as a Crown Colony of Britain in 1842. On June 30, 1997, the colonial rule ended and sovereignty was returned to China, and Hong Kong became a SAR of China, officially known as Hong Kong SAR. English and Chinese are Hong Kong's two official languages. Because the majority of the population in Hong Kong is ethnic Chinese, the Cantonese dialect is "the language of the home, the street and the entertainment media" (Education Commission, 1994, p.15).

When Hong Kong was still a British colony, English played a predominant role in the government, business, professional sectors, and in higher education as well. Therefore, English was considered a "symbol of power" (Cheung, 1984, p. 278). Its unusual status was referred to by Luke and Richards (1982, p. 55) as an "auxiliary language," being neither a second nor a foreign language. With the increasing importance of Chinese and Putonghua after the political change of Hong Kong from a British colony to an SAR of China, it has been argued that English is increasingly a foreign language in Hong Kong (Falvey, 1998). Nonetheless, given Hong Kong's strategic position as an international center, it is unlikely that English will diminish in its importance. English still plays an important role in the business sector, in the workplace, and especially in higher education.

HISTORY OF ENGLISH LANGUAGE TEACHING (ELT) IN HONG KONG SAR

The beginning of English language education in Hong Kong dates back to 1842, the year in which Hong Kong was ceded to Britain, when the Morrison Education Society School was established. The Morrison School, which aimed to provide bilingual education for the Chinese, was founded on the belief that English education was a "central element in the development of critical and creative thinking" (Evans, 1998, p. 23).

In the first 100 years of British colonial rule (1842 to 1941), Hong Kong schools were divided into two streams: the Anglo–Chinese stream and the Chinese stream. The Anglo–Chinese stream provided English-medium education based on a Western style, whereas the Chinese-medium stream offered a "Chinese" style of education similar to that of the mainland. Since the introduction of English- medium education in Hong Kong, there has existed a better balance between the English and Chinese streams at the secondary than at the primary level (see Education Department, 1955–1997). In 1955, for example, 54% of secondary schools were English-medium while only 10% of primary schools were English-medium (Education Department, 1955–1997). Between the 1950s and 1990s, more and more secondary schools switched to English as their medium of instruction. The Education Department's[1] survey findings (1955–1997) show that the percentage of English-medium secondary schools increased from 54% in 1955, to 68% in 1965, to 80% in 1975, to 91% in 1985, and to 94% in 1997. At the primary level, the situation was reverse, because there was a slight decrease in the percentage of English-medium schools from 10% in 1955 to 7% in 1997. Nonetheless, a great deal of importance has been attached to the learning of English at primary level, because a good command of English is regarded as a prerequisite for entry into English-medium secondary schools. In fact, the majority of parents opt for English-medium education for their children (Evans, 2000; So, 1992).

Ironically, despite the expansion of English-medium instruction, there have been more and more complaints about students' falling English standards since the 1980s. Grave concerns have been expressed by the government, business and commerce sectors, and educational bodies about the declining English-language standards. One culprit often quoted in the 1980s was the substitution of mixed-code teaching for English-medium teaching in a large number of secondary schools: that is, teachers switching between and mixing English and Cantonese in classroom instruction and interaction (see Johnson, 1983; Johnson & Lee, 1987).

---

[1]The Education Department in Hong Kong is currently referred to as the Education and Manpower Bureau.

The 14,000 English language teaching force in Hong Kong is notorious for its overall lack of training (see Coniam & Falvey, 1999b; Falvey, 1995). Recent surveys of the qualifications of English language teachers in Hong Kong show that only about 14% of secondary teachers of English are both subject and professionally trained (see Coniam & Falvey, 1996, 1999a, 1999b; Tsui, 1993), this is, possessing a relevant English degree and a Postgraduate Diploma/Certificate in Education majoring in English. In primary schools, a large number of English teachers are nondegree holders (see Lee, 1996). About 43% of them have no relevant degree and no relevant teacher training (Standing Committee on Language Education and Research; SCOLAR, 2003). However, it was only in June 2003 that an announcement was made about entry qualifications of new English teachers starting from September 2004 (SCOLAR, 2003). A professionally qualified English teacher, according to the announcement, would have to possess either a Bachelor of Education degree, majoring in English, or a relevant English major degree plus a Postgraduate Diploma or Certificate in Education majoring in English.

In line with its policy to upgrade the English teaching profession in Hong Kong, the government has also introduced the idea of language benchmarks, referred to as the Language Proficiency Requirement (LPR), to set the standards of language proficiency expected of English teachers. The objective of LPR is to make sure that all English teachers possess the minimum proficiency to teach English (i.e., Level 3 out of 5 levels), and to encourage them to strive for higher levels of language proficiency (i.e., Levels 4 and 5). It is expected that from the 2000–2001 school year, all new teachers will be required to meet the LPR. By 2006, all serving language teachers must also have met the LPR (Education Department, 2001).

Since 1988, the government has encouraged the hiring of native English teachers, under the Expatriate English Teachers' Scheme (EET), to teach English in secondary schools in Hong Kong. In 1997, in response to local teachers' falling English standards and in order to enhance the quality of English language teaching, the government began to invest more money in the recruitment of native speakers to teach English in Hong Kong. The EET scheme was renamed as the Native-English Speaking Teachers Scheme (NET), and a greater number of native-English speaking teachers, known as NETs locally, have been recruited to teach English in secondary schools (Education Department, 2002). The main aim of the NET scheme is to upgrade students' English language proficiency. Now each secondary school has one NET recruited by the government (or more hired by schools of their own accord). In 2000, 20 NETs were recruited to 40 primary schools to help implement a Primary Schools English Development Pilot Project. In the project, the NETs collaborated with local teachers in teaching and organizing English activities, and they contributed to materials writing and school-based teacher development programs. In September 2002, the NET scheme was extended to all primary schools in Hong Kong, with two primary schools sharing one NET.

Other expatriates playing a significant role in ELT in Hong Kong are from the British Council (BC). The BC serves both English teachers and the general public. It organizes seminars and workshops for local English teachers to help enhance their teaching competence. The BC English Language Center, which was established in 1976, provides English language courses and related services for the general public, mainly focusing on practical communication skills. The Council also collaborates with the Hong Kong Institute of Education to enable student teachers of English to go on a short study trip to England. Although Hong Kong is no longer a British colony, the British Council is likely to play an important role in ELT in the territory.

THE ELT CURRICULUM

In Hong Kong, English is an important part of the school curriculum from kindergarten. Students start learning English when they enter preschool. In primary and secondary schools (6 years and 7 years, respectively), English is taught as a compulsory subject. The universities in Hong Kong adopt English as their official medium of instruction, with the exception of the Chinese University of Hong Kong, which is the only bilingual university in the territory. At university level, English language-enhancement programs are provided for university students irrespective of their majors to help strengthen their English skills. The following section focuses on the primary and secondary curriculums in Hong Kong.

Within each school, there is an English subject panel headed by the panel chairperson. In secondary schools, there are usually two panel chairpersons, one in charge of lower forms and the other in charge of senior forms. In primary schools, the planning of the English language subject is more of a collaborative effort of the school head, the panel chairperson, level coordinators and all other English teachers in the same school, although the panel chairperson is the one who carries out the actual implementation with the assistance of level coordinators and all English teachers (see Curriculum Development Council, 1999).

The Education Department recommended seven to eight periods per week to be allocated to the teaching of English at secondary level (each period lasting 40 to 45 minutes; Curriculum Development Council, 1999). For primary schools, the minimum number of lessons recommended for Primary 1 to Primary 6 range from five to eight periods (each period being 35 minutes long), but schools can increase or decrease the number of lessons according to their students' needs (Curriculum Development Council, 1997). In many schools, the learning of English is rigidly compartmentalized into different components, such as dictation, oral, listening, grammar, reading and writing.

The majority of schools adopt commercially available course books for English language teaching. In fact, Hong Kong teachers have been criticized as heavily textbook-bound, because many teachers rely only on course books (see, e.g., Morris et al., 1999). The government encourages a wide variety of resources for English language teaching. In 1997, the Education Department set up the Hong Kong Extensive Reading Scheme (HKERS), which enables schools to buy a variety of English books, magazines, and multimedia reading materials to en-

courage extensive reading. The Education Department also encourages the incorporation of information technology (IT) in English language teaching. Schools
are provided with funding to purchase computers and educational software to
promote IT in English language teaching.

Assessment is very much part of the curriculum in Hong Kong schools. The
Hong Kong Certificate of Education Examination (HKCEE) was introduced in
the 1930s for students at the end of Form 5 (grade 11). Those who achieve better
results go on to Form 6 (grade 12). At the end of Form 7 (grade 13), students take
another public examination called the Hong Kong Advanced Level Examination
(HKALE), which is the university-entrance examination. In both examinations,
the English language is a crucial subject. The assessment of the English language
subject is demanding, as students are required to take separate examinations in
speaking, listening, writing, and an integrated paper that tests the integration of
skills. In Hong Kong, the washback effect of public examinations is that teachers
busy themselves with 'covering the syllabus' and preparing students for public
examinations by giving them a large dosage of examination practice, model answers, examination tips, and so forth. It is felt that any innovative approaches are
doomed to failure because of the exam-oriented learning culture, not to mention
other debilitating factors such as large class size and English teachers' heavy
workloads (see, e.g. Evans, 1996).

The exam-oriented culture in the classroom is exacerbated by the fact that students in Hong Kong adopt an extremely passive approach to learning. Teaching
and learning is characterized by a focus on knowledge transmission, where classroom interaction is largely dominated by the teachers. In English lessons, teacher-
fronted presentations and explanations are predominant. In lower-band schools,[2]
English lessons are often conducted in a mixture of English and Cantonese, while
students almost always interact in Cantonese. Outside the classroom, English is
rarely used, perhaps except in some English-medium schools where a conscious effort is made to create an ethos of speaking English. Therefore, English is perceived
as a dry and boring subject learnt for instrumental purposes, chiefly to pass examinations. There exists a wide gap between the ideal represented by the official policy
recommended by the Education Department on one hand, and actual classroom
practices, on the other.

The English language curriculum in primary and secondary schools is drawn up
by the Curriculum Development Council (CDC), whose membership includes
heads of schools, lecturers from tertiary institutions, officers of the Hong Kong Examinations Authority and staff from different divisions of the Education Department. The teaching of English in Hong Kong schools is based on the English
language syllabuses recommended by the CDC.

---

[2]According to the Secondary School Places Allocation System, students were previously allocated
to secondary schools divided into 5 bands based on their academic performance, but the 5 bands have
been reduced to 3 bands to avoid the labeling effect.

In the 1960s and 1970s, the teaching of English in Hong Kong was characterized by a form-focused approach. The English syllabus for secondary schools (Curriculum Development Committee, 1975) advocated an oral-structural approach that emphasized the repetitive drilling of structural patterns, with the focus shifted from the written to spoken form. In the 1980s there were major attempts to revise the English language syllabuses (see Curriculum Development Committee, 1981, 1983) to incorporate communicative language teaching (CLT) into the curriculum. The revised syllabuses, which were implemented in the late 1980s, were the result of a realization that focusing on language forms failed to help students use the forms appropriately in real situations, and that "meaningful use of the language for the purpose of communication represents an essential element in successful language learning" (Curriculum Development Committee, 1983, p. 15).

The major shift of emphasis from the traditional teacher-centered approach to a communicative approach, however, has been criticized as inappropriate and unduly imposed on teachers without adequate support from local research. In reality, the CLT syllabuses are put aside by teachers, as many schools prefer to "concentrate on the formal features of the language at the expense of encouraging students to use the language" (Education Commission, 1994, p.25). Overall, the impact of CLT can be described as negligible (Evans, 1996). Within the exam-oriented education system in Hong Kong, learning English through a communicative approach is regarded as time consuming and unproductive.

Despite teachers' failure to realize the theoretical ideal of CLT at the classroom level, another major curriculum reform was initiated by the government in the early 1990s. Known as the Target-Oriented Curriculum (TOC), the new curriculum has been regarded as "the most comprehensive and radical attempt at curriculum reform ever taken in Hong Kong" (Cheung & Ng, 2000, p. 112). Under TOC, the English curriculum (together with Chinese and mathematics) has been reconceptualized to include 'targets' as its major focus: to develop students' ever-improving capability to use English to (a) think and communicate; (b) acquire, develop, and apply knowledge; and (c) respond and give expression to experience. (see Curriculum Development Council, 1997, 1999). TOC advocates a task-based approach, which emphasizes "learning to communicate through purposeful interaction in the target language" (Curriculum Development Council, 1999, p. 41).

The new curriculum also promotes holistic, learner-centered learning, and criterion-referenced assessment to replace the long-existing academic, teacher- and textbook-centered approach to learning that is dictated by competitive and norm-referenced assessment. The entire TOC is divided into several key stages covering Primary 1 (U.S. grade 1) to the Sixth Form (Grades 12 and 13), with each stage being developed from the previous stage and leading on to the next. Key Stages 1 and 2 (Primary grades 1 through 3 and 4 through 6) lay the foundation of English language development through engaging students in interesting activities, while Key Stages 3 and 4 (Secondary grades 1 through 3 and 4 through 5) enable students to apply English for everyday, learning, and developmental purposes. The

Sixth Form focuses on preparing students for the language they need for further study at tertiary level and in the workplace.

Although TOC has been gradually introduced into primary and secondary schools from 1995, local research indicates that the implementation of TOC has met with innumerable obstacles, such as lack of teacher support, teachers' limited understanding of TOC, inadequate in-service teacher education, and a unrealistic implementation schedule (see Carless, 1997; Cheung & Ng, 2000; Lam, 1996).

In spite of the minimal impact of curriculum policy at the implementation level, the wheel of English language education reform has continued to turn. After the oral–structural approach in the 1970s, communicative language teaching in the 1980s, the TOC that advocates task-based teaching in the 1990s, Hong Kong is heading for another major English language education reform in the new century. In a new consultative document, *Learning to Learn,* published by the CDC in 2000 (see Curriculum Development Council, 2000), it is stated that the English language education curriculum should provide learners with "learning experiences to develop their *knowledge, skills, values, and attitudes* [my emphasis] so as to enable them to interact with people and cultures effectively in English and to prepare them for lifelong learning" (Curriculum Development Council, 2000, p. 10). In the new curriculum framework, still target oriented, English teachers are expected to take on a wider range of responsibilities, including helping students develop general and linguistic knowledge and lifelong learning skills, inculcating positive values and attitudes through English language learning. Indeed, the implications of the proposals are profound and far reaching.

BECOMING AN ENGLISH TEACHER

The beginning of my teaching career is neither remarkable nor memorable. At university, I majored in English literature and linguistics, and thinking that there was no other option left for an English major, I decided to become a teacher. I obtained my first teaching job in a Band 1 secondary school in Hong Kong. Although the English syllabus at that time advocated communicative language teaching, I had no inkling of what it entailed. I received my primary and secondary schooling at a time when the emphasis of ELT in Hong Kong was on the form and structure of the English language. Therefore, I learnt English in a very traditional manner—primarily by doing mechanical drills and exercises, and learning and memorizing grammar rules.

Initially, my teaching approaches were based entirely on how I had learnt English as a student. I can still remember how my English lessons were dominated by explanations of vocabulary and grammar and the dictation of meanings of words and grammar rules. Teaching was fine but not exciting; my only consolation came from knowing that my students liked me and thought that I was a good teacher. Seeing the need to upgrade myself, I took a 2-year part-time Diploma in Education course at the Chinese University of Hong Kong in my third year of teaching. The course provided me with opportunities to study new subjects like psychology, sociology, and children's development. In sessions for English majors like myself, I had chances to examine my own teaching philosophy through discussions and I deepened my understanding of English language teaching. In the same year, I attended a British Council summer school for secondary teachers of English and obtained a lot of useful tips on how to organize communicative activities. I began to develop a better grasp of communicative language teaching and how it could be realized in the classroom.

After teaching 5 years at the secondary school, I obtained a job lecturing at the Education Department's Institute of Language in Education (ILE) (currently Hong Kong Institute of Education), which organized in-service refresher courses for primary and secondary teachers. My entry into the ILE marked a significant turning point in my teaching career. My transition from a secondary teacher to a teacher educator was, however, initially difficult and painful. When I first started the job, I was struck with horror at my own ignorance of ELT. I therefore started reading ELT books and articles in ELT journals, and made a great effort to upgrade my knowledge of recent developments in the field. Through self-study, observation of my colleagues' teaching, interactions with in-service teachers, and school visits, my understanding of ELT was immensely enhanced and my horizons greatly broadened.

After working 1 year at the ILE, I decided to do a master's course in Applied Linguistics to upgrade myself professionally. I had a real thirst for knowledge and felt that I was a different teacher than before. I enrolled in the M.A. in Linguistics (TESOL) course provided by the University of Surrey and completed it in a distance-learning mode. I was fully absorbed in the course and derived tremendous pleasure from it. My M.A. supervisor later told me that I completed the course in 'record time'.

After working 4 years at the ILE, I joined the Hong Kong Polytechnic University (HKPU), which marked another turning point in my career. At the HKPU, I taught service English to undergraduate students as well as the M.A. in the ELT course. I began to become more interested in classroom-based research and how I could construct knowledge by researching into my own practice. I decided to enroll in a part-time Ph.D. program at the University of Hong Kong. My doctoral research on the topic of coherence in writing emanated from a genuine problem I faced as a writing teacher. Aside from working on my Ph.D. research, I obtained grants from the HKPU to do some small-scale research projects, all classroom based. I became a determined teacher–researcher, believing in the symbiotic relationship between research and practice (see Smagorinsky & Smith, 1998). As a university teacher, I was convinced that one of my goals was to conduct research on new pedagogy to inform practice. At the HKPU, I continued to develop my expertise in ELT and pursued academic research and publications.

For family reasons, I left the HKPU after 3 years and emigrated to Canada. Although I had a secret wish to pursue my academic career, knowing that I still had a doctoral thesis to finish writing, I knew that at best the kind of job I would be able to get was perhaps an ESL teaching job. One month after I arrived in Canada, I applied to a community college and obtained an ESL teaching job there. My success in the job interview was amazing to a lot of people, given I had no international teaching experience and I was such a new immigrant, not to mention the fact that I am a non-native speaker (NNS) of English. In my third year in Canada, I found another ESL teaching job at Simon Fraser University (SFU), where again I was the only NNS on the small teaching team.

Teaching ESL in Vancouver turned out to be more challenging than teaching in Hong Kong, mainly because students were more assertive and motivated, and hence more demanding. Another reason, in my own case, was that I was the only NNS in my workplace, and so I was in the real minority. Once I was challenged by an Iranian student in a writing class. To cut the story short, I was made to read aloud a sentence by the student illustrating the use of 'however': "Icy is a good teacher; however she has a Chinese accent". This incident was extremely embarrassing but unforgettable and significant in my teaching career because it started me thinking of my own professional identity and my contributions as a NNS (see Lee, 1999). Instead of having a sense of inferiority, I felt more and more certain of my own professional status and contributions as a NNS.

My 3 years in Canada was not eventful in terms of academic pursuits because of the lack of opportunities in the work environment. However, because I had less work and more spare time than before, I was able to complete my doctoral dissertation in a shorter time than I originally expected. Thanks to my professional contacts, I had opportunities to engage in freelance work like writing pedagogical materials for Hong Kong students, reviewing articles for academic journals, and acting as an external examiner for M.A. theses in a Singaporean university.

After 3 years in Canada, I returned to Hong Kong fresh and invigorated. The 3-year absence provided me with the time and space to revitalize myself as a teaching professional. My professional ideals have been renewed and I feel imbued with indefatigable enthusiasm for the profession. I am confident that as a NNS educated and brought up in Hong Kong with a diversity of academic and professional experience, I have a lot to offer to teachers of the new generation. Now as a teacher educator at one of Hong Kong's most well established universities, I firmly believe that I can be a useful agent to help create positive changes in other teachers' lives.

CONCLUSION

In this chapter, I have portrayed EFL teaching in Hong Kong by examining the history of EFL teaching and the structure of the English curriculum, and through depicting my own history and development as an English language educator. Indeed, EFL teaching in Hong Kong is increasingly a challenge fraught with intractable problems. As this chapter has shown, declining English standards of students, falling English standards, and lack of training among English teachers, the controversial benchmarking test, education reforms that call for drastic restructuring of the curriculum, and mounting pressure faced by English professionals have meant that English language teaching is becoming more and more taxing and demanding, especially for frontline educators. Given the strategic importance of English in the territory, Hong Kong simply cannot afford continuing failure in its English language education. I believe that long-term investment must be put to strengthen the entire ELT profession in Hong Kong so that our English language educators are well equipped to brace themselves for the many challenges that lie ahead.

REFERENCES

Carless, D. (1997). Managing systemic curriculum change: A critical analysis of Hong Kong's target-oriented curriculum initiative. *International Review of Education, 43*(4), 349–366.

Cheung, D., & Ng, D. (2000). Teachers' stages of concern about the target-oriented curriculum. *Education Journal, 28*(1), 109–122.

Cheung, Y. S. (1984). The uses of English and Chinese languages in Hong Kong. *Language Learning and Communication, 3,* 273–283.

Coniam, D., & Falvey, P. (1996). *Setting language benchmarks for English language teachers in Hong Kong secondary schools.* Advisory Committee on Teacher Education and Qualifications: Hong Kong.

Coniam, D., & Falvey, P. (1999a). The English language benchmarking initiative: A validation study of the classroom language assessment component. *Asia Pacific Journal of Language in Education, 2*(2), 1–35.

Coniam, D., & Falvey, P. (1999b). Setting standards for teachers of English in Hong Kong: The teachers' perspective. *Curriculum Forum, 8*(2), 1–27.

Curriculum Development Committee. (1975). *Provisional syllabus for English (Forms I-V).* Hong Kong: Government Printer.

Curriculum Development Committee. (1981). *English (Primary 1-6).* Hong Kong: Government Printer.

Curriculum Development Committee. (1983). *Syllabus for English (Forms I-V).* Hong Kong: Government Printer.

Curriculum Development Council. (1997). *Syllabuses for primary schools: English language.* Hong Kong: Education Department.

Curriculum Development Council. (1999). *Syllabuses for secondary schools: English language.* Hong Kong: Education Department.

Curriculum Development Council. (2000). *Learning to learn. Key learning area: English language education. Consultation document.* Hong Kong: Government Printer.

Education Commission. (1994). *Report of the working group on language proficiency.* Hong Kong: Government Printer.

Education Department. (1955–1997). *Annual summary/enrolment survey.* Hong Kong: Government Printer.

Education Department. (2001). Language proficiency requirement for teachers. Available at http://www.ed.gov.hk/aid/english/language/teacher/planning.htm (May 1, 2001).

Education Department. (2002). *Native-speaking English teachers (NET) scheme.* Hong Kong. Available at http://www.ed.gov.hk/chi/highlights.asp?sid=16&cid=71 (July 19, 2002).

Evans, S. (1996). The context of English language education in Hong Kong. *RELC Journal, 27*(2), 30–55.

Evans, S. (1998). The Morrison Education Society School and the beginning of Anglo-Chinese education in Hong Kong. *Hong Kong Journal of Applied Linguistics, 3*(1), 17–40.

Evans, S. (2000). Classroom language use in Hong Kong's English-medium secondary schools. *Educational Research Journal, 15*(1), 19–43.

Falvey, P. (1995). The education of teachers of English in Hong Kong: A case for special treatment. In F. Lopez-Real (Ed.), *Teacher education in the Asian region. Proceedings of International Teacher Education Conference* (ITEC) '95 (pp. 107–113). Hong Kong: Department of Curriculum Studies, The University of Hong Kong.

Falvey, P. (1998). ESL, EFL and language acquisition in the context of Hong Kong. In B. Asker (Ed.), *Teaching language and culture: Building Hong Kong education* (pp. 73–78). Hong Kong: Addison Wesley Longman.

Johnson, R. K. (1983). Bilingual switching strategies: A study of the modes of teacher-talk in bilingual secondary school classrooms in Hong Kong. *Language Learning and Communication, 2,* 267–285.

Johnson, R. K., & Lee, P. (1987). Modes of instruction: Teaching strategies and student responses. In R. Lord & H. Cheng (Eds.), *Language education in Hong Kong* (pp. 99–121). Hong Kong: Chinese University Press.

Lam, C. C. (1996). *Target-oriented curriculum* (Education Policy Studies Series No.1 in Chinese). Hong Kong: The Chinese University of Hong Kong, Hong Kong Institute of Educational Research.

Lee, I. (1996). Hong Kong primary teachers' perspectives on ELT. *Regional English Language Centre (RELC) Journal, 27*(2), 100–117.

Lee, I. (1999, February/March). Can a nonnative speaker be a good English teacher? *TESOL Matters,* p. 19.

Luke, K. K., & Richards, J. (1982). English in Hong Kong: Functions and status. *English World-Wide, 3,* 47–64.

Morris, P., Adamson, R., Chan, K. K., Che, M. W., Chik, P. M. P., Lo, M. L., Mo, P. Y., Kwan, Y. L. T., Mok. A. C., Ng, F. P., & Tong, S. Y. A. (1999). *Target oriented curriculum: Feedback and assessment in Hong Kong primary schools. Final report.* Hong Kong: University of Hong Kong, Faculty of Education.

Smagorinsky, P., & Smith, M. W. (1998). Editors' introduction: Announcing the Alan C. Purves Award: On the impact of educational research. *Research in the Teaching of English, 39*(1), 5–9.

So, D. (1992). Language-based bifurcation of secondary schools in Hong Kong. In K. K. Luke (Ed.), *Into the 21st century: Issues of language in education in Hong Kong* (pp. 69–95). Hong Kong: Linguistic Society of Hong Kong.

Standing Committee on Language Education and Research (SCOLAR). (2003). *Action plans to raise language standards in Hong Kong: Final report of language education review.* Hong Kong: The Printing Department.

Tsui, A. M. B. (1993). *Report to the Hong Kong Language Campaign.* Hong Kong: Hong Kong Language Campaign.

5

FACTS AND BEYOND—
TEACHING ENGLISH IN HUNGARY

Péter Medgyes
Ministry of Education, Hungary

Hungary is a landlocked country in Central Europe, occupying almost the whole of the Carpathian Basin on an area of 35,920 square miles. Because the territory of present-day Hungary has always been a busy crossroads, it has been attacked repeatedly by foreign invaders. Two of the invaders who had major influence were the Turks, who occupied Hungary for 150 years in the 16th and 17th centuries, and the Austrian Hapsburgs. Patriotism, however, could not be suppressed: Hungarians have a history of heroic but tragic uprisings, including the Revolution and War of Independence in 1848–1849. Hungary gained autonomy in 1867, and full independence in World War I.

As a consequence of that war, however, in 1920, some two thirds of the territory of Hungary was annexed to neighboring countries. Hoping to reclaim its lost land, Hungary sided with Nazi Germany in World War II. After the defeat of the Axis powers in 1945, the Soviet liberation army stayed in the country, forcing a communist takeover and the proclamation of the Hungarian People's Republic in 1949. A revolution broke out against dictatorship in 1956, only to be crushed by Soviet tanks. Between 1956 and 1988, Hungary gradually adopted liberal policies and was known popularly as "the happiest barracks behind the Iron Curtain." In 1989, Hungary's communist leaders voluntarily abandoned their monopoly of power, thus facilitating a peaceful shift to a multiparty democracy and free market economy. Since then, there has been an exceptionally long democratic period in the history of Hungary.

Hungary has a population of slightly more than 10 million. Hungarian is spoken by nearly 98% as a first language and, with the exception of foreign nationals residing in Hungary, it is spoken by the entire population. Thus, Hungary may be regarded as a monolingual country where minority languages play an insignificant role (Fenyvesi, 1998).

Hungarian belongs to the Finno-Ugric family of languages and, as such, occupies a unique place in Central Europe; in all the surrounding countries, languages of Indo-European origin are spoken. Thus, Hungarians are not able to communicate with their non-Hungarian neighbors unless they have learnt to speak foreign languages. It is small wonder, therefore, that the knowledge of foreign languages has always been held in high esteem in Hungary; as a Hungarian proverb puts it, "You are as many persons as the number of languages you can speak."

However, according to recent statistical data (Medgyes & Miklósy, 2000), a mere 11.2% of the population aged 18 or above claimed at least to "get by" in one foreign language. The same report also revealed that 90% of secondary-school graduates and 59% of university and college graduates did not manage in any foreign language, a clear indication of the ineffectiveness of foreign-language education. It can only be hoped that, with Hungary's accession to the European Union, the process of growth in foreign language competence will accelerate.

HISTORY OF ELT IN HUNGARY

The teaching and learning of foreign languages in Hungary is deeply rooted in and determined by the political and economic structure of the country. Although Hungary has never had a well-designed language policy, foreign languages have been invariably offered at school, in accordance with overarching national interests.

Because Hungary was under the influence and domination of German-speaking countries until the end of World War II, German was the compulsory foreign language in all schools until the late 1940s. In addition to the "pride of place" granted to German, grammar schools, which catered to students with academic interests, offered two classical languages, Latin and Greek. In vocational schools, on the other hand, which were attended by students who did not intend to go on to higher education, the classical languages were superseded by modern languages, primarily French, followed by English and Italian.

After the country had unwillingly joined the community of Soviet-style dictatorships, Russian was decreed to be the compulsory foreign language in public education. This coincided with the virtual expulsion of all other modern languages from schools, while classical languages were pushed to the periphery. In connection with a process of liberalization after 1956, Western languages gradually crept back into the curriculum, even though their status was "low bordering on subversive" (Gill, 1993, p. 15). With respect to English, this implied that, even in the last year of communist rule, less than 3% of primary (ages 6 to 14) and 16.5% of secondary (ages 15 to 18) school students had access to instruction, in spite of the upsurge of interest in English (Medgyes, 1993).

The methodology of foreign-language teaching in Hungary followed the universal pattern, albeit with some delay. The proverbial swing of the pendulum brought in a series of methods and approaches, with communicative language teaching bringing up the rear in the late 1970s. Although still centrally designed, the curricula produced in the last 10 years of communist rule were increasingly devoid of ideology. Similar signs of "loosening up" showed up in the course books written in Hungary, while glossy teaching materials imported from the United Kingdom not only became increasingly available but also managed to marginalize their less attractive Hungarian counterparts.

And yet, foreign-language teaching and learning was in a pathetic state. Ironically, Russian was the worst off: Despite over 30 years of mandatory Russian instruction, a mere 1.2% of the Hungarian population claimed to speak Russian in the late 1970s. Nevertheless, Russian instruction imperturbably dragged on, depriving other foreign languages of the room they needed for more dynamic development.

Beginning in the early 1980s, in an effort to offset the shortcomings of state-sector education, private and semiprivate language schools were allowed to admit adult and teenage learners. They were immediately flooded by customers who attempted to make up for what they had lost during their formal schooling. Not surprisingly, the most sought-after languages were English and German.

No sooner had Communism collapsed in Hungary in 1989 than the Russian language was officially stripped of its privileged status. Since then, it has been possible for schoolchildren to learn any foreign language they wish, as long as there are teachers available to teach it (I will say more about this later). As a result, the distribution of foreign languages throughout the education system has changed irrevocably: Russian has nose-dived and English and German have risen rapidly. The proportion of Russian learners dropped from 100% to .7% in primary schools, and from 100% to .8% in secondary grammar schools between 1989 and 2000. Currently, German and English are the two most dominant foreign languages, studied by approximately 90% of learners. German is preferred in primary schools, whereas the order is reversed in secondary grammar schools. With regard to the situation in higher education, the gap between English and German is much wider in favor of English (51.4% vs. 27.7%, respectively), these two languages accounting for nearly 80% of all language instruction offered (Statistical Report, 1989–2000).

As centripetal forces brought Hungary closer to the mainstream of Europe, foreign language education became a buzzword. While the three consecutive governments seem to have disagreed on most political issues, they have been vociferous in their support of foreign-language teaching and learning. However, this support has repeatedly failed to materialize in clear-cut policy decisions, with the consequence that the average Hungarian youth still does not speak foreign languages. Hartinger (1993) was right in saying that "it was easier to pull down the barbed wire on the border than it has been to cross the language barrier" (p. 33).

THE ELT CURRICULUM

The National Core Curriculum (NCC), which was first issued in 1995, has been the key component of the Hungarian educational reform since the change of regime in 1989. It is the basic document for public education, determining the objectives, content, and requirements of education for the 10 years of compulsory schooling (up to grade 10). NCC broke with the traditional approach of detailed central planning and overregulation of the curriculum. In its original form, it advocated a two-tier system, with NCC representing the higher and compulsory level, upon which the lower level, that is, the local curriculum, was to be built. Many teachers and other education experts appreciated the privilege of autonomy and the opportunity of professional development required through the production of local curricula—and just as many voiced their concerns. The critics argued that teachers in Hungary lacked expertise in curriculum writing and, more importantly, were too overburdened and underpaid to be expected to perform such duties.

Paying heed to the opponents, the present Ministry of Education decided to launch a three-tier system by interposing the frame curricula between the national and the local levels. Developed by professional curriculum writers, several frame curricula are currently available for each subject, and schools are free to choose one of them and adjust it to their local context. While it is true that this policy has relieved teachers of extra work, it may also be regarded as a return to a more centralized system of education (Medgyes & Nikolov, 2002).

Within the framework of NCC, English is listed under the chapter "Modern Languages". This chapter specifies objectives, content, and requirements in general, without specific reference to any of the languages offered in Hungarian schools. The task of identification for particular languages is thus left to the discretion of frame curriculum writers, local educational authorities, schools, language departments, and teachers. The document is predicated on a pragmatic concept of *foreign language education,* emphasizing that the main objective of teaching foreign languages is to provide learners with practical language skills, and only passing references are made to secondary objectives, such as familiarity with the values of different cultures, personality enhancement, and the development of cooperation skills. Foreign language instruction in Hungary aims to be *euroconform,* similar to the instruction that takes place elsewhere in Europe, which implies the adoption of humanistic and communicative principles of language education.

NCC in its modified version lays down the following criteria:

- Obligatory foreign language instruction must start in grade 4 at the latest;
- Foreign-language study must be maintained until graduation (grade 12);
- Students in secondary grammar schools must learn two foreign languages;
- Each foreign language must be studied in a minimum of 3 hours per week;
- Group size for the foreign-language class must not exceed 16 pupils;

- Provision must be made for a free choice of languages; and
- Special measures must be taken to prevent the regression of foreign languages other than English and German.

With respect to English, euroconform instruction is also warranted by determining the level of the language proficiency Hungarian students are expected to achieve in relation to the European reference levels (Common European Framework, 2001). Thus, in their first foreign language, secondary-school students should reach a level between A2 (waystage) and B1 (threshold) by the end of grade 10, and a level between B1 and B2 (vantage) by graduation (grade 12). Expected output in a second foreign language is one level lower. In other words, the Hungarian secondary school graduate is expected to speak one foreign language at the intermediate and another at the basic level.

In conjunction with the creation of NCC, a new system of examinations, still in development, was envisaged. The principal aim of this system is to modernize the school graduation examination and reestablish its prestige (Nikolov, 1999). From the perspective of foreign-language education, the traditional exam not only fails to provide reliable feedback on students' proficiency, but also assesses formal knowledge rather than practical skills. As a consequence, teachers are thrown into a very confusing situation: after they have been teaching real-life communication for several years, they are advised to switch into a traditional testing mode a few months before the school graduation examination.

According to the reform, foreign languages will play a central role in the school-leaving examination (SLE): one of the four compulsory subjects is a foreign language, but candidates may also sign up for a second foreign language as an optional fifth subject. The SLE is also designed to alter the relationship between foreign-language instruction and the State Foreign-Language Examination (SFLE).

Organized by a semigovernmental body, the SFLE may be taken from the age of 14 on three levels: basic, medium, and superior. Hungarians have been anxious to pass the SFLE for decades, and for good reasons too. An SFLE certificate entitles the holder to be the beneficiary of several advantages: it is worth extra points at university entrance examinations and is a compulsory condition for graduation from higher education, it entitles civil servants to language allowances, and so on. Not surprisingly, in the year 2000, more people took the SFLE for English than for all the other languages combined (56.4%), whereas 37.7% took the exam for German. In the same year, about 80% of all successful candidates came from secondary schools, and an additional 10% were university students (State Foreign Language Examination Board, 2001). This is reassuring because it shows that the importance of foreign-language learning is increasingly recognized by the younger generation.

Today, students who have passed the SFLE are exempt from having to attend language classes, and are granted a waiver at the SLE in that foreign language.

Once the school reform has been introduced, these privileges will be revoked, but candidates who achieve high scores on the advanced level SLE will automatically be awarded an SFLE certificate as well.

Traditionally, secondary-school teachers of English are trained in a 5-year degree program, whereas primary school teachers are trained in a 4-year nondegree program. Both types of training have an academic rather than a practical profile. Students are required to obtain a thorough knowledge of literature and linguistics, and a fair command of English. Methodology courses, which are regarded as add-ons, are followed by only a brief spell of actual teaching practice. The philosophy underlying this pattern of teacher training posits that teachers should be, first and foremost, highly erudite in the humanities, and should acquire the necessary teaching skills while on the job.

A major change in teacher education resulted when Russian ceased to be the compulsory first foreign language in 1989. The resulting interest in the study of English and German necessitated the training of some 10,000 English and German teachers to supplement the existing supply of approximately 5,000 teachers. The situation was aggravated by the fact that, due to low teacher salaries, thousands of qualified teachers of English and German were siphoned off to more lucrative jobs offered in private language schools, business, commerce, banking, and tourism (Medgyes, 1993).

To alleviate the shortage of English and German teachers, school principals were prepared to hire almost anyone who claimed to have a smattering of English, even young native English-speaking backpackers, whose native command of English was often believed to make up for their lack of training and experience (Medgyes, 1999). However, the most welcome candidate to alleviate the shortage was the Russian teacher whose work had suddenly become superfluous. Russian teachers were even offered the chance to become fully qualified teachers of English or German, provided they succeeded in completing a government-sponsored program, called the Russian Retraining Program.

One government initiative was the establishment of teacher-training centers within existing universities and colleges. The main aim of these centers was to run fast-track preservice teacher training programs, mostly in German and English. Their profile was different from that of traditional programs in that they were shorter (3 years in duration), and practical methodology and teaching practice were granted a much larger scope in their curriculum than was customary in philology tracks (Malderez & Bodóczky, 1999; Medgyes & Malderez, 1996; Medgyes & Nyilasi, 1997). Despite their remarkable achievements, the fast-track programs have always been considered as a stopgap measure, and now that the teacher shortage problem has eased, the centers are about to be closed down or merged into traditional programs. It is a moot point whether their innovative features can be saved in prevailing conservative university environments.

BECOMING AN ENGLISH TEACHER

I was born on August 6, 1945, on the day when the nuclear bomb was dropped on Hiroshima, Japan. By the time I reached nursery-school age, communists had seized power in Hungary, nationalized *bourgeois* property, and banned all foreign languages other than Russian. Nevertheless, I was lucky enough to attend a private nursery school in Budapest, where the language of instruction was half Hungarian, half English. It is unbelievable how Aunt Ida's school managed to remain private and teach English in the bargain. Be that as it may, it was there that I made my first acquaintance with Humpty Dumpty and others in the treasure trove of English nursery rhymes.

Throughout my school education, my parents hired private English teachers for their two sons. I can remember three of them quite vividly. Aunt Franciska was a soft-spoken former nun whose contribution to my education ended when my mother saw me turning Hungarian somersaults instead of practicing English grammar. Another teacher was Aunt Ila, a lady of half Indian descent, who presented our family with a mahjong set from China. The third one was ex-privatdocent, Dr. Koncz, a relic of the old regime, whose sternness only softened when he asked me once a week to fill in his lottery ticket at the end of the lesson.

Why English, I often wondered. After all, we were a family rooted in and surrounded by German language and culture. In fact, my grandmother spoke German as her first language and never learned proper Hungarian. My father, too, spent many an hour on brushing up his broken command of German, keeping a German vocabulary book even by his deathbed, as if it were his umbilical cord to life. And yet, my parents insisted that their two sons learn English before German, because Great Britain was their ideal of freedom, sophistication, and wealth, and they were convinced that English was the language of the future.

As a child, I took my English studies for granted. I must have been around 10 years old when my elder brother decided to give up his piano lessons. I immediately wanted to follow suit. My mother said "All right. You may also quit the piano, but only if you promise never to quit English." That was a deal.

I never learned English at school, even though, by the time I reached secondary school age, English was gradually allowed back into the curriculum. Instead, my parents sent me to a class that specialized in two languages. One of them was Latin, because my father belonged to a generation capable of reeling off the long list of Latin prepositions backward and forward. The other language had to be Russian, because, as a realist, my father knew that a good command of Russian was an asset in a communist Hungary.

Upon graduation from secondary school, I went to study English and Russian at Eötvös Loránd University in Budapest. My parents loathed the idea of their son becoming a teacher, "a slave of the nation", as Hungarians would put it. In vain I tried to assure them that teaching was the last thing I intended to do. My lofty goal was to become a man of letters—whatever that meant.

It was at university that I met the first native English speakers in my life. Miss Galton, an elderly instructor sent by the British Council, began her first tutorial by asking our study group which English-language newspaper we were in the habit of reading. When we unanimously said that it was the *Morning Star,* the daily of the British Communist Party and the only English-language paper available in Hungary, she was flabbergasted—and left Hungary at the end of the first term. Her successors were more open-minded, and enjoyed the privilege of being pampered by the affection, and quite often, the adulation, that Hungarians feel is due to samples of a rare species. Some of these native English teachers got so carried away as to marry Hungarians and permanently settle here, adding to the tiny British expatriate community.

Foreign-language majors were obliged to do their school practice in the final year of their studies. Internships at that time included a month's practice in a provincial town. I happened to land in a lovely town near the Austrian border. My teaching duties involved two groups of secondary-school students with an overwhelming majority of girls. Their eyes were glued on me, a strapping young man to replace Aunt Aliz, who would doze off as soon as I started the lesson, only to wake up for the bell and say "Splendid! You're a born teacher, Peter." Because my experience in a Budapest school called Radnóti turned out to be just as exhilarating, my fate was sealed. On graduation, I was offered as many as seven teaching jobs; this had much less to do with my excellence than with the fact that I was a male in a female profession, and that English from the late 1960s was more and more in demand. I accepted the job in Radnóti.

Initially, I was teaching from the one and only mandatory course book written by Hungarian authors—and I found it deadly boring. A couple of years later, I supplemented the Hungarian book with British material. My pupils and I enjoyed the imported books so much that, soon enough, I decided to chuck the Hungarian books altogether and use British books only. One day I was summoned by the school principal. He said that my illegal use of foreign books had been brought to the attention of authorities in the Ministry of Education. My heart sank. Then he asked, "Do you find those books any better than the compulsory ones?" I stammered that I did. "Well, you should know. You're the professional," the principal said. "Carry on. I'll take care of the rest." And I carried on as before, unruffled under his protective wings.

I had been a teacher for 5 years when I visited Britain for the first time. That British Council summer course for teachers of English was an unforgettable experience: I was suddenly faced with the harsh reality that my listening comprehension skills were far too limited to understand accents like the one heard in the north of England. My subsequent trips confirmed that, indeed, English was spoken with an accent throughout the world.

I was in my late twenties when I was commissioned to write my first course book, which was followed by several others designed respectively for primary- and secondary-school students. To be fair, my work was not hindered by political dictates; although I was never forced to include specific content, I instinctively knew what *not* to include. The most serious objection of a political nature was raised by an editor who insisted that I delete the word "godfather" from my text, because it had religious connotations. I complied.

However, even in the era of political and economic liberalization (nicknamed "goulash Communism") in the 1980s, English teachers were considered a suspicious lot. Typically, when I applied to the Hungarian Ministry of Education with the idea of establishing an English teachers' association, I was flatly rejected. In retrospect, I realize that my case was considerably weakened by the unfortunate choice of an acronym—ATAK.

Meanwhile, I gave up my teaching job at the school for a lecturer's post in the English Department of my alma mater. I soon realized that the English Department was as liberal politically as it was conservative professionally. In the eyes of most of my colleagues, the phrase "teacher education" was anathema. I shall never forget when a highly-respected literature professor came up to me after one of the staff meetings and said: "You're right, Peter. There's no point in teaching methodology in just one course." As I beamed, he added: "So I'd bring down the number of courses to zero." Frustrated, I felt like going on holiday, when I received a Fulbright grant in 1988.

Although my stay at the University of Southern California in Los Angeles, in the United States, was a most rewarding experience, it robbed me of the opportunity to witness firsthand the most exciting year in the recent history of Hungary. By the time I arrived home in 1989, communism was all but dead, and the Russian language had lost all its prerogatives. At the behest of the Minister of Education, I quickly set about conceiving the retraining program for Russian teachers and the new fast-track preservice training program. A year later, I was appointed the founding director of the Centre for English Teacher Training, the 3-year program in Budapest previously described.

At the Centre, we knew right from the start that we were created as a stopgap measure and our lifespan was limited. So we moved along in the fast lane: rapid growth, wonderful professional opportunities, plenty of unpaid work, close involvement in the establishment of ATAK, now known as IATEFL Hungary, and a Ph.D. program in language pedagogy, the first in its kind in Hungary and in the whole region. Our happy moments were saddened by the fact that about half of our graduates chose not to go into teaching, and many of those who did dropped out after a year or two. Why? Well, simply because, as one of them admitted, they couldn't afford to stay in such a terribly underpaid profession.

And now it looks as if we have come to the end of the road: The Ministry of Education decided to discontinue the fast-track programs as of 2002. The burning question at the moment is: Will the University wish to retain our expertise with the program itself gone? And if yes, under what conditions?

On a personal note, in an effort to keep myself in shape as a teacher, last year I undertook to teach a group of 15-year-olds in the school where I started my career more than 30 years ago. No sooner had I come to this decision than I was attacked by doubt. Would I be able to cope as an ordinary schoolteacher after such a long gap? Would teenagers still accept me? What would students be like these days, anyway? What would their attitude to English be? And, because I was not able to find conclusive answers to my queries, I decided to complete another year in the school.

CONCLUSION

Today, the English language is omnipresent in Hungary. What was once forbidden fruit, today is staple diet, especially for youngsters. It is a virtual obligation to speak English—and obligations are seldom loved. Think of the sad story of Russian. Indeed, it looks as though the juggernaut of English is trampling down every other language—except German, perhaps. Is that the goal we wish to achieve?

Where do I stand on this issue, as an English teacher and teacher educator? Should I develop a bad conscience because, as an ELT professional, I am contributing to the relentless expansion of English—or should I rather rejoice? Where do my moral responsibilities begin, and where do they end?

Indeed, what is my attitude to the English language? Well, English certainly is far more than a means of earning a living or a tool of communication. My house is adorned with English dictionaries, big and small. I never miss a chance to improve my command of English. And this was the case well before English picked up speed in Hungary. When in my youth, there was nobody to talk to in English, I soliloquized. For me, English has always been the most rewarding form of self-actualization and my most loyal companion. For better or for worse, I am desperately in love with it.

REFERENCES

Common European Framework of Reference for Languages: Learning, Teaching, Assessment. (2001). Cambridge: Cambridge University Press.
Fenyvesi, A. (1998). Linguistic minorities in Hungary. In C. B. Paulston & D. Peckham (Eds.), *Linguistic minorities in Central and Eastern Europe* (pp. 135–159). Clevedon: Multilingual Matters.
Gill, S. (1993). Insett (inservice teacher training) in Slovakia: Past simple, present tense, future perfect? *Perspectives, 2,* 15–21.
Hartinger, K. (1993). Why language learning difficulties are not always linguistic. *Perspectives, 1,* 33–35.
Malderez, A., & Bodóczky, C. (1999). *Mentor courses: A resource book for trainer-trainers.* Cambridge: Cambridge University Press.

Medgyes, P. (1993). The national L2 curriculum in Hungary. *Annual Review of Applied Linguistics, 13,* 24–36.

Medgyes, P. (1999). *The non-native teacher* (2nd ed.). Ismaning: Hueber Verlag.

Medgyes, P., & Malderez, A. (1996). *Changing perspectives in teacher education.* Oxford: Heinemann Educational Books.

Medgyes, P., & Miklósy, K. (2000). The language situation in Hungary. *Current Issues In Language Planning, 1*(2), 148–242.

Medgyes, P., & Nikolov, M. (2002). The interface between political and professional decisions. In R. B. Kaplan (Ed.), *Handbook of applied linguistics* (pp. 195–206). New York: Oxford University Press.

Medgyes, P., & Nyilasi, E. (1997). Pair-teaching in pre-service teacher education. *Foreign Language Annals, 30,* 352–368.

Nikolov, M. (1999). *English language education in Hungary: A baseline study.* Budapest: The British Council.

State Foreign Language Examination Board (2001). Statistical Data, 2000 [Mimeo]. Budapest, Hungary: Author.

Statisztikai tájékoztató [Statistical Report]. (1989-2000). Budapest, Hungary: Ministry of Culture and Education.

6

ENGLISH LANGUAGE TEACHING IN INDIA: COLONIAL PAST VIS-À-VIS CURRICULAR REFORM

Premakumari Dheram
Osmania University College for Women, India

India, *Bharath* in Indian languages, has a rich cultural heritage. The country was invaded and ruled by different colonizers and the British rule lasted for nearly 300 years. So, when India became an independent democracy in 1947, it had become the home of various religious and linguistic groups. Although 78% of its people adopt the Hindu way of life, others follow Buddhism, Christianity, Islam, Jainism, and Sikhism. Most of the 28 states in India are formed on the basis of language. With an area of 3.3 million square kilometers, India has a population of 1 billion.

In India, there are 18 official languages and 350 other languages that are recognized as major languages. Hindi is the official language of the Union, and the regional languages are the official languages of the States. English enjoys the status of associate official language, and the Central and State recruitment boards conduct examinations and interviews in Indian languages as well as in English. English is the language of higher education, and the *lingua franca* across state boundaries. Cable television and the information technology industry have encouraged Indians to appreciate the instrumental, regulative, interpersonal, and imaginative purposes the English language can serve (Kachru, 1983). Most importantly, English is the language of India's national and international business, and the opening up of the economy to multinational companies in the 1990s has increased the demand for English education.

HISTORY OF ELT IN INDIA

The history of English language teaching in India makes a powerful study in sociolinguistics. Even a quick reading of the letters, travel diaries, and official records of the last 400 years draws attention to the singularly utilitarian nature of the approach adopted by the British and the Indians toward the language. The official history of English in India, however, begins at the end of the 18th century with the "observations" of Charles Grant, the then Director of the East India Company. His 1797 treatise is considered to be the first blueprint of English language and education (Tulsi, 1983). Grant recommended the establishment of "places of gratuitous instruction in reading and writing English" to "insure its diffusion over the country" (cited in Aggarwal, 1993, p. 33).

However, most members of the British Parliament were afraid that Christian missionaries' preaching of the gospel might antagonize the Hindus, and that education would encourage them to fight for independence. Ten years later, Lord Minto, the Governor General of India from 1807 to 1813, recommended "oriental learning" for the "natives" (Sharp, 1920, p. 19). Subsequently, the East India Company (Charter) Act of 1813 (known as the Charter), which came to be called "the foundation stone of the English educational system in India," ordained that "a sum of not less than one lakh rupees" (i.e., 100,000 Indian rupees) be set apart each year "and applied to the revival and improvement of literature and the encouragement of the learned natives of India, and for the introduction and promotion of a knowledge of the sciences among the inhabitants" (Sharp, 1920, p. 22). In fact, it was missionaries who first established schools to preach Christianity and educate the natives in English. The Charter gave the missionaries the freedom that had hitherto been denied, and they established English schools all over the country.

However, the Charter could not resolve the differences among the natives who were divided into orientalists and Anglicists. While the former demanded that the government support instruction in Sanskrit and Arabic, the latter insisted on English education. In 1823, when the Government used the annual educational grant for the establishment of oriental colleges and translations, Raja Rammohun Roy, an Indian scholar and reformer, submitted a memorandum in protest, recommending a "more liberal and enlightened system of instruction, embracing mathematics, natural philosophy, chemistry and anatomy" (Sharp, 1920, p. 101). He believed that only Western education would bring about a cultural reform by bringing the best of East and West together.

Therefore, when Thomas Macaulay came to India in 1834, in his capacity as a legal member of the Governor General's Executive Council and President of the General Committee of Public Instruction, the stage had been set (Mayhew, 1928). Macaulay had strong administrative and political reasons, which were in line with the policy of the British government, and personal prejudices founded on an inadequate understanding of the Indian languages, especially Sanskrit, for his advocacy of an educational policy that encouraged only English. He said that "a single shelf of a good

European library was worth the whole native literature of India and Arabia" (Macaulay, 1972, p. 241), and highlighted the need "to form a class who may be interpreters between us and the millions whom we govern; a class of persons, Indians in blood and color, but English in taste, in opinions, in morals, and in intellect" (p. 249). Not surprisingly, Macaulay is called the Father of English education in India.

Macaulay's policy was accepted in principle by the Governor General William Bentinck in a resolution that directed that "the native population [be imparted] a knowledge of English literature and Science through the medium of the English language" (Aggarwal, 1993, p. 57). This proved to be a turning point in the history of education in India, as later developments, such as the Indian policy of education, and the structuring of the aims and materials of English courses, testify.

A series of Acts, during 1837 through 1847, provided various incentives for the study of English. Many career and employment opportunities were made available to the Indians who studied English. Persian as the Court language was replaced by English and Indian languages in the higher and lower courts respectively. Preference was given to Indians with a knowledge of English in all departments of the government. By 1852, there were 1,185 mission schools with 38,000 students in the Madras Presidency alone, and, by 1854, there were 169 government secondary schools with 18, 335 pupils (Zaidi, 1973).

In 1854, Woods' Educational Despatch (Aggarwal, 1993) declared that the objective was "to extend European knowledge ... by means of the English language in higher branches of institution, and by that of the vernacular languages of India to the great mass of the people" (pp. 58–59). The Despatch contributed to the growth of educational institutions in the country between 1854 and 1902. In spite of the directives of the Despatch, by 1902, the indigenous schools (*pathasalas*) had disappeared almost completely, and only the new educational system "whose ideal was to spread Western knowledge and science through the medium of English" had progressed (Naik & Syed, 1974, pp. 157–158). Secondary schools were forced to introduce English as a subject and as the medium of instruction because doing so would enable students to pursue university education (Zaidi, 1973).

The 20th century began with the Viceroy Lord Curzon's attempts to reform Indian education. In 1902, he appointed the Indian Universities Commission, and the Indian Universities Act came into force in 1904. It ordained that the universities "shall provide for postgraduate teaching, study and research in the faculty of Arts and Science" (Report of the Government Grant Committee, 1922, p. 8). The universities were no longer merely examining bodies. By 1937, modern Indian languages were developed as media of instruction at the primary- and secondary-school levels and English continued to be the medium at the high-school and university levels (Naik & Syed, 1974). The syllabi echoed the opinion of people like Grant and Macaulay that English literature was the only means to improve the morals of the Indian. The textbooks at various levels were more or less the same as earlier ones. The authors they presented included Shakespeare, Milton, Pope, and Wordsworth (Sinha, 1978).

When the British left in 1947, their language (and religion) had become a part of the Indian social, emotional, and intellectual heritage. English had been the official language since 1835. Indeed, one of the key issues before the Constituent Assembly was the question of the official language. After independence, states were formed on a linguistic basis, and they were authorized to adopt Hindi or any other modern Indian language for official transactions. However, whenever the states opted to draw up bills or acts in a language other than English, they were required to publish relevant translations in English. It was also decided that the official language of India would be Hindi, with English being used for official purposes for 15 years after independence (Sinha, 1978). However, the non-Hindi speaking southern states preferred the continuation of English and protested against the imposition of Hindi in the 1960s because they feared that the Hindi-speaking northern states would have an advantage over them if it became the federal language. Consequently, the Official Language Amendment Act of 1967 "assured to English the status of an associate language without any ambiguity whatsoever until such time as the non-Hindi states may decide otherwise" (Tulsi, 1983, p. 287).

Similarly, when the Universities Education Commission (UEC) met in 1948, the medium of instruction was no longer just an academic question but a social one. English had been the medium of higher education for nearly 100 years. The UEC adopted a practical approach and decided that English would continue as the medium of instruction in higher education. Whereas Woods' Despatch had adopted a two-language policy (regional language up to the secondary school level, and English at the higher secondary and university levels), the UEC evolved a three-language policy according to which students at the higher secondary and university levels would study the regional language, Hindi/or a Southern language, and English.

THE ELT CURRICULUM

In 1990–1991, the number of Government secondary schools was 59,468, and the number of higher secondary schools, 19,151 (Ministry of Human Resource Development, 1992). The secondary stage (up to grade 10) is the stage of general education and the higher secondary stage (grades 11 and 12) is marked by diversification and specialization. In most Indian states, English is introduced in grade 5, and it continues to be a compulsory subject up to the second year of undergraduate studies. The state boards may offer instruction in English and the regional language. Most private schools, however, have English medium instruction only. They may be affiliated with either the national or the state boards. The two national school boards are the Central Board of Secondary Education and the Indian Certificate of Secondary Education (ICSE).

The National Council of Educational Research and Training (NCERT) develops the common core curriculum for grades 1 through 12, and designs the syllabus and textbooks as well. In accordance with this framework, the states and union territories formulate their policies and prepare instructional material. In many schools, English is taught for five to six periods per week, each period lasting 40 to 45 minutes. A school may prescribe a text prepared by the NCERT or the State Council of Educational Research and Training (SCERT) or a commercial course book. The materials include a reader, a workbook and a supplementary reader. Prose, poetry and short stories form the basic material, with a number of exercises focusing on grammar, vocabulary, reading comprehension, and composition.

For example, the 2000–2001 ICSE grade 10 syllabus includes works by William Shakespeare and Ernest Hemingway, poems by Robert Southey, Lewis Carrol, W. H. Auden, Benet, Ted Hughes, T. S. Eliot, D. H. Lawrence, Katherine Mansfield, Rudyard Kipling, John Milton, Henry Louis Vivian Derozio, Toru Dutt, Kamala Das, Rabindranath Tagore and Vikram Seth; and short stories by Mark Twain, Guy de Maupassant, O. Henry, Isaac Bashevis Singer, Barry Pain, Anton Chekhov, Leo Tolstoy, H. H. Munro, Liam O' Flaherty, Oscar Wilde, Keki N. Daruwalla, Chakravarti Rajagopalachari, Pritish Nandy, and Gulzar. Explication, dictation, and drill continue to be the most common classroom techniques. There is an increasing awareness of the importance of pair and group work among the teaching and learning communities. Finally, a student is tested on knowledge of English and the content of the prescribed texts.

India has many states, and I present the ELT curriculum in one state, Andhra Pradesh, for the sake of brevity here. Andhra Pradesh adopts a structural syllabus for both English- and Telugu- medium classes. The English-medium student studies English as a compulsory subject from grade 1 through grade 12, and the non-English medium student from grade 3 through grade 12. In accordance with the national curriculum, the SCERT and the Andhra Pradesh Department of School Education formulate the curriculum and the syllabus.

What follows is a brief description of the teaching of English in the context of non-English medium classes. In grades 3 and 4, learners become familiar with the basics of the language through informal activities. The activity book is completed in the first 30 sessions, and the workbook in 120 to 130 subsequent sessions. Each session is 40 minutes in length. Guidance for the teacher and instructions for the student are incorporated into the lessons themselves. Suggestions for parents, in English and Telugu, are included in the workbook as well.

The state adopts a 6-year syllabus beginning in grade 5. Nearly 100 structural and functional items, including sentence patterns, structural words, and formulas are graded and distributed over grades 5 through 9. The instructional material in grade 10 consolidates the structural content learnt in the earlier grades. The lexical syllabus for grades 5 to 7 includes nearly 1,000 vocabulary items, and the syllabus of grades 8 to 10 includes 2,000 vocabulary items.

The English Reader consists of stories, poems, and reading passages followed by exercises. Each unit includes material for various learning activities such as listening, speaking, reading, writing, drawing, role-playing, pair-drilling, dictation, spelling, and recitation. Discoveries, inventions, festivals, legends, national and international events form part of the thematic content of the texts. Genres such as autobiography, biography, essay, letter, story, and travelogue are equally represented. Poetry is also given a great deal of importance and the nature and length of the poems are specified in the syllabus. The theme and the language of the text are considered to be more important than the popularity of the author.

There are two supplementary readers for each grade from grade 7 on. Usually, one of them is a simplified novel and the other is an anthology of short stories. Except for a few stories by Indian writers, the narratives are by native speakers of English. However, translations of literature in Indian languages into English are becoming increasingly popular. In addition to the general guidelines, there are suggestions to the teacher at the beginning of every unit in the reader. The workbook contains exercises for language practice and model question papers for unit tests and terminal examinations. It also includes guidance on administering and scoring the tests. The syllabus is completed in roughly 170 periods.

In 1990–1991, there were 176 state universities, 7,121, colleges and over 4.4 million students in Andhra Pradesh (Ministry of Human Resource Development, 1992). In addition, there are five open universities and four open schools. The University Grants Commission (UGC) develops the policy for university education. Apart from professional and vocational courses, most Indian universities offer a 3-year undergraduate course in arts, commerce, and sciences. The undergraduate curriculum includes a 2-year compulsory course in general English that aims to equip the student with study skills in English. "The prevalent pattern for the course seems to be the prescription of reading texts ... along with some exercises on reading comprehension, vocabulary, grammar and composition" (Report of the Curriculum Development Centre in English, 1989, p. 17). However, recent developments include the introduction of genre-based courses in English for Specific Purposes (ESP) in some universities. Special English, a literature-based elective, is offered in most universities, and most of the students who opt for it go on to study for an M.A. in English.

A quick review of the master's course in different Indian universities highlights the fact that it is predominantly literature oriented. It covers American, British, and Commonwealth literature from Chaucer to the present day, literary criticism, and literary theory. The study of the English Language for nonliterary purposes is yet to be recognized as part of an M.A. program in English. Although a great deal of work is done in the literary genres, the attention given to ESP, and especially the popular nonliterary genres such as advertisements, features, and news reports, does not correlate with the spread of English in the Indian context. This is so, despite the fact that these genres address a larger audience than their literary counterparts and enrich the original models to suit the multilingual and sociocultural Indian context. However, the process of accommodating ESP in the bachelor's and master's programs in English has begun, and a full-fledged curricular reform in this direction will raise the Indian users' awareness of the nativization of English (Kachru, 1996) and encourage them to contribute consciously, and more actively, to the process.

Although the use of computers for teaching and learning English is still rather restricted, radio and television transmissions have reached even the rural classroom. The Central Institute of Educational Technology and the State Institutes of Educational Technology have been producing curriculum-related programs. In higher education, the UGC has established 15 educational media research centers and audiovisual centres, whose programmes are transmitted on the national television network. Educational technology is also an integral part of in-service teacher training.

Eligibility criteria for schoolteachers include teacher training certificates and bachelor of education degrees. For college and university teaching, a score of 55% or higher on the master's examination and a pass in the national eligibility test held by the UGC are required. The National Council of Teacher Education and the District Centres take care of the in-service training of schoolteachers. Language institutions such as the Central Institute of English and Foreign Languages in Hyderabad and the Regional Institute of English in Bangalore train school and college teachers.

Unlike schoolteachers, college and university teachers do not receive any training in pedagogy. For this reason, when the Curriculum Development Centre highlighted the need to train students in study skills and teachers in communicative language teaching methodology in its 1989 report (Report of the Curriculum Development Centre in English, 1989), the UGC established 48 academic staff colleges and identified 200 university departments to offer in-service training.

Established in 1948, the British Council plays an active role in both cultural and academic spheres. Its activities include library services in 11 centres, and training programs all over India. The Council is associated with Project Action Plan for Teachers in training the preuniversity teachers of 60 districts in South India. Under the sponsorship of the Hornby Trust, it organizes ELT summer schools for teachers. Its ELTeContact Scheme for facilitating electronic networking among ELT practitioners and policymakers in India has been very effective.

BECOMING AN ENGLISH TEACHER

In this section, I reflect on the three phases in my growth from a teacher into a reflective practitioner. The first phase is marked by my identification of gaps in my approach to teaching and my development of a complete understanding of the profession. It also indicates how the opportunities to work with professionals in ELT enabled me to achieve this understanding. The second phase shows how as an international student of TEFL (Teaching English as a Foreign Language) in England, I became aware of my peripheral status as a nonnative English-speaking teacher in the world of ELT. The final and present phase presents my efforts to move toward the center in an attempt to be an active participant in the ELT discourse community.

I obtained an M.A. in English from the Central University of Hyderabad and a Postgraduate Diploma in the Teaching of English from the Central Institute of English and Foreign Languages. I began my career as a part-time lecturer in an undergraduate college soon after completing my M.Phil. course work at the Central Institute. I taught for nearly 10 years at various colleges in Hyderabad. Simultaneously, I worked on CLT methodology for my M.Phil. dissertation, and later on, cultural nationalism as a mode of self-affirmation in the novels of the Nigerian author, Chinua Achebe, and the African American writer, Ralph Ellison, for my doctorate at Osmania University in Hyderabad.

I firmly believed that the communicative approach was the cure for all ills. In fact, until 1991, I used to look for miracles in the classroom. I wrote volumes of material and tried it out in various classrooms. No classroom was ever unmanageably large or stifling. Pair work, group work, and oral tests were more the norm than the exception. Every course meant supplementary material, and I enjoyed writing materials. Therefore, when I met Kate Mulvey, I had already had a long relationship with CLT. The meeting marked the end of the first phase of my career, and the beginning of the second.

Kate came to the ELT Centre at Osmania University 2 months after I had joined it as an assistant professor, in 1988. The Centre had been conducting a key English language teaching project in collaboration with the British Council. The project aimed to improve the study skills of the university postgraduate students and Kate was the project leader. Very soon, I found myself discussing material, methods, and classroom activities with her. I had always been critical of my work but never did I have an opportunity to analyze my work professionally. Our discussions forced me to look for answers to questions such as: Why did it work? Why did it not work? Where did it go wrong? Thus I began to reflect and the first phase of my career ended. In fact, when Kate discussed my classes with me and Robert Bellarmine, the British Council's English studies officer, they encouraged me to write for a feature titled "It Works" in the Council's *Focus,* we were actually laying the foundation for the rest of my career, because classroom research has been my passion ever since.

Of equal importance were the project-related workshops, where I saw professionals, such as Alan Davies, Alan Maley, Esther Daborn, Joan Allwright, Kate Mulvey, Maggie Jo St.John, Rob Nolasco, Rod Bolitho, and Tricia Hedge, in action. I exercised my skills in classroom observation, and when the first phase of my career ended, I was a reflective practitioner who could discuss her critical awareness using the register of the international ELT community. Incidentally, the workshops also gave me an opportunity of a practical nature. They helped me master the vote of thanks.

The second phase began in 1991 to 1992. I went to Reading University, in England, on a British Council scholarship for an M.A. in TEFL. During that year, my understanding of culture, history, and heritage acquired new dimensions; neither my M.Phil. in ELT nor my doctoral work on African American and Nigerian writing had prepared me for the culturally alien academic objectives. The grades I received for my assignments never rose beyond a B, and, if these grades are the yardstick, I did not learn anything in that year; but I did. The international composition of the M.A. in TEFL class introduced me to various perspectives and enriched my understanding of ELT as a global concern, with the nonnative English-speaking student at its center and the nonnative English-speaking teacher at its periphery. As teachers, the aims of native English-speaking and nonnative English-speaking teachers are similar; however, our circumstances and hence our approaches may be different. Yet, we all seem to draw inspiration from the same set of theories that forms the basis of our teaching practices. In our own ways, we nonnative English-speaking teachers add to these theories, although most of us care little about publishing. Is this because we are aware of a discourse barrier? I read Swales (1990) 2 years after I had published my first international article in 1995, and John Flowerdew's (1999) interview with Sandra McKay on nonnative speaker writers only a few months ago.

During one classroom discussion, I became aware of the question: Why do nonnative speakers of English not publish? I am not sure if anyone else was as troubled as I was by the question. I needed to publish an article in the *English Language Teaching Journal* more than I needed the M.A. in TEFL degree. My thesis was ready by the end of August, and I began to carve an article out of it. I dropped the article in the mailbox at Heathrow airport in London just before boarding the flight back to India at the end of September. If you say that I wrote the article to comfort my wounded ego, you may be right. Thus, the second phase of my professional development ended on an insecure but confident note. I had made my first move towards the center of the ELT world.

The urge to write, publish, and belong to the international discourse community marks the third and present phase. There may be institutions where the research article is a component of the M.A. syllabus but I had to learn the genre on my own. I am sure the experiences of my native English-speaking and nonnative English-speaking colleagues are not any different. I wrote my first published international article, the one for the *English Language Teaching Journal* in September, 1992. It took me 3 more years to appreciate the nonprototypical genre of the research article, thanks to the *English Teaching Forum*. My experience of publishing articles with *Focus, the English Language Teaching Journal* and *Forum* between 1989 and 1997, though quantitatively minimal, has been invaluable in terms of its contribution to my growth.

Between 1993 and 1998, I lived a full professional life. I was holding down a full-time position at the ELT Centre. In addition, I organized workshops on communication for management students and corporate trainees, and wrote Open University lessons in business communication and English for Science and Technology. But this phase is more significant for other reasons. I conducted two workshops at international conferences. The first one, on strategies for revising drafts (Dheram, 1994), was at the Regional English Language Center in Singapore.

I was pleasantly surprised to find that 36 participants chose to attend my session. They had never heard of me, nor had they ever seen my name in print. I nearly choked when I introduced myself to Ms. Alison Hoffman, the chairperson. The second one, on value-oriented communication (Dheram, 1997), took place at the Third International Conference on Language in Development in Malaysia. It was born of my experience of training management students in business communication. I have learnt that at any conference there are always some teachers who are guided by topics and themes rather than by names, and it is the presenter's responsibility to rise to their expectations.

In 1994, I was transferred from the ELT Centre to the Osmania University College for Women, where I now teach English language and literature to the undergraduate and postgraduate students and supervise doctoral research in ELT.

CONCLUSION

In this chapter, I presented a brief but comprehensive introduction to the ELT context in India, highlighting the curricular challenges created by its roots in the colonial past. I also reflected on the varied learning opportunities the ELT situation created for me as an English teacher, enabling me to grow into a professional and make my modest contribution meaningful.

To return to the status of the English language in India, the process of nativization continues at a rapid pace. As Kachru (1996) pointed out, "the greater the number of functions and longer the period, the more nativized [English] variety" (p. 59). Although a great deal of attention has been paid to the literary genres of this nativized variety of Indian English, the nonliterary genres have largely escaped a similar degree of scrutiny. This is ironic because these nonliterary genres address a larger audience in India than their literary counterparts. There is a strong case for exploring them in order to understand how the multilingual and sociocultural context of India enriches the original models. Such explorations must include the pedagogical implications of Indian English so that the teaching and learning communities will appreciate their role in decolonizing English language education. Curricular reform in this direction will not only raise the Indian users' awareness of the nativization of English but also encourage them to contribute consciously and more actively to the process.

REFERENCES

Aggarwal, J. C. (1993). *Documents on higher education in India (1781–1992): Selected educational statistics: World overview.* Delhi, India: Doaba House.

Dheram, P. (1994, April). A process approach to writing: Strategies for revising drafts. Workshop conducted at the Regional Seminar on Reading and Writing Research: Implications for Language Education, Regional English Language Center, Singapore.

Dheram, P. (1997, July). Value-oriented communication in interpersonal relations, with focus on clear thinking. Workshop conducted at the Third International Conference on Language Development, Langkawi, Malaysia.

Flowerdew, J. (1999). *TESOL Quarterly* and non-native speaker-writers: An interview with Sandra McKay. *Asian Journal of English Language Teaching, 9,* 99–103.

Kachru, B. (1983). *The Indianization of English: The English language in India.* Delhi, India: Oxford University Press.

Kachru , B. (1996). Models for non-native Englishes. In B. Kachru (Ed.), *The other tongue: English across cultures* (pp. 48–74). Bombay, India: Oxford University Press.

Macaulay, T. B. (1972). *Thomas Babington Macaulay: Selected writings.* In J. Clive & T. Pinney (Eds.), *Chicago and London* (pp. 237–251). Chicago: The University of Chicago Press.

Mayhew, A. (1928). *The education of India: A study of British educational policy in India, 1835–1920, and of its bearing on national life and problems in India to-day.* London: Faber & Gwyer.

Ministry of Human Resource Development. (1992). *Programme of action: National policy on education.* New Delhi, India: Author.

Naik, J. P., & Syed, N. (1974). *A student's history of education in India (1800–1973).* Delhi, India: Macmillan.

Report of the Curriculum Development Centre in English. (1989). New Delhi, India: University Grants Commission.

Report of the Government Grant Committee. (1922). Calcutta, India: Calcutta University Press.

Sharp, W. H. (1920). *Selections from Educational Records, Part I* (1789–1839). Calcutta, India: Government Printer.

Sinha, S. P. (1978). *English in India.* Patna, India: Janaki Prakashan.

Swales, J. (1990). *Genre Analysis: English in academic and research settings.* Cambridge: Cambridge University Press.

Tulsi, R. (1983). *Trading in Language: The story of English in India.* New Delhi, India: GDK.

Zaidi, Q. H. (1973). A historical survey of secondary education in India. In K. G. Saiyidain, V. Prakasha, P. Nath, & C. L. Sapra (Eds.), *The fourth Indian year book of education* (pp. 1–50). New Delhi: National Council of Educational Research and Training.

7

TEACHING ENGLISH AS A FOREIGN LANGUAGE (TEFL) IN INDONESIA

Junaidi Mistar
University of Malang, Indonesia

The linguistic situation in Indonesia is complex because more than 400 local languages with thousands of dialectical varieties are spoken as first languages (Nababan, 1982). The national language, *Bahasa Indonesia,* unifies the various ethnic groups with different languages and cultural backgrounds into an Indonesian nation and it serves as an official language at the national level. To equip Indonesians with an ability to communicate at the international level, English is the first foreign language officially taught to students from junior secondary school.

This chapter discusses English teaching in Indonesia and covers three main issues, including the historical development of the teaching of English, the structure of English curriculum, and my personal experience in developing a career as an English teacher.

HISTORY OF ELT IN INDONESIA

The teaching of English in Indonesia can be classified chronologically into three major phases. The preindependence phase covers the period before 1945, and the early independence phase includes the years 1945 to 1950. The third phase, the development period, covers the years from 1950 onwards.

Starting from the early 1600s, the Dutch ruled Indonesia, formerly called the Netherlands East Indies, for about three and a half centuries. The teaching of English, however, can only be traced from early 1900s when there was a move to abolish French as a subject in the *Europesche Lagereschool* (European primary schools) and to replace it with English (Groeneboer, 1998). English was also taught to students in the *meer uitgebreid lager onderwijs* (MULO, or junior secondary schools) as a compulsory subject for three to four classes a week. The teaching of English at this time was successful in the sense that many of the MULO graduates could speak, read, and write good English. One reason for the success was the small number of students in the classroom, as only children from families with a middle- and upper-class social status were allowed to go to school (Sadtono, 1997).

In early 1942, the Japanese armies ousted the Dutch. As a result, the teaching of Dutch was banned in the entire archipelago, as was that of English (Thomas, 1968). Books and other materials written in Dutch or English were burned. Instead, the Malay language, later on called *Bahasa Indonesia,* was taught extensively in addition to the Japanese language. Thus, during this period, no formal teaching of English took place. In some places, however, Dutch as well as English instructions were still carried out clandestinely (Groeneboer, 1998).

On August 17, 1945, Soekarno and M. Hatta proclaimed the independence of the Republic of Indonesia. On the following day, the constitution, called the 1945 Constitution, was proclaimed. Chapter XV, article 36 of this constitution declares that the language of the state is the *Bahasa Indonesia* (Ministry of Information, 1966).

The selection of a foreign language to serve Indonesians for international communication, however, was not yet decided. The choice eventually fell on English, not Dutch, despite the fact the decision makers at that time had been educated in Dutch language schools (Huda, 1999). One reason for the choice of English was that not long after the proclamation of its independence, Dutch troops had returned to Indonesia to reclaim the new country only to be met by Indonesians resistance. Consequently, when the decision about which foreign language to choose was to be made, Indonesian leaders were not prepared to adopt the language of the enemy (Thomas, 1968).

During this early period of independence, however, the teaching–learning process in schools was not effective and in many cases the schools were closed for some periods because the students joined the revolutionary battles under a body called *Tentara Pelajar* (Student Soldiers; Mestoko, Bachtiar, Sunityo & Arif, 1986). Only after the Netherlands government acknowledged the sovereignty of the nation on December 27, 1949, did the students return to schools.

One important step taken by the Ministry of Education was the establishment of an Inspectorate of English Language Instruction in charge of the supervision of the English language teaching (ELT). Mr. Frits Wachendorff, a Dutchman who remained in Indonesia, was appointed to head the body and he first spelled out the objective of TEFL in Indonesia: English was to be a foreign language and it was not and would never be either a social language or a second official language in Indonesia (Sadtono, 1997).

A sharp increase in school enrolment from the early 1950s raised at least two major problems for the teaching of English: the shortage of qualified teachers and the inadequate availability of English instructional materials (Sarumpaet, 1963; Soedijarto et al., 1980; Thomas, 1968). To address the first problem, second-year university students of any major were recruited to teach in secondary schools (Sarumpaet, 1963). In addition, 2-year evening courses, B-1 courses as they were named, were established in a number of cities throughout the country in August 1950 with financial and technical assistance from the Ford Foundation. The courses were to train noncertified teachers who had been teaching in junior secondary schools to become certified teachers. In 1954, Standard Training Centres (STC) were established in Jogjakarta (Central Java) and Bukittinggi (Sumatra), with the aim of producing more qualified English teachers. The students were taught English literature in addition to the English language itself (Thomas, 1968). In the same year, the Ministry of Education and Culture (MEC) also launched the regular formal day classes called *PGSLP* and *PGSLA* (*Pendidikan Guru Sekolah Lanjutan Pertama* and *Pendidikan Guru Sekolah Lanjutan Atas* respectively). The former trained the students to be teachers for junior secondary schools and the latter, for senior secondary schools (Mestoko et al., 1986).

At the tertiary level, also in 1954, three programs called *perguruan tinggi pendidikan guru* (state teacher training colleges) were set up in Malang, Bandung, and Batusangkar. By 1961, each of these colleges became a *fakultas keguruan dan ilmu pendidikan* (FKIP; faculty of teacher training and education) when linked to the nearest university. At this time, too, all types of teacher education including the B-1 courses, STC, *PGSLP* and *PGSLA* were integrated to the faculty of teacher training and education (Ministry of Education and Culture, 1970).

Also in 1960, another project called the English Language Teacher Training Program was set up at the Airlangga University's FKIP in Malang. The primary objective of this project was to create a corps of English language teachers who would constitute the pillars of ELT in Indonesia. Participating students were selected from the top graduates of the FKIP's bachelor's program from all over Indonesia. Upon completion of the program, the students were entitled to teach at the college level (Sadtono, 1997).

In order to deal with the lack of instructional materials, a committee was formed to develop English syllabi and a manual for secondary schools, with assistance from the Ford Foundation. These were published in 1956 for the first year and in 1958 for the second and third years of the junior secondary schools. Drafts for the senior secondary school level had largely been completed but never published (Thomas, 1968).

In the mid-1960s, however, attention to the teaching of English in Indonesia declined markedly due to an unfavorable political climate, when the communists were powerful. The concern for improving ELT in Indonesia regained its momentum when the new regime took control of the country after the failure of the Indonesian Communist Party's coup in September 1965. In 1967, the MEC issued a decree stating the aim of English teaching in Indonesia (Huda, 1999). In 1968, an English Language Project was set up consisting of two sub-projects: the English Teachers Upgrading Project, which was to upgrade the secondary school teachers of English, and the English Materials Development Project, which was to prepare materials for the upper secondary schools. Since then, several projects on in-service English teacher upgrading have come and gone (Sadtono, 1997).

Concern for the quality of ELT in Indonesia also inspired some Indonesian academics to set up a forum for teachers of English to share ideas regarding ELT. An association called Teachers of English as a Foreign Language in Indonesia (TEFLIN) was launched in 1973 at Gajah Mada University in Jogjakarta. Since then, TEFLIN seminars and conferences have been conducted throughout the country and in the last few years, the conferences have been attended by teachers and experts from neighboring countries such as Malaysia, Singapore, Thailand, and Australia.

The curriculum was standardized in 1975, and updated in 1984 and 1994. Revisions have been made to the instructional objectives, the teaching approach, and the syllabus design. The teaching of English under these curricula is discussed in the next section.

The latest development in ELT in Indonesia is the teaching of English to primary school students. The 1994 curriculum allows the teaching of English to primary school students starting from their year 4 if it is deemed necessary, provided that qualified teachers, instructional materials, as well as other resources are available. Unfortunately, a survey indicates that teachers assigned to teach English in primary schools are, in fact, rather incompetent (see Suyanto, 1997).

THE ELT CURRICULUM

In this section, I focus on the teaching of English in Indonesian general secondary schools by referring to the current curriculum in particular. The previous curricula are also referred to in order to show how English teaching policies have evolved over time. The discussion emphasizes three areas: the objectives, the teaching approach and syllabus design, and the results and challenges for improvements.

The objective of English teaching in Indonesia, as first spelled out by Frits Wachendorff, was not elaborated until 1967, when the MEC issued decree number 096/1967 (Huda, 1999). This decree stipulates that the objectives of English teaching in Indonesian secondary schools is to equip the students with language skills that enable them to

- Read textbooks and reference materials in English, which constitute 90% of all available reference materials;
- understand lectures given by foreign lecturers as part of the affiliation programs with universities abroad or to communicate with individuals and students from overseas;
- take notes of lectures given by foreign lecturers, and to introduce the culture of Indonesia to international communities;
- communicate orally with foreign lecturers, individuals and students in oral examination and discussions (Ministry of Education and Culture, 1967, cited in Huda, 1999, p. 127).

These objectives represent an order of priorities of the four macrolanguage skills, with reading skills being on top, followed by listening, writing, and speaking. This priority order was maintained in the 1975 curriculum and the 1984 curriculum, except that the skills were no longer limited to academic purposes only. The 1975 curriculum, for example, described the function of English teaching in secondary schools as the facilitation of the development of advanced science, technology, culture, and arts, as well as to enhance international relationships (Ministry of Education and Culture, 1975a, 1975b). In addition, the number of vocabulary items that students should master in order to develop these four language skills was specified: 1,500 words for the junior secondary school (Ministry of Education and Culture, 1975b, 1987) and 4,000 words for the senior secondary school (Ministry of Education and Culture, 1975a, 1986).

In the 1994 curriculum, a slight change occurred in the priority order of the writing and speaking skills. In earlier syllabi, writing was placed third, after reading and listening, and speaking was last. In the 1994 syllabus, the order was reversed, with speaking placed third and writing placed last. This change was intended to meet the needs of students and parents as expressed in a survey (Huda, 1999). Moreover, the expected number of vocabulary items was substantially reduced to 1,000 words for junior secondary school and 2,500 words for science and social science streams at senior secondary school. A target of 3,000 words was set up for the students of senior secondary school majoring in the language stream. Grammar and other elements of language, such as pronunciation and spelling, were to be taught only to support the acquisition of the four language skills, not for mastery of the language elements (Ministry of Education and Culture, 1993a, 1993b).

The 1975 curriculum specified that English should be taught with the audio–lingual approach with an emphasis on the teaching of linguistic patterns through habit-formation drills. As such, the syllabus was created mainly on the basis of structure. Structural items were presented according to the degree of complexity and frequency of use (Ministry of Education and Culture, 1975a, 1975b).

The teaching approach was changed when the use of the communicative approach was introduced in the 1984 curriculum. However, not enough information of the teaching procedures was available to the teachers, with the result that the approach was misinterpreted and implemented incorrectly. One serious misinterpretation was that the communicative approach meant a focus on the acquisition of oral communicative competence (Huda, 1992).

However, many classroom teachers still emphasize the teaching of English structure. Two factors may be responsible for this: the final national examination, which still gave greater emphasis on grammar mastery, and the syllabus (Huda, 1992). The syllabus was designed in such a way so that each instructional unit consisted of seven components: structure, reading, vocabulary, speaking, writing, pronunciation, and spelling. The fact that the structural component was placed at the beginning of each unit led to the impression that structure was still the emphasis of English teaching. To resolve the problems, the curriculum was again revised in

1994, and this version is still in use. In the revised curriculum, the teaching approach is called the meaningfulness approach (*pendekatan kebermaknaan*), but this is nothing more than the communicative approach redefined to suit the situations of ELT in Indonesia.

The syllabus design adopts a variable focus model (Ministry of Education and Culture, 1993a, 1993b) in which structure, notions, functions, and situations are the guiding principles of organization (Huda, 1990). At the junior secondary level, the linguistic forms are the organizing principle; notions and language functions are presented to provide contexts of use of the presented structural items. At the senior secondary school level, the notions and language functions gain greater emphasis and the linguistic forms are gradually deemphasised.

Another significant feature of the new syllabus is the integration of language components and language skills. Unlike the 1984 syllabus, in which language skills and language components—structure, vocabulary, and spelling—were taught separately, the 1994 syllabus integrates them in the form of themes. Thus, themes are the central components that tie language components and language skills together. In addition, the syllabus also contains recommended topics derived from the listed themes, functional skills to be developed, examples of communicative expressions, and lists of vocabulary items to be taught. The teachers are then free to design their own instructional materials for classroom teaching. After being used for a few years, the curriculum was found to have three major weaknesses: some communicative expressions were not in line with the theme, several functional skills overlapped, and a number of the stated teaching objectives were vague. In response, a slight revision of the syllabus was carried out in 2000 (Ministry of National Education, 2000).

Despite the high expectations placed on the English curriculum, the time allocated for teaching English is minimal. In junior secondary school, it is taught in four sessions of 45 minutes long per week for the three class levels (Ministry of Education and Culture, 1993a). In senior secondary school, it is also taught in four sessions of 45 minutes per week for the first and second year students. For the third year students, it is taught in five sessions a week for the students of science and social science streams and 11 sessions a week for the students of the language stream. Each session lasts 45 minutes (Ministry of Education and Culture, 1993b). As a result, some students receive little exposure to English communicative situations, which in turn leads to poor results of the overall teaching–learning activities.

Despite the ideal guidelines on what and how to teach English prescribed in the syllabus, the students' achievement of the stated objectives is still far from satisfactory. In the final examination of the year 2000, for example, the national average score of the junior secondary school students was 5.27 on a scale of 0 to 10. At the senior secondary school level, average scores of 5.04, 4.08, and 4.65 were obtained from the students of the science, social science, and language streams respectively (Directorate General of Primary and Secondary Education, 2001). Apart from the weaknesses of the test materials (Alwasilah, 1997) leading to a dispute of the validity and reliability of the results, which in turn led to a recommendation for the abolition of the examination (*Ebtanas,* 2001), these figures indicate that the teaching of English in Indonesia is not yet successful.

Several causes have been cited for the poor results. In addition to the limited time allocated for English teaching as discussed in the previous section, another serious problem is the low competence of teachers. A survey carried out in 1990 indicated that 37% of English teachers at junior secondary schools in Indonesia were senior secondary school graduates without any training in TEFL (Huda, 1999). In-service training must be provided for them. Also, preservice teacher training institutions should produce secondary school teacher candidates who are competent in both the English language and teaching skills. To do this, institutions must improve the professionalism of their lecturers so that they can train their students to be competent teacher candidates. In the next section, I turn to what I have done to improve my role as an English teacher as well as an English teacher educator.

BECOMING AN ENGLISH TEACHER

My senior secondary school was a vocational school called *Sekolah Pendidikan Guru (SPG)* that trained the students to be elementary school teachers. However, the fact that I was judged the best graduate of 1986 motivated me to take a state university entrance test instead. I chose the undergraduate program of the English Department of the Institute Keguran dan Ilmu Pendidikan (IKIP) Malang as my preference for study. That meant that I would teach English at either the secondary school or the university level. I was one of only 29 students accepted out of 1,099 applicants.

The first semester of learning English in this department, however, was a real nightmare for me. I thought I would be taught English like at secondary school, where the Indonesian language was used as the medium of instruction. I was wrong. The lecturers used English in the classroom all of the time and I did not understand a word they said. When I was at the *SPG,* English was taught only twice a week, for 45 minutes, and only during the first and second years. For this reason, I was really inferior to the other IKIP students in my class in English language skills. I was quite frustrated and told my academic adviser that I wanted to change my major. She did not agree and asked me to stay on, while advising me that changing a major from English was not a wise decision. She also assured me that I would be able to overcome the problem in one or two semesters.

My academic advisor was right. I started to enjoy learning English in the second semester. To overcome my poor speaking and comprehension abilities, I shared a house with other students in the English department so that I could study with them and practice speaking English. As a result, I began to improve, and made very good progress beginning in the third semester of my studies.

During my studies, I learned both the English language and language teaching methods. The course outline for the English Department at *IKIP* Malang dedicated the first 2 years of undergraduate study to building up the students' language competence. Consequently, the only subjects taught were the skills of listening, reading, speaking, and writing in English. Each skill was taught separately. English structure and vocabulary were also taught in the first half of the 4-year study period, and the last 2 years was for developing the students' mastery of English linguistics and literature as well as theories of language teaching and learning.

The curriculum of *IKIP* Malang at that time also offered two elective streams for undergraduate students: thesis stream or nonthesis stream. The students choosing the thesis stream were required to take some additional courses related to research methodologies and thesis-writing processes, whereas those choosing the nonthesis stream were not. On completion of their studies, students in thesis group were qualified to pursue careers as lecturers at the university level, while students in the nonthesis group became teachers at the secondary school level. I decided to take the thesis stream, and I received my undergraduate degree after 4½ years of study.

With an undergraduate diploma in hand, I started looking for a job as an English teacher. I applied to be a lecturer at a newly established private university called the Islamic University of Malang. The university has an English department under the Faculty of Teacher Training and Education that trains students to be secondary-school teachers. I was accepted, and started my English teaching profession there in 1991. Although I had obtained a formal qualification to be an English teacher, I was not automatically a good one. Practical experiences in teaching contributed to the improvement of my professional skills to a great extent. In addition, to further develop my career, I attended regional, national, and international seminars and conferences, and in some cases I presented papers on these occasions.

As a young teacher, I also wanted to develop my professional career by pursuing a master's degree. The rector of the university where I was teaching supported my ambition, and suggested that I apply for a scholarship to study for a master's degree at *IKIP* Malang. I received the scholarship to study for 2½ years starting in September 1994. Consequently, I had to leave all teaching tasks so that I could concentrate on my studies. In the master's degree program, I learned more about quantitative and qualitative research approaches, advanced English linguistics, applied linguistics, second-language acquisition, instructional designs, and English-teaching approaches. Beyond my expectations, I was judged the best graduate because I had the highest grade point average (GPA) of the graduates in 1997.

As a reward for my academic achievement, I was offered another scholarship, this time to study for a doctorate degree at the same university. I began my doctoral work, but at the same time, I applied for a scholarship from the Australian government to study in Australia. In 1998, I was granted a scholarship to study for a Ph.D. degree at an Australian university. Consequently, I terminated my doctoral studies at *IKIP* Malang after a year of study, and went to Australia to study at Monash University in Melbourne. I finished my Ph.D. thesis on January 17, 2002, and returned to Indonesia to resume my teaching career at the Islamic University of Malang.

With these qualifications, I hope I can contribute my expertise to the improvement of the quality of English teaching in Indonesia, and the training of more qualified secondary-school teachers of English. That should be the best thing I can contribute to my beloved country.

CONCLUSION

English has been described as the first foreign language in Indonesia and it is officially taught to students in the secondary schools. The history of English teaching in Indonesia is actually traceable to the early 1900s when modern schooling was first introduced. Efforts to improve its teaching have been made since the arrival of Indonesian independence in 1945; these efforts have included the standardizations of the curriculum carried out in 1975, 1984 and 1994. The most recent curriculum, the 1994 one, is still in use. It advocates a teaching approach called the Meaningfulness Approach.

However, an evaluation of teaching to date indicates that it is not yet successful. This fact stands as a great challenge for every one dealing with ELT in Indonesia. For this reason, effort to improve the quality of English teaching is highly appreciated, in particular the improvement of the professionalism of English teachers.

REFERENCES

Alwasilah, A. C. (1997). *Politik Bahasa dan Pendidikan* [Politics of language and education]. Bandung, Indonesia: PT Remaja Rosdakarya.

Directorate General of Primary and Secondary Education. (2001, January 10). *Rata-rata NEM propinsi dan nasional: Hasil ebtanas 1999/2000* [Provincial and national average scores: The result of 1999/2000 national final examination]. [Electronic version]. Retrieved on August 13, 2001, from http://www.websamba.com/infoebtanas/ebta2000.htm

Ebtanas belum berfungsi sebagai "Quality Control" [National final examination has not functioned as a quality control]. (2001, October 31). [Electronic version]. Retrieved on November 31, 2001, from http://www.pdk.go.id/go.php?a=1&to=f250

Groeneboer, K. (1998). *Gateway to the west: The Dutch language in colonial Indonesia 1600-1950* (M. Scholz, Trans.). Amsterdam: Amsterdam University Press.

Huda, N. (1990, March). *Syllabus design for secondary schools.* Paper presented at the 35th Teachers of English as a Foreign Language in Indonesia (TEFLIN) Conference, Fakultas Pendidikan Bahasa dan Sastra-Institute Keguran dan Ilmu Pendidikan Semerang, Semarang, Indonesia.

Huda, N. (1992). The 1994 English syllabus for secondary schools: Issues and problems. *Jurnal Bahasa dan Seni, 21,* 1–12.

Huda, N. (1999). *Language learning and teaching: Issues and trends.* Malang, Indonesia: Institute Keguran dan Ilmu Pendidikan Malang.

Mestoko, S., Bachtiar, S., Sunityo, & Arif., Z. (1986). *Pendidikan di Indonesia: dari jaman ke jaman* [Education in Indonesia: From era to era]. Jakarta, Indonesia: CV. Manggala Bakti.

Ministry of Education and Culture. (1970). *25 tahun pendidikan dan kebudayaan* [25 years of education and culture]. Jakarta, Indonesia: Department Pendidikan dan Kebudayaan.

Ministry of Education and Culture. (1975a). *Kurikulum sekolah menengah atas: Garis-garis besar program pengajaran, mata pelajaran Bahasa Inggris* [Curriculum for senior secondary school: Syllabus for English subject]. Jakarta, Indonesia: Balai Pustaka.

Ministry of Education and Culture. (1975b). *Kurikulum sekolah menengah pertama: Garis-garis besar program pengajaran, mata pelajaran Bahasa Inggris* [Curriculum for junior secondary school: Syllabus for English subject]. Jakarta, Indonesia: Balai Pustaka.

Ministry of Education and Culture. (1986). *Kurikulum sekolah menengah tingkat atas: Garis-garis besar program pengajaran, bidang studi Bahasa Inggris* [Curriculum for senior secondary school: Syllabus for English subject]. Jakarta, Indonesia: Departemen Pendidikan dan Kebudayaan.

Ministry of Education and Culture. (1987). *Kurikulum sekolah menengah tingkat pertama: Garis-garis besar program pengajaran, bidang studi Bahasa Inggris* [Curriculum for junior secondary school: Syllabus for English subject]. Jakarta, Indonesia: Departemen Pendidikan dan Kebudayaan.

Ministry of Education and Culture. (1993a). *Kurikulum pendidikan dasar: Garis-garis besar program pengajaran sekolah lanjutan tingkat pertama, mata pelajaran Bahasa Inggris* [Curriculum for basic education: Syllabus for junior secondary school, English subject]. Jakarta, Indonesia: Departemen Pendidikan dan Kebudayaan.

Ministry of Education and Culture. (1993b). *Kurikulum sekolah menengah umum: Garis-garis besar program pengajaran, mata pelajaran Bahasa Inggris* [Curriculum for senior secondary school: Syllabus for English subject]. Jakarta, Indonesia: Departemen Pendidikan dan Kebudayaan.

Ministry of Information. (1966). *The 1945 constitution of the Republic of Indonesia* (Special Issue No. 001/1966). Jakarta, Indonesia: Department of Information.

Ministry of National Education. (2000). *Penyempurnaan/Penyesuaian kurikulum 1994 SMU (Suplemen GBPP)* [Revision of the 1994 curriculum for senior secondary school (syllabus supplement)]. Jakarta, Indonesia: Department Pendidikan Nasional.

Nababan, P. W. J. (1982). Indonesia: the language situation. In R. B. Noss (Ed.), *Language teaching issues in multilingual environments in Southeast Asia.* Singapore: SEAMEO Regional Language Centre.

Sadtono, E. (1997). ELT development in Indonesia: A smorgasboard. In E. Sadtono (Ed.), *The development of TEFL in Indonesia* (pp. 1–19). Malang, Indonesia: Institute Keguran dan Ilmu Pendidikan Malang.

Sarumpaet, J. P. (1963, December). Indonesian secondary schools. *The Secondary Teacher,* 12-15.

Soedijarto., Moleong, L., Suryadi, A., Machmud, D., Pangemanan, F., Tangyong, A. F., Nasoetion, N., et al. (1980). In T. N. Postlethwaite, & R. M. Thomas (Eds.), *Schooling in the ASEAN region: Primary and secondary education in Indonesia, Malaysia, The Philippines, Singapore, and Thailand.* Oxford: Pergamon Press.

Suyanto, K. K. E. (1997). Teaching English to young learners in Indonesia. In E. Sadtono (Ed.), *The development of TEFL in Indonesia* (pp. 166–172). Malang, Indonesia: Institute Keguran dan Ilmu Pendidikan Malang.

Thomas, R. M. (1968). Indonesia: The English-language curriculum. In R. M. Thomas, L. B. Sands, & D. L. Brubaker (Eds.), *Strategies for curriculum change: Cases from 13 nations* (pp. 279–322). Scranton, Pennsylvania: International Textbook Company.

8

ENGLISH TEACHING IN ISRAEL: CHALLENGING DIVERSITY

Ofra Inbar-Lourie
Beit Berl College, Israel

Israel is a Middle Eastern democracy with a population of 6,600,000 that is predominantly (80%) Jewish. Since its establishment in 1948, the country has absorbed Jewish immigrants from all over the world, and, as a result, about 40% of the population consists of veteran or new arrivals in the country. The largest non-Jewish minority group is the Arab community, which numbers 1,195,000. Smaller minorities are the Druze (106,000), the Bedouins (about 60,000) and the Circassians (3,000; Central Bureau of Statistics, 2002).

The linguistic scene in this small country is dynamic, constantly shaped and reshaped by new influxes of immigration. The 1990s were characterized by two major waves of immigration that had a significant impact on Israeli society: approximately 900,000 immigrants from the former Union of Soviet Socialist Republics and 65,000 immigrants from Ethiopia (Ministry of Immigrant Absorption, 2003). In addition, approximately 250,000 foreign workers from Asian, African, and European homelands (Knesset Research and Information Centre, 2003) have recently arrived in Israel, leaving their mark on the local demographic landscape.

Although Hebrew and Arabic are both official state languages, Hebrew, the language of the Jewish majority, enjoys prominent status and is more frequently used. The Hebrew language has gone through a remarkable rejuvenation in the last century, from the ancient language of the Jewish scriptures to a modern language used in all spheres of life (Fishman, 1991). Arabic, the language of the Moslem and Christian Arab community in Israel, serves as the medium of instruction in schools in the Arab sector.

The melting-pot ideology, prevalent in the country until recently, perceived Hebrew as one of the major cornerstones for establishing a cohesive Israeli society, and for this reason a monolingual language policy was advocated. Nonnative speakers of Hebrew were strongly endorsed to use the language and to abandon their mother tongues; this often resulted in the loss, and sometimes extinction, of heritage languages (Shohamy, 1994). Currently, grassroots endeavors toward language maintenance are evident, as well as the introduction of an educational language policy that promotes multiculturalism and the retention of immigrant languages (Ministry of Education, 1996).

Languages taught in the school system besides Hebrew and Arabic as mother tongues are English, Arabic for Hebrew speakers, and Hebrew for speakers of Arabic, French, Russian, Yiddish, Spanish, and, to a lesser degree, 16 other languages, including Amharic, the major language of the Ethiopian immigrants.

HISTORY OF ELT IN ISRAEL

English is by far the most important foreign language in Israel. It is used extensively in the media, for academic publications, and as a gatekeeper to higher education. Furthermore, English is the language of the largest Jewish diaspora (that of North America), and immigration from English-speaking countries has provided a considerable supply of native English-speaking teachers.

English was used for government during the British conquest and subsequent rule of Palestine from 1917 to 1948. Arabic and Hebrew, however, retained their statue as official languages and languages of instruction, whereas English was taught as a foreign language in both Arab and Jewish schools. The teaching was not guided by an official curriculum and strongly emphasized British literature and the promotion of British culture rather than language use (Spolsky & Shohamy, 1999). After the state was established in 1948, a centralized educational system was gradually formed, divided into a Jewish and an Arab sector, the Jewish sector being further split into secular and religious schools. Attitudes toward English were unenthusiastic, reflecting the animosity of the local population toward the former British Mandate rule. Beginning in 1960, English was made a compulsory school subject from grade 5 on. The predominantly literary-based studies taught in crowded classes to students from diverse linguistic backgrounds were far from successful and came under severe criticism by language-teaching experts (Spolsky & Shohamy, 1999). A major curricular innovation in English teaching occurred in 1968, when a gradual shift from a culture-based curriculum to a more functional approach occurred. Like other curricula in the centralized Israeli school system, the curriculum for English teaching has always been top–down and prescriptive, its implementation supervised by local district inspectors for English teaching.

With the increasing spread of English and the emergence of the communicative approach to language teaching, the need for changes in the national curriculum for English teaching arose. According to the curriculum introduced in 1988, English should be taught as an international "world language" for practical communication purposes rather than for cultural integration with an emphasis on "cultural and educational values" (Ministry of Education, Culture, and Sport, 1988, p. 5).

One of the basic underlying premises for the design of the 1988 curriculum was that English language acquisition was confined to school settings. This assumption was becoming less realistic towards the end of the 20th century, with the extensive use of English in the media and in technology, and with evolving globalization phenomena. Thus, yet another curricular innovation in English teaching took place in the year 2000, with the implementation of a standards-based curriculum.

THE ELT CURRICULUM

The new national curriculum introduced in 2000[1] is a standards-based document that sets as its goal "to achieve achievable standards of excellence for the teaching of English as a Foreign Language in Israeli schools" (Ministry of Education, Culture, and Sport, 2001, p. 1). Drawing on constructivist theory, it views knowledge as the individual's construction of reality, and perceives teachers and students as collaborative partners in the learning process. Because the Israeli population is extremely heterogeneous in terms of linguistic, cultural, and ethnic backgrounds, the curriculum encourages teacher empowerment and local decision making with regard to the introduction of topics, language structures, and lexis.

The curriculum consists of four interrelated domains of language knowledge: social interaction, access to information, presentation, and appreciation of culture, literature, and language. Progress in each domain is indicated by standards and benchmarks that set goals for the end of primary school, the end of junior high, and the end of high school. The teacher is expected to navigate within these general frameworks, designing school- and class-based programs according to the students' needs and previous knowledge. Principles for language learning and teaching, as well as choice of materials and assessment procedures, are likewise stipulated.

The move from the prescriptive 1988 curriculum to a more descriptive, autonomous framework presupposes teaching expertise and teachers' willingness to take an active role in the decision-making process. Critics of the curriculum consider both assumptions somewhat unrealistic, especially in view of the present teacher shortage, which sometimes results in the placement of untrained teachers. Another major obstacle to the implementation of the curriculum is without doubt the apparent paradox of promoting local autonomy within a centralized, top–down educational system. One of the crucial factors that may bridge this gap is a revision in the school graduation assessment procedures, whereby teachers are also empowered to take a more active, accountable role in assessing facets of language knowledge that are not tested in the national end-of school matriculation examination now described.

---

[1]An official draft version of the curriculum was first introduced in 2000, followed by the final version published in 2001.

According to the curriculum, English is to be taught in the school system from age 10 to graduation at age 18 in both the Arab and Jewish sectors for 2 to 5 hours weekly in the elementary school, and 4 to 6 hours weekly in junior high and high school. Due to public demand and current ministry policy, however, teaching usually starts earlier. Although the English curriculum is uniform for both Hebrew and Arabic speakers, achievement scores on national tests in the Arab sector are far lower than those in the Jewish population. Amara (2001) attributed these results to a number of factors: (a) the fact that English constitutes the third school language after Modern Standard Arabic and Hebrew; (b) the limited exposure to English in the Arabic-speaking community, especially in the more remote Arab villages; (c) the lack of trained English-speaking teachers; and (d) the unsuitability of English-language textbooks that represent the Jewish culture and are not attuned to the needs of Arab students.

All Israeli students sit for their matriculation exam at the end of their studies in the twelfth grade. The test has a major impact on English studies, particularly in the higher grades, where it totally overshadows teaching in terms of content and assessment, often becoming the de facto curriculum. Because the washback effect of the test is tremendous (Shohamy, Donitsa-Schmidt & Ferman, 1996) the test has often been used to promote what the English Inspectorate perceives as desirable curricular innovations (Spolsky & Shohamy, 1999).

The examination is offered in three different levels, with only the top two levels accepted as university-entrance criteria. The written test includes a listening comprehension section (broadcast over national radio during test administration), reading comprehension, a writing task and a language component. The highest percentage of the score is allotted to reading comprehension (50%), versus 8% for listening, 12.5% for writing, and 12.5% for language. Speaking is tested separately in the schools by the test taker's teacher and an external tester (a teacher from another school), and constitutes 17% of the grade. About 60,000 students take the exam annually. According to data published by the Ministry of Education on the year 2000 examination (Ministry of Education, Culture, and Sport, 2001), about one fifth (22%) of the testees took the lowest level exam, one third (35%) the medium level, and 43% the highest level. Of the students who took the examination in 2000, 93% passed (Ministry of Education 2001). Although the test is a high stakes examination, no piloting is conducted, and only minimal psychometric analysis is performed on students' scores as an aftermath, thus seriously jeopardizing the validity and reliability measures of the test.

Israeli EFL teachers are trained in two principal modes: a 4-year program at one of the 19 teacher training colleges for a bachelor's degree in education focusing on English teaching, and a teaching certificate for academics with a first degree in English, granted at one of the five universities in the country. The training programs require a high level of English proficiency and draw on the disciplines of linguistics, literature, education, and pedagogy. In addition, teachers are encouraged to join in-service training programs conducted under the auspices of the Ministry of

Education in various parts of the country. Because the demand for English teachers far exceeds the supply, there is a chronic shortage of teachers.

Most English teachers are employed by the Ministry of Education or by local municipalities. Due to the growing demand for English instruction, the number of English teachers in Israel is constantly on the rise, with the total number estimated in 1996 at 6,000 (Spolsky, 1996). One of the reasons for the lack of English teachers is the staggering dropout rate; a large percentage of the novice teachers leave in the first years of teaching. Among graduates of teaching programs, close to 50% do not even set foot in the classroom. This is due to low pay, a nonexistent career ladder, overpopulated classes, and the teachers' inability to cope with discipline problems, as well as the possibility of pursuing more lucrative career opportunities open to proficient English speakers.

The English teaching sector in Israel is a tightly knit, well-informed professional group, reputed for collaboration both nationally and locally (Horovitz, 1997; Spolsky & Shohamy, 1999). English teachers have an active teachers' organization, the English Teachers Association of Israel, with a membership of 1,200 teachers (Horovitz, 1997) and a dynamic Internet site (ETNI). The fact that only locally produced textbooks are approved for classroom use has created a vigorous, competitive textbook-publishing market that produces a wide selection of attractive and pedagogically sound books for all levels.

Even though Israel is not defined as an inner- or even an outer-circle nation (Kachru, 1985), an estimated 35% of the English teachers are considered native English speakers, having their roots in inner-circle countries, "a figure probably not matched in other educational systems anywhere" (Spolsky, 1996, p. 6). These are first- and second-generation members of the English-speaking community permanently residing in the country, whose families having arrived in Israel as immigrants at different periods.

Not only is the Israeli English teaching population unique in term of the relatively large number of native English-speaking teachers, but its nonnative English-speaking teaching population is also highly unusual because it consists of both Israeli-born teachers and new or veteran immigrants, many of them from the former Soviet Union. Because Israeli ideology and national policy promote the absorption and integration of new immigrants, special care is taken to retrain these teachers and assist them in joining and supporting the workforce of local English teachers. No clear preference is officially indicated for either native or nonnative English-speaking teachers, although, as a result of the shortage of English teachers, native speakers of English may become teachers of English without having received any training or certification, and may or may not enroll in training programs after they are hired (Spolsky, 1996).

Research findings have shown that native English-speaking teachers perceive themselves as superior to the nonnative English-speaking teachers, whereas the nonnative English-speaking teachers do not acknowledge such differences (Inbar-Lourie, 1999). The number of prominent power positions held by native English-speaking teachers (inspectors, department coordinators in secondary schools, counselors, and material developers) is far disproportionate to their relative percentage in the overall English teaching population. All of the above does not apply to the Arab sector, however, where native English-speaking teachers are scarce.

Job dissatisfaction is more common among native than nonnative English speakers, perhaps because many became English teachers merely because of their language knowledge rather than as a result of teaching aspirations. The group of nonnative English-speaking teachers who immigrated to Israel from the former Soviet Union was found to have distinct negative perceptions of the superiority of native English-speaking teachers, and distanced relations with Israeli students (Inbar-Lourie, 1999).

It is worth noting that the local student population likewise consists of individuals with diverse linguistic and cultural backgrounds. Since 1989, about 147,000 immigrant students have enrolled in Israeli schools, mostly from the former Soviet Union (77%), but also from Ethiopia (9%) and other countries (14%), some of which are English speaking (Levine et al., 2002). Thus, the teaching situation is further complicated because native and nonnative English-speaking teachers (who are native and nonnative speakers of Hebrew) must teach English to native and nonnative speakers of Hebrew, some of whom are native speakers of English.

BECOMING AN ENGLISH TEACHER

My childhood home, like so many other Israeli homes, was potentially multilingual. My mother immigrated to Israel from Germany before World War II. German was her mother tongue, but, being a gifted and avid language learner, she managed to master English and French in addition to gaining nativelike proficiency in Hebrew. My father immigrated to Israel from Russia as a young child. Russian was his home language, but, because he had no formal schooling in the language, his knowledge was limited to basic communicative exchanges. Thus when it came to choosing a home language, Russian did not present a viable option, and German was not a favorable one, due to the strong negative feelings it evoked in Holocaust survivors. Moreover, the ideological belief that Hebrew should predominate regardless of personal linguistic background excluded the possibility of multilingualism. I therefore grew up in a monolingual Hebrew household, with the other languages looming in the background.

English was seldom heard or used. There in fact did not seem to be any external stimuli that would motivate young Israelis to study English; television had not reached Israel yet, the only radio channel was a Hebrew one, and visiting foreigners were scarce. Furthermore, English had been stigmatized as the language of the conqueror following 30 years of British rule.

School instruction in English began at the age of 10. On reaching that ripe age, I was ready to start the English-acquisition journey. The only obstacle to my mastering the language was my pregnant English teacher, who missed most of the classes. After a year of study, my English knowledge was rather meager. Fortunately, some relatives and their children from the United Kingdom arrived for a visit and stayed with us for a few days. Because they knew no Hebrew, I had an obvious linguistic advantage with my vocabulary load of 20 isolated English words. We managed to carry on a basic conversation using content words. "Ball" and "catch" were sufficient to facilitate a ball game. Sentence structure and tense seemed irrelevant for we had established a comprehensible channel of communication.

When I was 12 years old, the whole family embarked on a 3-year sojourn to Toronto, Canada, accompanying my father on a mission on behalf of the Israeli Ministry of Foreign Affairs. Arriving in a foreign land and attending a local school were greatly complicated by my almost complete lack of English. While my parents were busy apartment hunting, I was left with a strange babysitter: the television set, an unfamiliar novelty. I was especially intrigued by the commercials, because they were short, eye-catching, and repetitive. Gradually I developed a special liking for some, particularly the ones that advertised detergents. English words floated magically from the screen, uttered in a tempting and cheerful intonation: *clean, refreshing, soft.* Feeding the squirrels later at the nearby museum gardens, I would try out my new acquisitions, repeating the words I had heard, imitating the accent and manner to my captive, patient audience. For a long while afterwards, when actually applying these words in conversation, I would still hear the original utterance in the back of my mind, and wonder whether my interlocutors were aware of the source of my knowledge.

The stay in Canada lasted 3 years. By the time we departed for Israel, my English proficiency surpassed my skills in my native Hebrew. Returning to Israel at the age of 15, I began my English teaching career. Israel was becoming internationalized, and foreigners were no longer an uncommon sight. A television station was making its debut, the radio broadcast English and American pop songs, and Israelis began to travel abroad for business and pleasure. English was suddenly heard and required everywhere. Thus, my English expertise was greatly in demand. I began assisting my classmates with homework and test preparation, teaching them the words of the songs on the hit parade, and simulating oral dialogues as preparation for trips abroad and for exchanges with visiting relatives. Following my high-school graduation, it seemed quite natural to proceed on the same track, and during my compulsory army service, I worked as an English tutor at the military academy. I tried to use the English language to give students who came from diverse backgrounds access to other sources of information and to encourage them to reach beyond their ethnocentric circles to discover other cultures, modes of behavior, and thought.

The road was paved. I taught children and adults of all ages and backgrounds. After receiving my first degree in English and American literature, and my teaching diploma, I was accepted as an English teacher in my old high school in Tel Aviv. The educational system had by then undergone a massive change. High-school education was no longer considered the right of the privileged few, and kids were bussed in from all over the city to study together in one class. Great gaps in knowledge were emerging among the learners, compelling teachers to use creative, adaptive teaching methods tailored to meet the needs of heterogeneous populations. Teacher-training programs were far removed from this new reality, however. Nothing had prepared me for my first day in school.

I stared in helpless disbelief as the children in my grade 8 low-level class jumped up and down on their desks screaming their heads off and throwing various articles at each other. Basically, what some of them were saying, either covertly or overtly, was that they had no interest whatsoever in English studies, and would I please go away and let them carry on with whatever it was that they were doing.

That was not quite the scenario I had anticipated. They were supposed to welcome me cheerfully, take out their neatly wrapped books and notebooks, and listen eagerly to what I had to say. I came home devastated. After crying my eyes out and saying that this was my first and last day at school, I decided to give it another try. I spent the whole night preparing games with basic English vocabulary. Armed with large colorful boards and card games I headed back to the scene of the crime. The kids were surprised to see me. Once I got their attention, we started to play. When the bell rang for recess no one left the room. They were totally engrossed in the Bingo game. What followed were dramatic simulations, a song competition, a fashion show, a book club, and a cake bazaar—all in English. During that year, I learnt a lot about teaching from these children and others, appreciating the infinite possibilities that English teachers have in terms of content and methods. I learnt about catering to different levels of learners and about the necessity of conducting a needs analysis and evaluating teaching on an ongoing basis. I did my homework: read the sports page, watched popular soap operas, learned about rock stars, and engaged the students in areas relevant to their age and interest. In return, they taught me about subject areas in which they had much greater expertise than I did, as well as about teaching methods such as how to introduce and foster autonomous learning.

In the early 1980s, British experts were brought over to Israel by the British Council to disseminate the emerging communicative approach by conducting local seminars. Feeling exhilarated after one such session that introduced the notion of a negotiated curriculum, I returned to my class of 16-year-olds determined to bridge the gap between theory and practice.

"What would you say, kids," I asked "if from now on we made joint decisions as to what to study, when and how, what your homework assignments should consist of, and whether you should have homework at all?" The students stared at me in disbelief. After recovering from their initial shock, they patiently explained that they did not want to be partners in making these choices because they wanted no share in the responsibility. So much for instantaneous self-regulated learning! As a result of our dialogue, however, a slow movement toward the target of autonomous learning, of making choices, and taking on responsibility gradually began.

In the years that followed, I obtained my Master's degree in language education, specializing in language testing and participating in various testing projects: a pilot for a new national speaking test and a project empowering teachers to provide their students' end-of-school English grades. The projects combined research and teacher training, both of which I found fascinating. Under the inspiring guidance and leadership of Elana Shohamy, I discovered the importance of assessing student progress and learned about test use and abuse. The need to provide teachers at all levels with a testing knowledge base was clear. I began teaching teachers, giving workshops and courses on the mysterious world of testing and alternatives in assessment, providing rationale as well as test samples, encouraging critique of existing tests and the integration of the assessment process with classroom teaching. Research was always an important component in the courses; reaching out to schools, trying new assessment formats, collecting evidence from students and teachers, and conducting action research in the English language classroom. My teaching career took a different turn.

In the years that followed, I gradually took on more teacher training responsibilities, along with becoming an English language inspector in charge of supervising the teaching of English in the city of Tel Aviv-Jaffa, one of the largest cities in the country. Visiting teachers and headmasters, I became mindful of the enormous power of the English language and of the difficulty of living up to public expectations and "delivering the goods" (i.e., high English proficiency) due to local constraints and student and teacher heterogeneity. I learned to be more tolerant of teaching methods, discovering that different teachers get things done in different ways. I also learned important lessons in discerning the local and national forces that shape language policies, as was manifested in the case of the lowering of the starting age for English teaching.

Although English studies are compulsory from grade 5 on, all schools began earlier, usually in grade 4, with the English Inspectorate strongly objecting to an earlier start. In 1993, the municipality of Tel Aviv was the first city to proceed with an experimental project whereby students began their English studies at the age of 8 rather than age 9 in five municipal schools. Although the findings presented in an evaluation report did not reveal advantages in terms of achievements among the younger students, the move towards "the younger the better" continued, sweeping over the whole city and other locations in the country as well. This was done in spite of the fierce protests of the English Inspectorate, clearly demonstrating how local stakeholders can overpower centralized forces and establish a local language policy.

My growing interest and involvement in the domain of language policy enabled me to widen my perspectives beyond the rather restricted English-teacher's view, realizing that English, though powerful and widely spoken, is but one language among many. I found out more about the complex array of variables that affect the teaching of different languages, about the interaction between language status and the language teacher (whether native or nonnative English speaking), about learner variables and school contexts, and about immigrant languages and local languages, in particular Arabic, each a world in its own. In my Ph.D. studies, I further delved into the power issues evident in the English language teaching profession, clearly manifested in societal and individual attitudes towards native and nonnative English-speaking teachers of English.

My experiential learning through the years has provided me with a keener understanding of the intricate challenges English educators face in our diverse, conflict-ridden society. In order to live up to the difficult yet rewarding feat of teaching English in such heterogeneous settings, I try to instill in the trainee and veteran teachers I work with a broad perspective on language teaching, an awareness of issues of equity and ethics, and a sincere appreciation of their students' ethnic, cultural, and linguistic backgrounds. I urge them to take risks, to keep an open mind, and, most important of all, to be constantly willing to learn from their students.

CONCLUSION

My personal English teacher story is intertwined with the history of English teaching in the Israeli state. Some facets of this history are unique to the local context, portraying the story of multilingual immigrants who initially strove for Hebrew hegemony, gradually realizing the national and personal assets of multilingual resources, in particular those of the English language. Other facets of this account are shared by English-teaching educators in other lands, reflecting the powerful role English plays in the life of every individual in terms of social mobility, academic recognition, and economic success. It is also the story of language professionals who are struggling to maneuver between local and global concerns, between providing access to a world language and preserving and respecting other linguistic and cultural resources.

REFERENCES

Amara, M. (2001). Arab language education in the Hebrew state. In R. L. Cooper, E. Shohamy, & J. Walters (Eds.), *New perspectives and issues in educational language policy in honour of Bernard Dov Spolsky* (pp. 155–170). Amsterdam: John Benjamins.

Central Bureau of Statistics. (2002). Web site. Jerusalem, Israel: Retrieved August 7, 2003, from http://www.cbs.gov.il/engindex.htm

Fishman, J. A. (1991). *Reversing language shift: Theoretical and empirical foundations of assistance to threatened languages.* Clevedon, England: Multilingual Matters.

Horovitz, N. (1997). From the chair. *The ETAI Forum, 8*(2), 2.

Inbar-Lourie, O. (1999). *The native speaker construct: Investigation by perceptions.* Unpublished doctoral dissertation, Tel Aviv University, Israel.

Kachru, B. (1985). Standards, codification and sociolinguistic realism: The English language in the outer circle. In R. Quirk & H. G. Widdowson (Eds.), *English in the world:*

Teaching and learning the language and literature (pp. 11–30). Cambridge, England: Cambridge University Press.

Knesset Research and Information Centre. (2003). Web site. Jerusalem Israel: Author. Retrieved August 7, 2003, from http://www.knesset.gov.il/

Levine, T., Shohamy, E., Spolsky B., Levy-Keren, M., Inbar, O., & Shemesh, M. (2002). *The achievements of immigrant students in Hebrew and math.* Jerusalem, Israel: Ministry of Education.

Ministry of Education. (1996). *Policy for language education in Israel.* Jerusalem, Israel: Office of the Director-General, Ministry of Education, Culture and Sport.

Ministry of Education. (2001). *English curriculum: Principles and standards for learning English as a foreign language for all levels.* Jerusalem, Israel: The Pedagogical Secretariat and the English Inspectorate, Ministry of Education, Culture and Sport.

Ministry of Education, Culture, and Sport. (1988). *English curriculum for state schools and state religious schools grades 5–12.* Jerusalem, Israel: Curriculum Development Division.

Ministry of Education, Culture, and Sport. (2001). *Policy for language education in Israel.* Jerusalem, Israel: Author.

Ministry of Immigrant Absorption (2003). Current immigration date. Jerusalem, Israel. Web site. Retrieved August 7, 2003 from http://www.moia.gov.il/english.netunim/stats/htm

Shohamy, E. (1994). Issues in language planning in Israel: Language and ideology. In R. Lambert (Ed.), *Language planning around the world: Contexts and systematic change* (pp. 131–142). Washington, DC: National Foreign Language Center.

Shohamy, E., Donitsa-Schmidt, S., & Ferman, I. (1996). Test impact revisited: Washback effect over time. *Language Testing, 13*(3), 298–317.

Spolsky, B. (1996). Multilingualism in Israel. *Annual Review of Applied Linguistics, 17,* 1–10.

Spolsky, B., & Shohamy, E. (1999). *The languages of Israel: Policy, ideology and practice.* Clevedon, England: Multilingual Matters.

9

ENGLISH LANGUAGE TEACHING IN JAPAN

Masaki Oda
Tamagawa University, Japan

Tomoko Takada
Gakushuin Girl's Junior and Senior High School, Japan

Japan consists of a chain of islands between the northern Pacific Ocean and the Sea of Japan, located to the east of the Korean peninsula. Its population was about 126 million in 2000, including around 10 million living in the Tokyo metropolitan area. Although Japan's official language is not declared, Japanese is considered the national language, and is used for law, education, media, and so on. Despite the monolithic image, there are various groups of linguistic minorities, including Korean and Chinese, living in Japan, as documented by Noguchi and Fotos (2001).

According to Koike and Tanaka (1995), over 10 million students were enrolled in lower- and upper-secondary schools. In addition, about 2.5 million students were enrolled in junior colleges, technical colleges, and 4-year colleges and universities. In junior secondary schools, a foreign language is mandatory; of the available options, English is preferred over Chinese, French, and German. A foreign language is required at most of the secondary schools, and, with few exceptions, English is the only foreign language offered at these schools.

In higher education, too, a foreign language had been a required subject until the national guidelines on higher education were revised in 1991 (see Oda, 1995). The main feature of the revision was the abolishment of the foreign-language requirement for graduation. As a result, it became possible for many nonlanguage majors to avoid taking foreign-language courses, including English. However, English is still a main subject of the entrance examinations for many universities, regardless of academic discipline. For example, at one private university in Tokyo, which has departments of agriculture, business, education, engineering, English and American literature, fine arts, and foreign languages, English is the only entrance examination subject required by all of the departments. In fact, this is typical of many institutions, which indicates the reason that a large number of secondary schools choose English as their primary foreign language.

As Yano (2001) described, English in Japan "is and will certainly stay a foreign language in that it will function only as a means of communication with non-Japanese in international settings" (p. 127). Although more Japanese travel overseas nowadays, especially to English-speaking countries, proficiency in English is not obligatory for daily life in Japan. This may make the readers wonder why so many students are learning English as their only foreign language. In the next section, a brief history of English language teaching in Japan will be presented in order to answer this question.

HISTORY OF ELT IN JAPAN

The history of English language teaching (ELT) in Japan is rooted in the early 19th century. However, very little has been documented in languages other than Japanese. In his comprehensive book on the history of ELT in Japan, Deki (1994) stated that the beginning of ELT in Japan was an accident. In 1808, the British battleship, Phaeton, came to the port of Nagasaki in order to capture Dutch ships. During that period, the Dutch were the only Westerners who were allowed to stay in Japan, and, for the Japanese, Nagasaki was the gateway to the Netherlands and the West. The British held the Dutch traders as hostages and the Japanese were forced to supply fuel, water, and food to the British in order to have the hostages released. According to Deki (1994), Matsudaira Yasuhide, a magistrate of Nagasaki, had to take responsibility and killed himself because, unable to understand English, he thought he had mishandled the case. This may have been one of the incidents that prompted Japan to seriously consider the importance of learning English for national defense purposes. The need for learning English increased when the Americans came to the shores of Japan in 1853. At that time, Japan made treaties with several countries and began to open its doors to the world.

There is evidence that, in the 1860s and 1870s, a sort of Japanese–English pidgin was used around the port of Yokohama where foreign ships visited. However, historians regard the establishment of the *Yosho Chosyo* (Institute for Western Document Research, later renamed *Kaiseisho*) in 1862, which is the University of Tokyo now, as an important event in the history of ELT in Japan. Deki (1994) also stated that Fukuzawa Yukichi changed his *Rangaku Juku* (Institute for Dutch Studies) to *Eigaku Juku* (Institute for English Studies) in the same year, and that this was a remarkable step for ELT in Japan. This institution is now called Keio University, and is one of the most prominent private universities in Japan.

English became even more important as increasing numbers of Japanese visited English-speaking countries and subsequently more Western ideas were imported. Another turning point for ELT in Japan in the early 20th century was the emergence of ELT as a profession. In 1937, the linguist, Okakura Yoshizaburo, published a collection of his lectures in ELT methodology titled *Eigo Kyoiku* (English Language Teaching; see Imura, 1997). According to Imura, Okakura clearly distinguished ELT professionals from those who simply knew English and appears to have stressed that ELT was a part of human development. Arakawa (1932) also suggested that Okakura used the term, *Ohyo Gengogaku* (Applied Linguistics), a synonym of ELT, around the same time. There is an anecdote concerning an argument between Okakura and Harold E. Palmer, who was another important figure in the history of ELT in Japan. According to Imura (1997), Palmer, who lived in Japan as an advisor for the Ministry of Education between 1922 and 1936, suggested to Okakura that the vocabulary of learners should be limited to 3,000 words at some point. However, Okakura strongly disagreed with him on the grounds that Japanese students wanted to learn 'full' English.

Without question, World War II was another turning point for ELT in Japan. During the war, the teaching of English was severely restricted and the use of loanwords originating from English was strictly prohibited because English was considered the language of the enemy. After the war, however, the educational system of Japan was restructured and English returned as a school subject. Although formally an elective, as stated earlier, it gradually became "virtually obligatory" (Koike & Tanaka, 1995, p. 17). At the same time, more people went abroad, especially to the United States, to receive trainings in ELT. In 1952, the first group of 293 students went to the United States on Fulbright Scholarships, and a group of 30 English teachers from the United States "participated in what became an annual exchange program" (Ike 1995, p. 6). It should be noted that many of these scholars later held important positions in ELT policymaking in Japan.

Since the 1960s, various ELT methods have been imported to Japan by scholars trained in English-speaking countries. The audiolingual methods in the 1960s and 1970s, and communicative language teaching (CLT) in the 1980s, were among them. However, these methods were used in the Japanese context without much evaluation (see Pennycook, 1989).

Between the mid-1980s and the early 1990s, the growth of the Japanese economy and its strong influence in the international market caused a boom in the learning of English. With the help of the mass media, the ELT industry grew dramatically. The Japanese were motivated to learn English for international communication, despite the fact that nobody was sure exactly what *international communication* meant. It was a period when many native speakers of English came to Japan to teach English because being a native speaker of English was highly valued. There were private schools known as English conversational schools in the vicinity of virtually every train station in the greater Tokyo area. Because of the severe shortage of English teachers, private schools usually did not require any qualifications for teachers. As a result, many teachers were employed solely on the basis of their status as native speakers of English.

A government-sponsored program was also launched during this period in response to the public demands for internationalization. The Japan Exchange Teachers (JET) program invites youth from overseas, mainly English-speaking countries, to assist in ELT at secondary schools. Most of the participants are native English speakers, another indication of how much native speakers are valued in ELT in Japan.

THE ELT CURRICULUM

In Japan, schooling starts at age 6. Children have to spend nine years in compulsory education, including 6 years at primary school and 3 years at lower secondary school. Although most elementary and lower secondary schools are administrated by local municipalities, there are private schools and a number of schools attached to national universities. In any case, schools are supposed to follow the national curriculum guideline (Ministry of Education, Sports, Culture, Science and Technology, 2003) and the textbooks used by the schools must be the ones approved by the Ministry of Education, Sports, Culture, Science and Technology.

Most students begin to learn English from the first year of lower secondary schools, at age 12. Except in some private schools, where foreign languages are taught at primary level, this is when English is introduced as a school subject to a majority of Japanese students. According to the recent survey by the Ministry of Education, Sports, Culture, Science and Technology (2003), 97% of lower-secondary-school graduates proceeded to upper-secondary schools in 2000, though the latter is not a part of compulsory education.

In both lower- and upper-secondary schools, a foreign language is mandatory. According to the national guidelines, each school decides which foreign language to teach, and most schools choose English. In order to teach English at secondary schools, teachers have to go through a teacher-training course at the college level and obtain a license. The training usually requires completion of course work in linguistics, literature, and comparative cultures, as well as in education. In addition, a few weeks of practicum is also obligatory. In the case of public schools, applicants must pass an examination administered by a prefecture board of education (with a few exceptions) in order to obtain a teaching position. There is no restriction on nationality for those who are licensed and given teaching positions; however, most of the teachers in this group are native Japanese speakers. Although some foreign teaching qualifications can be transferred to their Japanese counterparts, thereby allowing foreigners to teach at Japanese schools, very few foreign teachers appear to be taking advantage of this regulation.

As mentioned earlier, there is another group of teachers involved in ELT at the secondary level. Since 1987, through the JET program, the Japanese government has invited youth from overseas, termed assistant language teachers (ALTs), to assist in the internationalization of education at secondary schools. In 2001, there were 5,583 ALTs, including 2,768 who had been in the program from the previous year. Although these ALTs represented 18 countries, 3,672 of them were from the United States or the United Kingdom (Ministry of Education, Sports, Culture, Science and

Technology, 2003). In order to participate in the program, one has to be a native speaker of the language involved and hold a bachelor's degree in any discipline.

In lower-secondary schools, English is taught for an average of four 45-minute class hours per week, using textbooks approved by the Ministry of Education, Sports, Culture, Science and Technology. Although the development of communicative competence is stressed, the grammar-translation method still plays a major role, for several reasons. First, class sizes are large, especially in urban areas. In public schools in the Tokyo area, each class may have up to 40 students; in private schools, the numbers can be higher. Second, there is very little opportunity for students to actually use English outside the classroom. On the other hand, English is a required subject for the upper secondary school entrance exams. Consequently, passing the exams is the only reason for many students to study English, and the third year of lower-secondary schools is heavily influenced by the entrance exams for the upper secondary level.

In the upper-secondary schools, the number of English class hours per week varies. Many public schools teach general courses such as English I and English II for their first 2 years, for four 50-minute class hours per week. In addition, subjects such as oral communication, which includes listening, speaking and discussion, reading, and writing are offered for 1 to 3 additional class hours per week in the first and second year of upper-secondary school, and intensively in the final year. Again, the entrance exams for universities have a significant influence on the curriculum and classes in the final year are often geared toward the exams.

In higher education, English courses are taught by both native and nonnative speakers of English; most of the latter are native speakers of Japanese. More institutions now recognize training in ELT as an important qualification for teaching English at the college level and hire instructors accordingly. However, in many universities, English courses are taught by specialists in literature or theoretical linguistics. These teachers, most of whom are native speakers of Japanese, may have had little formal training as language teachers.

Another problem is that many university ELT programs still consider native speaker status as the most important qualification for a teacher of English. As a result, to cite one instance, a foreign teacher who was not a native speaker of English, but was highly proficient in Japanese and had a Ph.D. in TESOL (Teaching of English to Speakers of Other Languages), was ranked on par with a monolingual English speaker with no teacher training and a B.A. in an unrelated discipline. Accordingly, some college-level, native English-speaking teachers may spend 20 years in Japan with no motivation to learn Japanese. Nevertheless, more and more institutions now recognize the importance of formal training and proficiency in both English and Japanese.

The ELT curriculum at the tertiary level is generally much more flexible than it is in secondary schools. Some institutions offer ELT programs in which teaching methods, materials, and evaluations are systematically coordinated. However, in many cases, teachers have more freedom in choosing what to teach and how to teach, as long as they stay within the performance objectives defined by the program. This can work both positively and negatively for the students.

BECOMING AN ENGLISH TEACHER

Tomoko Takada embarked on her first teaching job at a private junior and senior high school in Tokyo immediately after her graduation from college. It did not take long for her to realize that the teacher training she received was inadequate to meet the demands of communicative language teaching (CLT), a new pedagogical approach. The CLT began to be accepted enthusiastically in Japan, at least conceptually, in the early 1980s. Tomoko had learned English in the 1970s through the grammar-translation method.

She implored help from whatever source and whomever was available to compensate for her lack of knowledge. She sought guidance from the experienced teachers at her school, and read professional journals and practical books. She jumped at any ideas that she thought would work in her classroom. Sometimes she was lucky to obtain positive reactions from her students. However, she never gained satisfaction, much less self-confidence. She was not a creative teacher; she was a consumer of other people's ideas. She began to realize that she could not survive professionally if she continued in this manner.

Around that time, Tomoko came across a short report in a teachers' magazine written by a Japanese who had earned a master's degree in TESOL at Boston University (BU). She immediately thought that such a degree was exactly what she needed because it would provide her with systematic knowledge instead of a hotchpotch of classroom tips. After a few years of preparation, she finally decided to pursue an advanced degree in the United States. Her school was supportive, offering her a 1-year leave and a scholarship. In August, 1987, she flew to Boston.

The TESOL program at BU revolutionized Tomoko's concept of teaching. Before BU, her interest had centered on what to teach and how to teach it. At BU, she became interested in what and how students want to learn. She learned that a language teacher should be a facilitator rather than a transmitter of knowledge. She also cultivated the ability to observe educational settings with a critical eye because she worked on projects that involved empirical observation. Later, this ability proved to be crucial to incorporating a research perspective into her teaching.

It was a blessing that Tomoko found role models in her professors. One professor read Tomoko's term paper draft every week, returning it to her with comments within 3 days. The message she got from the professor was "Be responsive to your students." Another professor regarded Tomoko's ethnic and linguistic background as a resource for class discussions and encouraged this quiet Japanese woman to speak out. The message she got from him was "Be sympathetic to your students." These professors were inspiring examples of dedicated teachers.

The year at BU transformed Tomoko from a consumer of practical ideas into a budding creative teacher, from a knowledge transmitter to a facilitator, and from

100% teacher to 70% teacher and 30% researcher. Her master's thesis was on teaching reading through a technique called reader–listener generated questions. She implemented this technique with a middle-school student regularly for one semester, recorded the student's reactions in a journal, and analyzed how the student's language developed. When Tomoko completed the project, she felt empowered. Years later, she had an opportunity to share this technique by co-authoring the teachers' manual for a high-school textbook.

Thus Tomoko broadened her perspective and redefined language teaching in the United States. Back in Tokyo, however, she confronted another challenge. As she strove to apply her updated resources to the Japanese educational setting, she found that teaching methods that were effective in the ESL context were not similarly effective in the EFL setting. In addition, there were administrative and budgetary restrictions; teachers had to use textbooks authorized by the Ministry of Education, for instance. Her struggle reflects how language teaching is dependent on social, political, cultural, and institutional contexts.

Tomoko was engaged in this battle for 5 years. The most difficult and paradoxical undertaking was to liberate herself from the framework of the prescribed textbooks without deviating from the guidelines they imposed. The typical high-school textbook was composed of a dozen reading selections drawn from a wide variety of topics. Teachers were expected to incorporate grammar instruction as well as listening, speaking, reading, and writing activities in each unit. This all-in-one concept of *language teaching,* which was presented in the 1980s as the antithesis of the grammar-translation method, blurred the focus of instruction; it aimed at a balanced development of all four skills, and led to an imperfect development of each skill.

Tomoko found two solutions to overcome this challenge. First, she started to use skills-based textbooks published in English-speaking countries as supplementary materials. Second, she created illustrative sentences, short passages, and mini-dialogues that reflected her students' personal, social, and cultural lives. Her intention was to diminish the psychological distance between the target language and the learner by including students' background in class instruction. This was exactly what she had learned at Boston University—to be sympathetic to your students.

Then came another turning point in Tomoko's career. Her family moved to the United States, and she started her doctoral studies in TESOL at New York University (NYU) in 1994. It was like entering a different world. A master's program in TESOL balances theory and practice; in contrast, a doctoral program in TESOL trains researchers in the social sciences. At NYU, one third of course requirements were allotted to research methodology. Tomoko had to switch her mode of thinking from being practical to being philosophical. It was a formidable challenge.

"Part of the art of being educated as a Ph.D. is cultivating healthy skepticism," said her advisor in one of the sessions with her. These words epitomize the education Tomoko received at NYU. One of the research methodology courses required students to read a journal article and to point out its strengths and weaknesses from methodological perspectives. This project perplexed this Asian student who was not used to questioning knowledge coming from authorities. She could easily point out some strengths of an academic paper written by a distinguished scholar, but how could she find its weaknesses? As she approached the end of the doctoral program, however, she understood that no study is free from weaknesses, and this is why we continue to conduct research. As her advisor said, "a healthy skepticism is a driving force for academic advancement."

Tomoko returned to Tokyo in 1997, just after she passed the defense of her dissertation proposal. She resumed full-time teaching at the junior and senior high school where she worked before, and she continued to work on her dissertation. She also started to teach part time at a college and a university. It was tough and stressful to teach 6 days a week, with every evening spent on writing her dissertation at home. Since she earned her doctorate in 1999, her workload has been as heavy as ever, with additional nonteaching obligations at school and with her new research for the doctoral dissertation.

Teaching college students is professionally rewarding, and it also provides deeper insights into language teaching at secondary schools. Because Tomoko's college and university students come from many parts of Japan, she can get an overview of how English is being taught at the secondary level throughout the country by observing her students' reactions to her teaching. Some students in her reading class get totally lost when she asks them to read one paragraph and tell her the gist of it. They do not understand her directions, even in Japanese, probably because their concept of *reading* is word-for-word translation. They may never have learned reading strategies. As she helps them develop language skills, she reflects on her own teaching at secondary school, thinking how she can better prepare her students for language learning at the college level.

Tomoko's current teaching responsibilities at three locations leave her limited time to conduct research and to get involved in the academic circle. Although at a very slow pace, she has been continuing her research and has made a few presentations at international conferences. Through this experience, she has learned that the TESOL profession is a collaborative endeavor. A researcher must be an independent thinker, but researchers need to be interdependent to grow professionally.

People ask Tomoko how she can juggle three teaching jobs while pursuing her research. True, her workload overwhelms her, but teaching simultaneously all levels of students from beginners to advanced, including returnees from overseas, gives her a unique ability to gain an overview of language learning in Japan through the lens of research perspectives she cultivated at BU and NYU. Tomoko believes that her varied teaching experiences will enable her to make contributions to the discipline of TESOL as she further refines her research skills. This conviction has been the source of her physical, mental, and spiritual energy.

CONCLUSION

In this chapter, we have described ELT in Japan through its historical and pedagogical aspects. We have shown that there is a difference in perception between the learners and the policymakers in terms of its objectives. Although many learners are motivated to study English in order to pass a college entrance examination or to obtain a good job, the policymakers continue to stress that communication and international understanding are the major purposes for learning English. This gap continues to create instability in the field of ELT in Japan.

This was also illustrated in Tomoko's personal story. She has shown how, as an ELT professional, she had to overcome various constraints, some of which are unique to the Japanese context. Her experiences remind us of the importance of customizing the ideas from abroad to a country's particular context of teaching so that the local learners will benefit more from them.

Japan continues to attract large numbers of native speakers of English as English teachers in Japan. As we have shown, this could be to the detriment of local English teachers. Despite a huge investment of resources in ELT, the evidence strongly suggests that English will remain a language used mainly for examination purposes within Japan and for interaction with foreigners outside.

REFERENCES

Arakawa, S. (1932). *Gairaigogaku Jyosetsu* [An introduction to loanwords]. Kobe, Japan: Hakubado.

Deki, S. (1994). *Nihon Eigo Kyoikushi ko* [A history of ELT in Japan]. Tokyo: Tokyo Horei Shuppan.

Ike, M. (1995). A historical review of English in Japan. *World Englishes, 14*(1), 3–12.

Imura, M. (1997). *Palmer to Nihon no Eigo Kyoiku* [Harold E. Palmer and teaching English in Japan]. Tokyo: Taishukan.

Koike, I., & Tanaka, H. (1995). English in foreign language education policy in Japan: Toward the twenty first century. *World Englishes, 14*(1), 13–26.

Ministry of Education, Sports, Culture, Science and Technology, (2003). Web Site. Retrieved August 1, 2003, from http://www.mext.go.jp/

Noguchi, M. G., & Fotos, S. (2001). *Studies in Japanese bilingualism.* Clevedon: Multilingual Matters.

Oda, M. (1995). The 1991 revised standards and the EFL profession in Japanese universities: Focus on teachers. *The Language Teacher, 19*(11), 47–49.

Pennycook, A. (1989). The concept of method, interested knowledge and the politics of language teaching. *TESOL Quarterly, 23*(4), 589–618.

Yano, Y. (2001). World Englishes in 2000 and beyond. *World Englishes, 20*(2), 119–132.

10

ENGLISH LANGUAGE TEACHING IN LEBANON: CHALLENGES FOR THE FUTURE

Kassim Shaaban
The American University of Beirut, Lebanon

The teaching of English in Lebanon has witnessed steady expansion since 1946, the year the government of the newly independent Lebanon introduced English as a foreign language (EFL) into the Lebanese public school system on par with French, the language of the former colonizer (Shaaban & Ghaith, 1999). However, during the last 25 years, English has been experiencing exponential expansion at all levels of education, primary, secondary, and tertiary. This new state of affairs has been motivated by the realization among all sectors of Lebanese society of the importance of proficiency in English for pursuing higher education and for getting better jobs in the modern world, where English is becoming the de facto universal *lingua franca* (Crystal, 1997; Heller, 1999; McArthur, 1998). Together with this phenomenal spread of English has come questions about the quality of English language education being offered and the preparation and professionalism of the English language-teaching community.

HISTORY OF ELT IN LEBANON

The teaching of EFL in Lebanon dates back to the middle of the 19th century, the time of the arrival and settlement in the country of Protestant missionaries from the United States and Britain. The aim of these missionaries "was originally a religious one, but later on there was a move from preaching to teaching in order to gain followers" (Bashshur, 1997, p. 20). Many evangelical schools were established around the country, using Arabic and English as the media of instruction; in 1883, there were 34 such schools in Lebanon (Bashshur, 1978). The most sig-

103

nificant event in connection with the teaching of English at the time was the establishment in 1866 of the Syrian Protestant College (now the American University of Beirut), which continues to have a great impact on education in Lebanon. The English-medium missionary schools were more popular than French-medium schools (around 24 in 1883) established by French Jesuit missionaries because the former were perceived as nonsectarian, whereas the latter seemed to cater mainly to Catholics (Shaaban, 1997).

This picture changed drastically after World War I, when Lebanon was placed under the French mandate in accordance with the Sykes–Picot agreement of 1916. The French introduced an educational system modeled after their own. The newly established Ministry of Public Instruction mandated that French and Arabic were the languages of instruction, with physical and social science subjects taught in French only. The English-medium schools had to adapt their curricula to the new system in order to allow their graduates the opportunity to join the public service sector, where French and Arabic were the languages of the administration. The teaching of French was thus introduced in grade 1 and English was put off until grade 4 (Mathew & Akrawi, 1949).

Independence from France came in 1943, and with it came a series of decrees to help establish the autonomous identity of the country in administration and education. Arabic was declared the only official language of the country and French was relegated to the role of a second language to be used in higher education and in the teaching of mathematics and sciences from the 7th grade on. Furthermore, schools were allowed to use English as the second language instead of French if they so desired (Mathew & Akrawi, 1949). This newfound status of English and the fact that it was dissociated from Lebanon's colonial heritage made it an attractive option, especially for Muslims. In 1946, the Lebanese government introduced an EFL curriculum that consisted of a general statement of the skills that were to be taught in the various grades, with emphasis on reading and writing. It also suggested a series of textbooks (Ghaith, 1991).

Despite the revival of English, French remained dominant due to the benefits associated with it in an administration that remained French in spirit and in practice. English schools accounted for about 27% of the schools. However, starting in the 1960s, there was a new realization of the importance of English for career advancement and for science and technology. As a result, many English-medium schools were established by the Catholic School Bureau in areas which had been exclusively French educated. More significant than this development was the introduction of English as a third language in all schools run by the French missions, a development dictated by the need to give students the opportunity to compete in a world that was more and more dominated by English, especially in the employment market of the Arabian Gulf (Bikar, 1998; Shaaban & Ghaith, 2000; Zakaria, 1992).

The 1946 curriculum continued to serve as the main guide for EFL instruction in Lebanon until 1968, when the Lebanese Ministry of Education developed new curricula. The new English language curriculum reflected the principles of structural linguistics and the teaching methodologies of the audiolingual approach. Emphasis in grade 1 through grade 9 was on developing basic communicative skills; the teaching of literature was emphasized in grade 9 through grade 11; and grade 12 stressed the study of psychology, ethics, and logic (Ghaith, 1991).

In 1971, the Center for Educational Research and Development (CERD) was established and entrusted with the mission of overseeing the implementation of the new curricula, producing textbooks, planning teaching methods, and defining requirements and objectives for official examinations at the end of grades 9, 11, and 12. It is worth noting here that, in addition to English language textbooks, textbooks for science and mathematics were produced in English for grade 6 through grade 12 (Bazzi, 1971).

In 1975, 4 years after the new textbooks were introduced, the Lebanese civil war erupted and continued unabated until 1990. The impact of the war on education was catastrophic, especially for public schools where educational standards declined sharply, and many of the EFL teachers either left the country or were lured away by the private sector. Many private schools were established during the war, most of them using the teaching of English as a main attraction (Bashshur, 1991). In 1984, the Hariri Foundation was established with the purpose of helping young Lebanese high-school and university graduates continue their education in universities abroad, mainly in the United States, England, and France. Because proficiency in English was a major condition for studying in English-speaking universities, the Foundation established the Special English Training Program, which lasted until 1995, in cooperation with the American University of Beirut.[1] Over 12,000 students passed through the program before being sent abroad or to local English-medium universities (Ghaith, 1991).

Another major development was the introduction of English as the main language of instruction in tertiary education. In fact, a few English-medium universities, such as Al-Manar University and the University of Balamand, were established in traditional French territory (Bashshur, 1997). In addition, some established universities, such as the Lebanese American University, expanded outside Beirut. Furthermore, many colleges and language centers grew into English-medium universities; the Ministry of Education recognizes the existence of about 43 such institutions (Abi Najm, 2003). As important as the establishment of English-medium universities was the incursion of English into Arabic- and French-medium universities (e.g., Beirut Arab University, St. Joseph University, and Universite Saint-Esprit Kaslik), which have added English language courses and some new programs and subject matter courses in English in order to ensure that their students are not left behind in a world increasingly dominated by English (Bashshur, 1997; Baydoun, 1998; Koussaifi, 1998).

---

[1]Personal communication with Shehadeh Abboud, Director of the SET Program during the period 1987 to 1993.

In 1997, the government introduced a new curriculum, and decreed that a second foreign language was mandatory. Thus, English was introduced in schools whose second language is French at the rate of 2 hours a week starting in the 7th grade. The new curriculum is thematic and content based, with skill integration and emphasis on the development of proper study habits, critical thinking, and cultural awareness, in addition to the traditional skills of listening, speaking, reading, and writing (Shaaban & Ghaith, 1997). Over a period of 3 years, EFL textbooks for all grades (1 through 12) were produced. The new curriculum and textbooks were received with a mixture of optimism and ambivalence. Some felt that they were too ambitious, setting objectives that schools would not be able to meet within the time allotted to English (Sayyed Kassem, 2001). On the other hand, EFL teachers in private schools felt that the curriculum was promising, but the textbooks were not as effective in addressing curriculum objectives as the ESL textbooks produced abroad (CERD workshop participants, personal communications, July, 1998).

The increased attention paid to English language education was perceived by many educators to be eroding the power of French in the Lebanese society (Smaily-Hajjar, 1996; Zakaria, 1992). Although CERD statistics still show that 73.5% of classes in Lebanese schools are French medium as opposed to 27.5% that are English medium (Smaily-Hajjar, 1996), there are many signs of the advances made by English. One such significant indication is the fact that, until 1996, 63% of French-medium schools were teaching English as a third language, as opposed to only 26% of English-medium schools teaching French as a third language (Smaily-Hajjar, 1996).

Another sign of the increasing importance of the role of English in Lebanon is the practices and the positive attitudes of the Lebanese people. For example, in her study of the attitudes of Lebanese university students, Smaily-Hajjar (1996) reported that only 30% of them often watched French television programs, as opposed to 73% who often watched English programs. As for radio programs, 33% listened to French-medium stations, as opposed to 45% who listened to English-medium stations. Only in the press is French ahead of English (15% as opposed to 5%). But, in reality, this difference is not significant because most Lebanese follow the local Arabic-language press. Abou, Kasparian, and Haddad (1996) found that 61.5 % of Lebanese believe that English is the most vital language for the future of Lebanon, as opposed to 31.8% who saw French as the most vital. In Ghaleb and Joseph's (2000) study, 67% of the subjects felt that English was the most important language for Lebanon as opposed to 31% who preferred French.

It is obvious from these findings that English is making remarkable strides as a language of education in Lebanon. Naturally, the teaching of English in Lebanon has undergone major changes in philosophy, methods, and techniques. The teaching of English as a third language has added a new dimension to the issue of teaching English; the methods and techniques are not necessarily the same as in ESL due to such factors as purposes, time, and domains of use of the language.

THE ELT CURRICULUM

EFL teaching in English-medium schools in Lebanon starts in preschool in private schools and in grade 1 in public schools. English is also the medium of instruction of science and mathematics beyond the 6th grade.

The new Lebanese English Language Curriculum assigns to teaching English the same number of hours assigned to teaching the native language, Arabic. Thus, the following periods of English appear in the weekly schedule: lower elementary (grades 1 through 3) 7 hours; upper elementary (grades 4 through 6) 6 hours; intermediate (grades 7 through 9) 5 hours; first secondary (grade 10) 5 hours; second secondary, 5 hours for Humanities and 3 hours for Sciences; third secondary, 5 hours for Humanities, 3 hours for Social Studies, and 2 hours for general and life sciences (Shaaban & Ghaith, 1999).

Moreover, two periods a week of English as a second foreign language are assigned to those French-educated students in grade 7 through grade 12. Two periods of translation between Arabic and English are also given to students in the second secondary and in the Humanities and Social Studies section of the third secondary (Shaaban & Ghaith, 1999).

In order to help deal with all the demands and pressures on the system, the Ministry of Education established the English Language Unit (ELU) in 1982 with the following functions: (a) organizing miniconferences, lectures, and seminars; (b) conducting in-service training; (c) classroom observation for purposes of identifying potential trainers; and (d) designing innovative programs. In the 1990s, the Unit was made part of the Directorate of Educational Guidance with little change in its function (Makram Haddad, Lebanese Ministry of Education, personal communication, March 12, 2001).

In addition to the ELU, there is the English Language Inspection and Supervision Unit, which is part of the Central Inspection Office. The Unit's personnel, who are mainly experienced teachers of English, are charged with the task of visiting classes in order to evaluate the performance of the teachers and provide them with immediate feedback. In another significant development, many schools have recently established English departments that consist of a coordinator and all the teachers of English. Members hold periodic meetings where they conduct teacher development activities, discuss examinations, or discuss problems (Makram Haddad, Lebanese Ministry of Education, personal communication, March 12, 2001).

As for instructional resources, schools may either use the CERD textbooks or choose any materials that go along with the philosophy, principles, and methods recommended by the curriculum. Most private schools, however, have opted for ESL textbooks produced in the United States and England because they believe that the local books are inappropriate for their students (CERD workshop participants, personal communications, July, 1998).

There is a basic awareness among ELT educators that the old system of evaluation, based on a combination of the grammar translation and the audiolingual approaches to language teaching, is no longer compatible with the new curriculum that professes to be learner centered and communicative. After lengthy deliberations, a competency-based system of evaluation was adopted (Ministry of National Education, Youth and Sports, 1999). The new system, put into effect in 2001, represents a radical move from testing rote memory and factual information only to testing critical thinking and higher-order comprehension skills as well. The recommended classroom evaluation system draws heavily on alternative assessment techniques such as observations, conferences, group projects, self-evaluation, peer evaluation, learning logs, dialogue journals, quizzes, homework, and portfolios (Shaaban & Ghaith, 1997). However, the problem remains in aligning national examinations with the curriculum objectives and these alternative assessment practices.

Although interest in EFL has been increasing steadily since the early days of independence, the country still has a shortage of teachers and facilities. ELT in all public and some private schools is carried out mainly by Lebanese teachers, but in many private schools there are significant numbers of Palestinian teachers and native English-speaking teachers.

Teachers' colleges and the Faculty of Education at the Lebanese University have contributed significantly to meeting the demands of the public sector. The American University of Beirut and the Lebanese American University, with their strong departments of education, have helped prepare English language teachers, mainly for the elitist private schools in Beirut. Furthermore, the recent mushrooming of new English-medium universities all over the country has helped fill part of the gap. All of the institutions mentioned do not only preservice, but also in-service EFL training. It is also worth noting that the Association of Teachers of English in Lebanon, the British Council, AMIDEAST, and commercial publishers carry out their own training activities.

Despite these efforts, the overall level of proficiency in English among English language teachers remains far from satisfactory. Most students who join English departments or TEFL programs are not proficient in English, but they are nonetheless employed by schools as the demand exceeds the supply. The Lebanese Ministry of Education has attempted in the past to arrange for enrichment English language classes for the less proficient teachers, but the attempt remained largely symbolic and ineffective.

As for expatriate teachers, there were, before the civil war, many native English speakers who taught in missionary and elitist private schools in all the educational cycles, from preschool to the end of secondary school. Basic English language courses at most universities were also taught by native speakers. The war drove most of those out of the country, and the local teachers and English-speaking housewives, who were given fast ELT training and sent to the field, had to spread themselves too thin in order to fill in for the departing expatriates.

English-speaking teachers are returning to the country now, many of them of Lebanese descent who fled the country during the war to go to England, Canada,

Australia, and the United States. Many of these teachers are taking EFL courses in Lebanon or abroad, mainly by correspondence, in order to gain the qualifications needed for teaching English.

BECOMING AN ENGLISH TEACHER

My first exposure to the English language was in 1959, at the age of 7, in the first grade in a private school in my hometown, Al-Marj, in the Bekaa Valley. My English teachers were Palestinians. Although Lebanon had decreed at the time that schools could use either French or English as a foreign language, there were not many Lebanese who were proficient enough in English to teach it because French was the dominant language of the land. In Palestine, on the other hand, English was the major foreign language taught in schools because the country had been under the British mandate since the end of World War I.

The most popular method of teaching EFL at the time was a local version of the grammar-translation method. Reading and translation were prevalent. The textbooks used were those produced by commercial British publishers. The texts were rich with simplified literary texts. Unfamiliar vocabulary was taught before reading, usually through synonyms in Arabic. The reading lesson itself took the form of reading aloud, which was intended for teaching and checking on proper pronunciation. After the text was read a few times by different students who were called on to read different parts aloud, comprehension questions were asked. The explanations were given in both English and Arabic. No attempt was made to teach language in context or to provide dialogues and conversations; no nursery rhymes and nursery stories were introduced. The official examination at the end of the 5th grade was a composition that was descriptive in nature.

In the intermediate school, the same approach was followed with slight modifications. Memorization of poems was introduced. I remember memorizing a Shakespeare sonnet without understanding what it meant. However, the thrust of the program was preparation for the official exam at the end of the 9th grade. The exam consisted of a composition on some serious topic such as patriotism, patience, or friendship. Students were made to memorize model compositions in the hope that the same topics would appear on the official examination.

In the secondary cycle, the emphasis was on literature. Of course, very little original literature was taught; the materials in the hands of students basically consisted of notes prepared by some Lebanese teachers. Students were asked to memorize the notes. There was much material to deal with (the Romantics, Victorians, Shakespeare, and others), and students usually emphasized one of the topics, most often Shakespeare, because there was always a question about him on the exam. The interesting thing was that the official examination questions usually related to the notes more than they did to the texts. I remember responding to the topic, "Write about an English literary figure who represents his age giving examples from his works." I wrote about Shakespeare and how his works reflected the Elizabethan age; my grade was one of the highest, 16 out of a possible 20, which made me very proud of my achievement and might have influenced my decision later on to study English.

In brief, the system of education that I studied under was characterized by teacher-centered classrooms, excessive use of the first language, and nonfluent teachers who code-switched heavily. It was based on unrealistic expectations set by the official curricula and the official examinations.

After graduation from high school, I joined the English language and literature program at the Lebanese University's Faculty of Education where I was one of 40 students. We studied for 4 years for the *licence d' enseignement* (teaching license) and an additional year for the teaching diploma. The license program included courses in education, language, and literature, with the first year dedicated mainly to the improvement of the students' own English. In the fifth year, we followed courses in methodology and practice teaching in secondary schools. Many of the professors in the department were Americans on Fulbright grants, and some were British and American professors at other universities who taught us on a part-time basis. Interaction with these native speakers helped improve my English language proficiency a great deal.

During my years in college, I taught on a part-time basis at two schools, and found myself using the same methods and techniques that my teachers used when I was a student. However, when one of our new professors started his methods course advocating the audiolingual method, I realized that I needed to introduce new elements into my teaching. I started to apply what I was learning in the methods course in my teaching. However, the excitement I had experienced with the new methods had to give way to stressing grammar and composition when I was asked to teach the 9th graders who were going to sit for the official examination. I felt that there must be more enjoyable and fruitful ways of teaching English and that I needed to explore them. And thus the idea of my traveling to the United States for a master's degree in the teaching of English was born.

I applied for and received a Fulbright-Hayes grant to study for the M.A. in TESL at the University of Texas at Austin. The experience was invigorating; new country, new educational setup, new teachers, new courses, and new educational philosophy. I discovered I was really hungry for knowledge and, as a result, I did extremely well in all my courses. After receiving a M.A., I continued my studies for a Ph.D. in applied linguistics, supported by the Fulbright grant. My interest in ESL continued, but I developed an equal interest in phonology and sociolinguistics.

Upon my return to Lebanon in 1978, I was appointed assistant professor in the English and Education Departments at the American University of Beirut. Two years later, I was appointed Director of the Center for English Language Research and Teaching. I have taught methods courses and supervised M.A. theses in the various areas of English language education. I have also helped design and coordinate major intensive English programs associated with the University. The most significant work I have done in this area was the introduction of an in-service teacher-training program in 1989 that continued for over 8 years and covered most of the regions in Lebanon. The training program was based on workshops held annually between 1987 and 1995 in Larnaca, Cyprus, for which TESL experts were brought from the United States to train 25 to 30 Lebanese teachers for 10 days in the summer. The major themes of these workshops were cooperative learning, communicative teaching, alternative assessment, content-based instruction, and specific skill training (for more information, see Shaaban & Ghaith, 1994).

Another major task I became involved in was the design of the English language curriculum that was put into effect in 1998, the first curriculum revision since 1968. I served as the coordinator of the project, working with a coordinating committee of 8 professors and 35 teachers from across the country. This gave me the chance to put all my knowledge, experience, and ideas into practice. Interacting with such large numbers of practitioners helped put things into perspective and give a practical touch to the curriculum. The curriculum is a thematic, content-based one that stresses skill integration, cooperative learning, autonomy in learning, cultural awareness, critical thinking, and study habits (for more about the Lebanese English language curriculum, see Shaaban & Ghaith, 1997). I also coordinated the teacher-training workshops for both public and private schools that followed the issuance of the new curriculum. Teacher-training handbooks were prepared and distributed to all participants (Shaaban et. al., 1998).

At present, I am still active in teaching, research, and development. I continue to be involved in teacher-training activities and in consultation work with schools and universities in Lebanon and the Arabian Gulf region. The consultation work I am involved in includes conducting needs analysis surveys, designing English language programs, evaluating programs, and training teachers.

CONCLUSION

This chapter provided an explication and analysis of the English language teaching situation in Lebanon. It presented a historical overview of the introduction and expansion of EFL in the Lebanese educational system, examined the structure and organization of the new English language curriculum, and discussed my development as an English language teacher, teacher trainer, and curriculum designer. The chapter also showed that the English language profession in Lebanon is under tremendous pressure to meet the increasing demands for English, both quantitative and qualitative, in the age of globalization and international communication.

In fact, the English language teaching scene in Lebanon is beset by many chronic problems, ranging from inadequate preparation and minimal professional development of teachers to the relatively low proficiency in English of students after they spend 12 years studying English, as attested by university English language admission tests (Shaaban, 1995), to inadequate technological and audiovisual facilities to go with the new curriculum, to lack of understanding among teachers of competency testing. Despite all of these shortcomings, ELT in Lebanon continues to thrive because the strength of the country depends on the strength of its tourism, financial services, and trade. These three bases of the Lebanese economy will be greatly enhanced if the Lebanese work force commands a high level of proficiency in English. The Lebanese government and the Lebanese population know this, and it is hoped that, in time, this knowledge will bring about a major reevaluation and reorganization of the various elements of the EFL teaching situation in the country.

REFERENCES

Abi Najm, T. (2003, July 27). Rumors about some universities precede facts and possible solutions remain elusive: Who applies and who violates the higher education regulations? *An Nahar,* 14.

Abou, S., Kasparian, C., & Haddad, K. (1996). *Anatomie de la Francophonie Libanaise* [Structure of the Lebanese Francophone]. Beirut: St. Joseph University.

Bashshur, M. (1978). *The structure of the Lebanese educational system.* Beirut: Center for Educational Research and Development.

Bashshur, M. (1991, March). Education: Conflict regulation vs. national building. Paper presented at the Comparative and International Education Society Conference, Pittsburgh, PA.

Bashshur, M. (1997). Higher education in Lebanon from a historical perspective. In A. Al-Amine (Ed.), *Higher education in Lebanon* (pp. 15–93). Beirut, Lebanon: Lebanese Association for Educational Sciences.

Baydoun, A. (1998, August 13). Language proficiency in our country is declining ... even in Arabic. *An-Nahar,* 14.

Bazzi, M. (1971). *An analytical study of English examination in the Lebanese Baccalaureate, part 1.* Unpublished master's thesis, American University of Beirut, Beirut, Lebanon.

Bikar, E. (1998, August 13). Using many languages in one sentence: A Lebanese identity that is unclosed and incoherent. *An-Nahar,* 14.

Crystal, D. (1997). *English as a global language.* Cambridge, England: Cambridge University Press.

Ghaith, G. (1991). *An analysis of teaching practices within the Hariri special English program in the Republic of Lebanon.* Unpublished doctoral dissertation, Indiana University of Bloomington.

Heller, M. (1999). Alternative ideologies of *la francophonie. Journal of Sociolinguisitcs, 3*(3), 336–359.

Koussaifi, M. (1998). What is new at Kaslik's Business School? *Campus,* 2, 6.

Mathew, R. D., & Akrawi, M. (1949). *Education in the Arab countries of the Near East.* Washington, DC: American Council on Education.

McArthur, T. (1998). *The English languages.* Cambridge, England: Cambridge University Press.

Ministry of National Education, Youth and Sports. (1999). *Evaluation teacher's guide: English language.* Beirut, Lebanon: National Center for Educational Research and Development.

Sayyed Kassem, K. M. (2001, September). *A preliminary proposal for revising the English language curriculum and textbooks.* Paper presented at the 2nd Educational Conference on the New Lebanese Curricula, Beirut, Lebanon.

Shaaban, K. (1995). Evaluation and testing of reading in ESL. *Educational Evaluation II: Measurement and Evaluation in English as a Second Language.* Beirut: Hariri Foundation.

Shaaban, K. (1997). Bilingual education in Lebanon. In J. Cummins & D. Corson (Eds.), *Encyclopedia of language and education, volume 5: Bilingual education* (pp. 251–259). Dordrecht: Kluwer Academic Publishers.

Shaaban, K., Ad-Daoud, N., Ghaith, G., Ghaleb, M., Ghosn, I., Iskandarani, R., & Khoury, M. (1998). *Teacher training handbook for English as a first foreign language.* Beirut: National Center for Educational Research and Development.

Shaaban, K., & Ghaith, G. (1994). Cooperative learning and staff development in Lebanon. *Cooperative Learning, 14*(3), 51–52.

Shaaban, K., & Ghaith, G. (1997). An integrated approach to foreign language teaching in Lebanon. *Language, Culture and Curriculum, 10*(3), 200–207.

Shaaban, K. & Ghaith, G. (1999). Lebanon's language-in-education policies: From bilingualism to trilingualism. *Language Problems & Language Planning, 23*(1), 1–16.

Shaaban, K., & Ghaith, G. (2000). Historical overview of the role of language in education in Lebanon. In K. Shaaban (Ed.), *Language and education* (pp. 17–45). Beirut: Lebanese Association for Educational Sciences.

Smaily-Hajjar, W. (1996). *Le francais et l'anglais langues etrangeres au Liban: analyse de leurs statuts actuel* [French and English as foreign languages in Lebanon: Analysis of their actual status]. Unpublished doctoral thesis, Universite de Nancy II, France.

Zakaria, M. (1992). Effectiveness of bilingualism. In *The teaching language in Lebanon: Proceedings of the Balamand University Conference* (pp. 70–94).

11

ENGLISH LANGUAGE TEACHING IN POLAND: TRADITION AND REFORM

Joanna Radwanska-Williams
Macao Polytechnic Institute, Macau

Liliana Piasecka
University of Opole, Poland

Poland is a country of approximately 38.7 million people and 312,685 square kilometers, in what the British historian Norman Davies (1984) called "the heart of Europe". The history of Poland reaches back over 1,000 years, to the beginning of Polish statehood in the 10th century. Poland lost its independence in 1795, and regained it after World War I under the Treaty of Versailles. After World War II, Poland fell into the Soviet sphere of influence as part of the Warsaw Pact until the collapse of communism in 1989. Since then, Poland has been a parliamentary democracy with direct elections for the parliament and for the presidency. In 1999, Poland joined NATO, and joined the European Union more recently.

The official language of Poland is Polish, a language with a strong literary tradition dating back to the Renaissance (Milosz, 1983). Since World War II, the population has been linguistically homogeneous, with only a small number of ethnic minorities. Polish is overwhelmingly the medium of communication in all aspects of everyday life, including education, government, and the media. English has traditionally been taught as a foreign language, alongside major European languages such as French and German. However, during the communist period, the teaching of Russian was compulsory at all levels of the educational system (primary, secondary, and tertiary). Since the political changes of 1989, English has replaced Russian as the most commonly taught foreign language. This emphasis on English language teaching, along with the teaching of other foreign languages, has been a part of a massive reform of the educational system.

HISTORY OF ELT IN POLAND

The history of English language teaching in Poland can be divided into the periods before and after World War II. Within this broad division, the earliest history (i.e., before World War I) is difficult to reconstruct, because the major issue at that time was whether Polish was to be permitted as the medium of instruction, especially in the Russian and Prussian empires, which enforced education in Russian and German. Thus, the status of ELT was not a focus of debate. By contrast, the status of ELT does enter into the overall picture of foreign-language teaching in the interwar period (1919–1939) and the communist period (1946–1989).

During the interwar period, the challenge of the educational system was to merge the three systems inherited from the foreign imperial partitions of the 19th century,[1] and to reestablish a predominantly Polish-medium education (with some exemptions, e.g., for Yiddish). The methodology of teaching foreign languages was widely discussed, including (a) whether schools should teach one or two foreign languages; (b) whether the teaching of foreign languages in schools should focus solely on communicative purposes or on educational purposes as well; (c) whether teaching should cover only matters relating to the language or also include geographical and cultural material; (d) what methods should be used in such teaching; (e) to what extent it should include the teaching of grammar; (f) what vocabulary should be taken into account, and so on (Grucza, 2001).

A professional association, the Polish Neophilological Society, was established in 1930 in Warsaw during the First Congress of Teachers of Modern Languages, together with the journal *Neofilolog,* which published "articles written by eminent practitioners and theoreticians of foreign language teaching" (Grucza, 2001, p. 63). University departments of neophilology (i.e., the study of modern languages and literatures) were established, and there was a close cooperation between the universities and the schools; "university professors did not spurn such practical occupations as writing foreign language textbooks for the schools" (Grucza, 2001, p. 63). The most commonly taught foreign languages were German, French, and English; a choice of one of these languages was compulsory starting at age 10 (Komorowska, 2001). These three languages, as well as Polish, were included in a project of the Institute of Phonetics at the University of Warsaw for the development of "handbook[s] which [were] meant to help in the teaching of pronunciation in Polish schools" (Grucza, 2001, p. 64). Thus, in the interwar period, there was a full-fledged development of language teaching as a profession, including ELT. Despite World War II and postwar repressions during the Stalinist period, the academic structures established before the war are still largely in place today.

---

[1]When the territory of Poland had been divided between Russia, Prussia, and Austria–Hungary.

During the communist period after World War II, Polish universities opened again, including the foreign-language departments. There was a brief flowering of interest in English immediately following the war; for example, the total enrollment in the English department at the University of Poznan in the academic year 1948–1949 was 300 students, about a tenfold increase over the prewar enrollment (Kielkiewicz, 2002). However, in 1948, Russian was introduced as the compulsory first foreign language at all levels of education. The privileged status of Russian would not be changed until 1990. During the Stalinist period, which peaked in 1950–1956, all Western foreign-language departments were closed down, except those at the University of Warsaw and the private Catholic University of Lublin, a unique institution in a communist country. These two universities were only allowed an enrollment of 20 students per year during this period (Grucza, 2001). Following the political unrest and thaw of 1956, the other foreign-language departments were gradually allowed to reopen.

In the 1960s and 1970s, the situation in the universities improved greatly. For example, at the University of Poznan, the English Department, which had been founded in 1919, reopened in 1965, with an initial first-year enrollment of 48 students. In 1968, it was converted into a School of English, with four departments: English language; English–Polish contrastive linguistics; teaching English as a foreign language, and English and American literature. Directed since 1968 by Jacek Fisiak, the school is internationally renowned, and houses four scholarly journals, including the international refereed journal, *Papers and Studies in Contrastive Linguistics.* The school has served as a leading center for English studies in Poland from 1965 to 1992, holding a summer school of English for third-year university students, with an annual enrollment of 300, and, since 1970, serves as the national center for the annual English language competition for secondary-school students, called the *olympiad* (Kielkiewicz, 2002). The olympiad is held in Poland in every subject, and the top contestants in the national competition are exempt from the university entrance examination in that particular subject.

Although it is safe to claim that the academic standard of English at universities was high during the communist period, the situation in primary and secondary schools was more complex. At the primary or basic school level, grades 1 through 8, starting at age 7, which was the level of compulsory education until age 14 (before 1965) or 15 (after 1965), little or no English was taught. Russian was the compulsory language from age 11 (grade 5). On the other hand, a second foreign language was required starting at the secondary-school level (grade 9 through grade 12). In the 1950s and 1960s, the second language was chosen from among English, German, French and Latin; in the 1970s, the selection expanded based on local conditions to include other West European languages, such as Italian and Spanish, and less commonly taught languages such as Hungarian and Swedish (Komorowska, 2001). The educational reform of 1965 also introduced, on a limited scale in the five largest cities, bilingual secondary schools with extended hours of foreign-language instruction and the teaching of other subjects through the foreign-language medium. Thus, there would be an English school, a German school, and so on. Since 1989, a larger number of these bilingual schools have been established and enjoy great popularity. Thus, it can be said that foreign-language education at the secondary school level during the communist period was of a sufficiently high standard to provide a foundation for the transition to the post-1989 period of democratic Poland.

THE ELT CURRICULUM

The changeover of the political system in 1989 brought about a series of swift and sweeping reforms in Poland, intended to transform it into a democracy and integrate it completely into the economic and political alliances of Western Europe. The educational system was reformed in 1990, and again in 1999. In the words of the Ministry of National Education:

> Since the moment of implementation in 1990, the reforms of the Polish education system have been designed to transform it in a way which ensures that the knowledge and competence acquired in Poland will allow a Polish pupil or student to continue or easily extend his/her education in other countries. (International Cooperation, 2002, Web site)

In the field of foreign-language education, this reform meant first and foremost that the compulsory study of Russian was abolished. Russian continues to be taught in Poland, but on an equal footing with Western European languages. At the primary-school level, one foreign language is required from age 11 (since 1999, from age 10). The most popular and most commonly taught language now is English: "In the school year 1999/2000 there were 4,573,314 pupils in the primary and lower secondary schools, of which 1,892,116 (41%) learnt English, 1,002,497 learnt German and 508,917 (11%) learnt Russian. Russian was taught mainly in the rural areas (20.6% of pupils), while in the urban areas it was taught to 4.7% of pupils only" (Komorowska, 2001, p. 7).

At the upper-secondary school level (before 1999, at grade 9 through grade 12, age 15 through age 18), two foreign languages are required, provided that the school can recruit enough teachers, which continues to be a problem in rural areas. Since the second reform of 1999, two foreign languages are being phased in also at the lower-secondary level (grades 7 through 9, with upper-secondary having been restructured as grades 10 through 12). The minimum number of hours for foreign-language instruction is 2 hours per week at the primary level, and 5 hours per week for both languages combined at the upper-secondary level. It is a common phenomenon that parents help to subsidize the school to hire teachers to offer extra hours. Schools are also encouraged to break up large classes (over 26 students) in order to ensure better delivery of language instruction (Komorowska, 2001).

The structure of the curriculum for foreign languages, including English, is governed by the dual principle of ensuring national standards and encouraging school autonomy. The core guidelines for the curriculum are articulated in documents published by the Ministry of National Education in 1997 and 1999, and based on recommendations by the Council of Europe. These specify general attainment and proficiency goals; for example, the general target for lower secondary is "acquisition of language skills enabling relatively efficient language communication on basic life matters in contact with foreigners" (Komorowska, 2001, p. 11). The goals are divided into several fields (Komorowska, 2001): communication (listening, speaking, reading, and writing, with "a certain degree of priority ... to oral skills"); grammar (pronunciation, grammar, lexis, and language awareness); sociocultural ("knowledge of others" and "understanding of others"); and cognitive and affective ("independent learning" and "personality development"). The latter two are innovations of the core curriculum; for example, the goal of knowledge of others "obliges schools to develop interest in the culture and civilization of the target language community", and recommended activities here are "correspondence and e-mail"; while "personality development" includes "supporting the feeling of self-worth and belief in the child's ability to acquire a foreign language", and recommended activities are "group work and project work" (Komorowska, 2001, p. 13). Overall, the core curriculum recommends the communicative approach and the use of authentic materials and new technologies.

Under the broad guidelines of the core curriculum, the Ministry of National Education approves the use of a variety of syllabi and language textbooks. The syllabi may be those developed and published by major academic publishers, or ones developed by individual schools and teachers. Each school is free to choose any syllabus or to develop its own, the latter to be approved by the Ministry. Secondly, the Ministry approves language textbooks that fit the goals of the curriculum. For example, the list for lower secondary school includes 43 textbooks for English, published by a variety of British, U.S., and Polish publishers. This compares with 64 textbooks for Polish, 19 for German, 7 for French and 7 for Russian (Ministry of National Education, 2003). This freedom of choice is radically different from the ideological control of the communist period, when only one or two textbooks per subject were approved for use at each grade level.

Curriculum reform and the development of ELT in Poland is aided by various Western programs and funding agencies and European programs (Komorowska, 2001, p. 3). For example, the British Council initiative, Support for Polish Reform in Teacher Education (SPRITE) provides teacher training and trainer training, with a focus on the methodology of teaching young learners (Pawelec, 2000). The British Council also sponsors nine university centers for English Teaching that offer teacher training at the major Polish universities. The Kosciuszko Foundation, a Polish-American cultural and academic organization, has sponsored a summer Teaching English in Poland program since 1991, in conjunction with UNESCO (United Nations Educational, Scientific and Cultural Organization). Over the 11 years of its existence, 1,070 American teachers have rendered service at 66 language immersion camps, which have reached approximately 6,600 students

(Kosciuszko Foundation, 2003). The Polish-American Freedom Foundation, a development agency founded in 1999, sponsors English language projects in rural areas, and has funded 58 projects benefiting 13,000 students and teachers (Polish-American Freedom Foundation, 2003). The challenges of development are great, but the number of initiatives gives cause for optimism.

In addition to development sponsored by funding agencies, ELT in English in Poland is being developed by professional associations. The most prominent of these is the Polish branch of the International Association of Teachers of English as a Foreign Language (IATEFL, Poland). The association has held an annual conference since 1991, and has a well-developed Web site, http://www.iatefl.org.pl, and special-interest discussion groups. The association provides a focus for networking and development to the ELT profession. Its existence is testimony to the maturity of ELT in Poland today.

BECOMING AN ENGLISH TEACHER

Liliana Piasecka was born in 1953—a very significant year for the people of Central Europe. That year, Stalin died, and new hopes rose high in Poland. Liliana was too young to understand what was going on around her at that time, but she remembers that people from her childhood looked happy, at least to her. She also remembers that her hometown Wałbrzych, a coal-mining town, was full of people who came from different parts of Europe. There were reemigrants from Northern France (Poles who had gone to France in the 1920s looking for a better life), Greeks who had left Greece after the 1948 civil war, Poles from eastern and central Poland, Jews who had survived World War II and came from various places, and local Germans. All these people managed to live together peacefully and each community maintained its unique identity. Her childhood playground was quite varied, but all the children spoke standard Polish; because there was no local dialect, they had no choice.

Liliana's first encounter with English took place when she was 12 and in the sixth grade of primary school. At that time, Russian was the only foreign language taught in primary school. However, the Association of Polish Teachers had organized an inexpensive afternoon course in English, and Liliana's parents enrolled her in it. Thus, Liliana started learning English around the age of puberty, and she was fascinated by the teacher, a beautiful young woman who spoke to the pupils in a friendly and reassuring manner. All of this teacher's female learners wanted to become her true image—independent, free, and beautiful. She also taught in a way the students were not used to, using a lot of pictures and situations. There were course books with pictures that the pupils cut out, manipulated, and talked about. This teacher was the first to introduce the concepts of the English present continuous, present simple, and present perfect tenses to Liliana.

After Liliana had completed primary school, she went to grammar school, where English was one of the compulsory school subjects. At this point, she was very lucky again because she had a wonderful teacher of English, a recent university graduate with a passion for the Beatles. This teacher and the teacher of physics had set up a language lab with a pair of headphones for every learner. When the pupils put the headphones on, it was like entering a different world. They heard people who spoke directly to them; the Beatles sang their songs for each and every one of them. Liliana believes she owes a lot to her teacher and to the Beatles, not only the unique spirit of the 1960s, but also an immense learning experience. She acquired a lot of vocabulary and grammar through their songs. She also listened to Radio Luxemburg, as did many of her friends, although the broadcast quality was very poor at times. She read everything in English she could place her hands on. Actually, not much was available. Novels and stories were not so difficult to obtain because Soviet Publishers published many of them in English and they were quite cheap. Newspapers and magazines were more of a problem. In fact, the *Morning Star,* published by the Communist Party of Great Britain, was the only newspaper available. By reading it, Liliana learned the English version of the slogan, "*Workers of the world, unite*".

After 4 years at grammar school, with the general certificate of education in her pocket, Liliana took the entrance examination to enter the Department of English Philology at Wrocław University. The exam itself was a traumatic experience, mainly because many of the candidates to whom she spoke before taking the examination had already visited English-speaking countries and taken private lessons. Liliana had not done so, and therefore she thought that her chances of passing the examination were close to zero. However, she passed the exam and became a proud student of English Philology.

The beginnings at the University were a trial for Liliana's mind and soul. In her first year, she had to read epic literature and to her horror, she discovered she did not understand a word. Fortunately, she had friends with the same problems who lived in the same student hostel, and together they devised strategies for approaching this challenge. They shared the work and they studied together, a method that proved to be very effective. Liliana's subsequent years at the University were an unforgettable experience. Her proficiency in English was rapidly improving due to the many excellent classes in practical English, and also due to the fact that the conversation classes were taught by native speakers of English. Actually, Liliana's first encounter with native speakers took place at the University. She also had to read a variety of texts by great English and American writers, literary critics, and linguists, and this reading contributed significantly to her knowledge of the language and her intellectual development.

After Liliana had completed her third year at the university, she went to Great Britain for the summer holidays. The year was 1975, and at that time it was extremely difficult for Poles to travel to capitalist countries. Everything was a problem—getting a passport, a visa, a train ticket. However, Liliana and her best friend overcame the problems, and one sunny July morning arrived at Victoria Station in London. It was their first time in Britain, and they were fascinated by everything because everything was so different from what they had experienced until then. They stayed in London for a while, then hitchhiked to Edinburgh and back to London. On the way, they visited such places as Oxford, Cambridge, Stratford-on-Avon, York, Glasgow, Manchester, Salisbury, Stonehenge, and many other points of interest. Liliana came back home very rich in life and linguistic experience and brought back a rucksack full of books, all in English.

During Liliana's years at the university, she took a great interest in literature, especially in poetry, which resulted in her writing her master's thesis on e. e. cummings. In 1977, she graduated from the university and the same year, in autumn, she started a regular job in Wroclaw as a teacher of English in one of the grammar schools, where at that time she was the only teacher of English.

With regard to Liliana's preparation for the teaching profession, at the university she had courses in pedagogy, psychology, and methodology of teaching English as a foreign language. She also went to local schools to observe the lessons taught by experienced teachers of English. After her fourth year of study, she had a 4-week-long teaching practicum in a secondary school in Jelenia Góra, where she had to teach regular lessons under the supervision of the schoolteacher of English who was to advise and support her in her teaching. In addition, beginning in her second year of study she gave private lessons to individual learners of various ages, which made her sensitive to a number of factors that influence the process of language learning.

Thus equipped, Liliana started her career. On average, she taught 28 hours a week and had three lessons a week with the students in each grade. The teaching load was quite substantial for a beginner, and Liliana worked hard to prepare and teach her lessons in an interesting way. She had wonderful pupils who were very eager to learn English, who responded positively to her experiments (e.g., they sang songs, listened to the Beatles and other pop groups of the day, read and wrote limericks), and who appeared to be very creative and imaginative. Two years later, however, Liliana's Wrocław moved to Opole, where she dropped anchor for good.

In Opole, Liliana first taught English in a technical secondary school of electrical engineering. This was a real challenge because she had 2 hours of English a week with each grade, there was a large number of pupils (about 40) per grade, and the pupils were not divided into groups for foreign-language lessons. Liliana learned how to maintain discipline, and how to focus the attention of energetic teenagers, mainly male, who did not care much about English. She even managed to teach them some basic expressions and structures.

In 1984, Liliana moved from the technical school to a grammar school in Opole, and this time she was very lucky. She taught within the so-called "extensive English program", which meant six lessons of English a week to groups of about 16 to 17 pupils each. The pupils were very highly motivated and hard working. They wrote novels in weekly installments. They managed to set up an English Language Theatre and produced a show based on *Tales from Arabian Nights,* called "Old Shoes". The pupils prepared interesting materials for the lessons. They also devised a very clever game, Risk-and-Travel, which relates to history, life, and institutions in the United States (Lisiuk & Piasecka 1989).

Liliana also implemented many new teaching techniques and ideas, which she had learnt during a summer school for teachers of English as a foreign language in Exeter, England, in 1985. The course, entitled "Interaction and the Individual in the Classroom," was organized by the British Council and staffed by experienced teachers with unconventional and creative ways of teaching English. After the course, which opened her eyes to new perspectives and possibilities in teaching, Liliana started writing articles for Polish teachers of English that were published in the bimonthly journal, *Foreign Languages at School.* The articles were practical. She wanted to share with others what she had learned, and also to suggest how new ideas could be applied in the classroom.

In 1988, Liliana won a contest for the post of an assistant (in Poland, the lowest rank of university lecturer) at the Institute of English Philology of the Higher Pedagogical School in Opole. She stopped teaching at the secondary level, moved to the tertiary level, and started doing her own research. At the beginning, she taught a variety of subjects: grammar, conversation, translation, and ELT methodology. Her research interests went into applied linguistics, and, more specifically, into studies on second and foreign language acquisition. At that time, thanks to the mediation of Professor Piotr Ruszkiewicz, she contacted Professor Hanna Komorowska of Warsaw University, who agreed to supervise her Ph.D. dissertation. The dissertation was based on the empirical research on the vocabulary learning strategies of Polish learners of English. In June 1996, she was granted a Ph.D. in applied linguistics.

Working at the Higher Pedagogical School, which then became a university, Liliana attended many national and international conferences, seminars, and workshops. In 1991, she received a Hornby Trust Scholarship to spend 3 months at the University of Birmingham, in England, where she carried out research and had a chance to meet many distinguished linguists. Liliana has also participated in the courses for teachers and teacher trainers that were organized within the SOCRATES, ARION and COMENIUS programs sponsored by the European Union.

Since 1992, Liliana has been working cooperatively with the Teacher Training College in Opole, where she teaches ELT methodology and runs diploma seminars. She has participated in the exchange program set up by the British Council to help the teacher training colleges that were established in 1990s to satisfy the growing demand for qualified teachers of English in Poland. Through this program, the Lower Silesia College Consortium, of which the Teacher Training College in Opole was a member, cooperated with the University of Reading, in England. Together, they worked out the form and standards for the final diploma examination that the Colleges now use. As an ELT methodology teacher in the Teacher Training College, Liliana visits schools and observes lessons that the trainees teach during their teaching practicum. She also has the opportunity to discuss various language-teaching-related issues with in-service teachers who supervise the trainees' teaching practice. She considers the needs of the in-service teachers when preparing training sessions for them, which she offers through the local In-Service Teacher Training Center in Opole.

CONCLUSION

Following the political changeover of 1989, foreign-language teaching in Poland has seen a rapid change, from an emphasis on Russian to an emphasis on English and Western European languages. In the near future, Poland expects to become a full member of the European Union. In the past 10 years, the Polish government has aggressively pursued a policy of educational reform in preparation for Poland's full integration into Western economic and political structures. At the same time, the present reform has been based on a solid tradition of education and scholarship. There is no doubt that, in the present configuration, English will be as important in Poland as it is in Western Europe, whatever the future will hold.

REFERENCES

Davies, N. (1984). *Heart of Europe: A short history of Poland.* Oxford: Oxford University Press.

Grucza, F. (2001). Origins and development of applied linguistics in Poland. In E. F. K. Koerner & A. Szwedek, (Eds.), *Towards a history of linguistics in Poland: From the early beginnings to the end of the twentieth century* (pp. 53–100). Amsterdam: John Benjamins.

International cooperation in education. (2002) Warsaw: Ministry of National Education. Retrieved on November 16, 2002, from http://www.men.waw.pl/english/education/educat_15.htm

Kielkiewicz, A. (2002). *The school of English: historical sketch.* Poznan: Adam Mickiewicz University. Retrieved on February 26, 2003, from http://elex.amu.edu.pl/ifa/history.html

Komorowska, H. (2001). *Supplement to Foreign language teaching in schools in Europe.* Warsaw, Poland: EURYDICE Foundation.

Kosciuszko Foundation. (2003). *Teaching English in Poland program.* New York: Author. Retrieved August 1, 2003, from http://www.kosciuszkofoundation.org/summer/English.html

Lesiuk, E., & Piasecka, L., (1989). Risk-and-travel-game. *English Teaching Forum, 27*(4), 37–39.

Milosz, C. (1983). *The history of Polish literature* (2nd ed.). Berkeley: University of California Press.

Ministry of National Education. (2003). Web site. Retrieved November 16, 2002, from http://www.men.waw.pl

Pawelec, D. (2000, June). *Country notes June 2000 Poland.* London: British Council. Web site. Retrieved August 1, 2003, from htttp://www.britishcouncil.org/english/eltecs/polandup00.htm

Polish-American Freedom Foundation (2003). Web site. Retrieved August 1, 2003, from http://www.pafw.pl

12

TEACHING ENGLISH IN THE KINGDOM OF SAUDI ARABIA: SLOWLY BUT STEADILY CHANGING

Khalid Al-Seghayer
Saudi Arabia

Saudi Arabia was first established in the early 18th century, and modern Saudi Arabia was founded in 1932 by King Abdul Aziz. It is the largest of all nations in the region, occupying approximately 863,730,000 square miles in the central Arabian Peninsula. It is bordered by the Red Sea, the Indian Ocean, and the Arabian Gulf. It has a population of 17 million people, of which about 4 million are noncitizens. All Saudi Arabians are Muslims and nearly 98% are Arabs who are bound together by their common mother tongue Arabic, strong family and tribal relationships, and adherence to Islam.

In the broader context, English performs only one of the four functions (regulative, instrumental, interpersonal, and imaginative–innovative) proposed by Kachru (1982) and later by Berns (1990). English performs the instrumental function as a medium of learning at various stages in the educational system of Saudi Arabia. This function is the central focus of this chapter.

HISTORY OF ELT IN SAUDI ARABIA

It is not clear how English was introduced in Saudi Arabia because Saudi Arabia has never been under a European power. In fact, it was the Saudi government that undertook the initial steps in introducing English to its people. Why did English become part of Saudi society in general and the educational system in particular?

Shortly after the establishment of the Kingdom of Saudi Arabia in 1932, the Saudi government realized the importance of training citizens who would be capa-

125

ble of communicating with the outside world. The great expansion of the oil industry crystallized the importance of developing a foreign-language program that
would train citizens to staff government and Arabian American Oil Company positions (ARAMCO, 1968). The early stage of oil production required Saudis who
could successfully communicate in English with interests outside the country and
with foreign experts (Alam, 1986). In addition, nearly 2 million Muslims from all
over the world visited the country annually to perform *umra* (a religious rite).
Therefore, it became essential for Saudis to be taught English so they could interact
with the large number of English-speaking visitors to their country.

The huge revenues generated by the oil industry enabled the Saudi government
to launch large-scale development programs by the early 1970s. The purpose of
these programs was to create an infrastructure that included transportation, tele-
communications, electricity, water, education, health, and social welfare. This required importing manpower, whose common language was English, and training
Saudis who could communicate with them. Thus, educational policymakers realized the importance of introducing English into the curriculum to prepare personnel who could fill positions requiring knowledge of English.

Researchers generally agree that the English language was introduced into the
Saudi Arabian educational system in 1927, a few years after the establishment of
the Directorate of Education in 1923 (Al-Abdulkader, 1978). English was regis-
tered as a subject at the secondary level along with French, but with no definite
learning objectives. When the intermediate level (grades 7, 8, and 9) was introduced to form a transitional stage between the elementary and secondary levels in
1959, English became an established subject with specific instructional objectives and syllabi (Jan, 1984). In 1960, the same was done at the already established secondary level.

English enjoys a high status in Saudi Arabia as the only foreign language taught
in public schools and in many private schools, universities, and industrial and government institutions. English is taught as a core subject in public intermediate and
secondary grades, all private school grades, and at all Saudi universities as either an
elective subject or a major field of study. Even non-English majors are required to
take an introductory English course. English is used as the medium of instruction in
most university technical departments and in science, medicine, and engineering.
King Fahad University of Petroleum and Minerals uses English as its exclusive medium of instruction. A number of technical and vocational institutes as well as military academies include English as a subject in their curriculums. The same is true in
various public and private organizations, which often have training centers that
teach English to their employees. This status also applies to other aspects of employment. Advertisements for job openings in private sector areas, such as industry, hospitals, and hotels stress the employers' preferences for potential employees
who can speak English.

The mass media is also a vehicle for the presence of English in Saudi Arabia.
One of the two national Saudi TV stations, channel 2, is the English channel. The

European language radio station, with programming mainly in English and some in French, transmits 24 hours a day. There are three English daily newspapers, the *Arab News,* the *Daily Riyadh,* and the *Saudi Gazette.*

THE ELT CURRICULUM

Education is not compulsory in Saudi Arabia except at the elementary level. However, the high rate of school enrollment (3,837,482 students in public education and 336,224 in higher education for 2001) shows that the majority of Saudis attend school beyond that basic level (Ministry of Higher Education, 2001; General Presidency of Girls Education, 2001). Education is free at all levels for all citizens. Although men and women are educated separately, they basically follow the same curriculum.

General education comprises five levels: kindergarten, elementary, intermediate, secondary, and higher education. Kindergarten includes three divisions for different age groups: infant, nursery, and preliminary. The elementary level spans grades 1 through 6, the intermediate and secondary levels are 3-year cycles, the former including grades 7, 8, and 9 and the latter grades 10, 11, and 12.

English is the only foreign language taught to intermediate and secondary students in Saudi Arabia. It is a required subject for grades 7 through 12 in both boys' and girls' schools. Thus, during their general education, Saudi students study English for a total of 6 years. Textbooks and teaching methods are the same in boys' and girls' schools, and all students have four 45-minute periods (3 hours) of English instruction weekly. Zaid (1993) noted that because reading and writing are considered most important in English teaching, more emphasis is placed on teaching the content of the language than on developing communicative competence.

It has been decided recently that the English curriculum be required at the elementary level beginning in the academic year 2002–2003. Among the proposed rationales for introducing English into elementary level is that the current low English-proficiency level of Saudi students has been caused by limiting English instruction to the intermediate and secondary levels (Al-Shithri, 2002). Furthermore, in 2000, the National Committee for the English Language suggested the incorporation of computer-based instruction in the EFL curriculum (Ministry of Higher Education, 2000).

The teaching of English in Saudi Arabia is centralized and controlled by the Ministry of Education (ME) and the General Presidency of Girls' Education (GPGE). English teachers at each grade level are required to adhere to identical syllabus guidelines and deadlines. Instructional materials are developed in the English-language sections of the departments of curriculum development at the ME and GPGE. The ME and the GPGE also assign and distribute ELT textbooks to intermediate and secondary students throughout the country.

According to Al-Hajailan (1999), the curriculum departments at the central offices of the ME and the GPGE undertake the tasks of developing guides, establishing standards, and planning instructional units. To further improve the curriculum, these departments rely on teachers' suggestions, supervisors' reports, and the contributions of language researchers. Although teachers are encouraged to submit recommendations for improving English teaching (especially textbooks), many do not take advantage of this option, possibly due to lack of knowledge about English-language curriculum development, planning, design, and evaluation (Zaid, 1993).

Over the course of 70 years, the curriculum for English as a foreign language in Saudi Arabia has undergone a number of developments. From 1927 through 1959, although English was taught in Saudi schools, there was no defined curriculum. The early 1960s witnessed the emergence of a comprehensive English curriculum, entitled *Living English for the Arab World* (Allen & Cooke, 1961), adapted from neighboring countries' curricula. Until 1964, a total of eight periods weekly were allocated to English language instruction. In 1971, the number of instructional periods was reduced to six and later to four (Ministry of Education, 1982). *Living English for the Arab World* remained in use until 1980. Al-Subahi (1988) argued that this program was feasible neither for Saudi education nor for the needs and interests of learners.

In 1980, the ME, in collaboration with Macmillan Press, introduced a new English program called *Saudi Arabian Schools English* at the intermediate and secondary levels (Field, 1980). This curriculum was believed to correspond better to the needs of learners and remained in use for almost 15 years.

In 1990, the Curriculum Department at the ME, in collaboration with some EFL specialists from King Fahad University, launched a new project to revise the English curriculum. The academic year 1995–1996 was marked for official implementation of the new curriculum, called *English for Saudi Arabia* (Centre for Statistical Data and Educational Documentation, 1991; Directorate of Curriculum, 1995), for teaching English as a core subject at the intermediate and secondary levels.

The new curriculum was developed around four major components: objective, content, teaching method, and student evaluation techniques. The main objective at the intermediate level is to enable Saudi students to speak, read, and listen with understanding to basic contemporary English discourse and to write a connected passage of up to half a page about a simple subject or incident. A further objective is to give pupils enough knowledge of the language to help them in their chosen vocations and introduce them to the outside world. These objectives are applied to the secondary level as well, with higher expectations and a more demanding focus on the four language skills—listening, reading, speaking, and writing.

These textbooks underwent many modifications during pilot experimentation in order to make them suitable for all students. During the selection of instructional material, the lessons and topics were examined to make sure they dealt with a variety of issues, met students' needs, and were interesting and easy to understand. They include discussion of local, Islamic, and international or target cultures. They were designed sequentially, introduced students to sufficient grammatical rules presented in an easy-to-grasp manner, and included vocabulary levels appropriate to students' educational progress.

In 1995, the entire series was completed and came under the ownership of the ME. These instructional materials consist of a teacher's guide and student textbook and workbook (Directorate of Curriculum, 1995). This set has been criticized for its lack of inclusion of some target elements of culture, such as lifestyle, family orientation, and names of places and people (Almulhim, 2001).

The methods used in teaching English in Saudi Arabia are the audiolingual method (ALM) and to some extent, the grammar translation method (GTM). Zaid (1993) noted that the ALM is the most popular method, and it is preferred by English teachers; however, all of the ALM's components are not incorporated. Most noticeably, the use of language laboratories is not included, although their use is essential to the method. Thus, Saudi students are not exposed to authentic spoken English. However, teachers do comply with the main tenet of the ALM, emphasizing the processing of stimulus and response situations. As a result, students are engaged in monotonous grammatical rule drills and repetition of words and phrases. Another commonly used teaching method in Saudi Arabia is the GTM. Teachers tend to rely heavily on explaining grammatical structures as the central focus of their teaching, as well as on memorization and vocabulary instructions (Al-Ahaydib, 1986). Further, teachers often use Arabic in teaching English or depend on translation (Abu-Ghararah, 1986, 1990).

The system just described, although built on sound pedagogical objectives, fails to produce learners who can carry on a basic conversation or comprehend a simple oral or written message. This is not a normal achievement level, especially after 508 mandatory hours of English study over the intermediate and secondary school years. There are a number of contributing reasons for low EFL proficiency among Saudi students, some that can be traced back to the teaching method employed, and others the result of student attitude and motivation. Almulhim (2001) attributed Saudi students' deficiencies in the four skills, especially speaking, to extensive use of Arabic in the classroom.

Because English is not immediately relevant to their needs, students usually do not pay serious attention to learning the language, and devote their efforts to acquiring the minimal competency needed to pass to the next grade level. They tend only to memorize grammatical rules, passages of written English, and vocabulary (Jan, 1984; Zaid, 1993). Intrinsic motivation is the key ingredient missing of most Saudi students, who are goaded by the extrinsic influence of the educational system.

English teachers in Saudi Arabia are trained to teach at the intermediate and secondary levels in the public schools in the English departments of different Saudi universities or in 4-year English programs at various colleges. Graduates of these programs are awarded a bachelor's degree in English. Prospective teachers enroll in an intensive program for one semester, then join the academic English program to take courses in linguistics, phonology, morphology, syntax, English literature, and teaching methods. The teacher trainees must take varying numbers of basic required education courses and courses prescribed by the department of English, along with elective courses. The total number of courses, and the number of courses in each of these categories, may vary from one institution to another. In the last semester of the preparation program, prospective teachers are assigned to teach for one semester in an intermediate or secondary school under the supervision of an advisor. Faculty members in the preparation programs are drawn from Saudi Arabia, the United Kingdom, the United States, Canada, Australia, and various Islamic and Arab countries.

Currently, eight universities offer foreign-language teacher preparation programs for both men and women, who receive bachelor's degrees in English. In 2000, the total number of graduates reached approximately 1,500 (Ministry of Higher Education, 2000). In addition, there are 4-year preparation programs that train female English teachers throughout the country. In 2000, 759 female English teachers had earned bachelor's degrees (General Presidency of Girls Education, 2001).

BECOMING AN ENGLISH TEACHER

I am a product of the English-instruction environment that has been described in the previous sections, first as a student and later as an English teacher. I began learning English at the age of 13, anticipating my English studies with both enthusiasm and trepidation. I was fearful because I had heard from other students how difficult the subject was, but excited due to the high ambitions I held for mastering the language. I was elated when I was introduced to the English alphabet on the first day of class, and went home that day proud that I could recite some English letters.

I proceeded well during the first year of the intermediate level, but my enthusiasm declined in the second and third years because of the way I was taught and the seeming uselessness of English. My zeal soon returned due to the teacher I had in grade 10 through grade 12, who stressed the importance and relevance of English to our educational and professional lives. In retrospect, my interest in English as a future profession developed in the 11th grade. This teacher inspired me and made me constantly consider the heart of the problem associated with learning English—the negative attitudes many of my classmates expressed.

On graduating from the secondary level, I was admitted to the English Department at the University of Imam and enrolled in the intensive language-improvement program for one semester. While in this program, I counted the days, looking forward to receiving training as an English teacher. I was disappointed when I realized that the central focus of the English Department was on English literature and linguistics. This put a gloomier face on the picture I had of myself as an English teacher who could simplify the process of learning English, and it seemed unlikely that I could achieve my goal. My enthusiasm for teaching English diminished greatly throughout my college years.

The last semester of study in English departments in Saudi institutions of higher learning offers teacher trainees an opportunity to practice teaching at a designated intermediate or secondary school. As I approached this stage, I again saw an opportunity to make a difference. I went to the classroom chiefly concerned with restoring students' motivation and teaching them so they could actually use English and not merely pass the final exam. Here I was, in a seventh-grade classroom where I could implement my beliefs.

I spent some time talking to the students about the relevance of English to their future, explaining that it was important because it was commonly used for international communication. When I felt students had developed a positive attitude toward learning English, I told them that their primary concern should be learning the language. If they would show signs of such interest, they would all pass the exam. Mindful of the fact that classroom atmosphere is affected by the teacher's attitude and behavior, I tried to create a friendly place where students felt free to express themselves without fear of being corrected and embarrassed. Students were given equal opportunities to contribute and were praised for their participation. I believe my class had a positive educational experience because the students did not raise the issue of the final exam for the remainder of the semester.

In 1993, I earned my bachelor's degree in Teaching English as a Foreign Language. At that time, my career objective was to teach English to intermediate or secondary school children. However, because of my high grade-point average, I was offered a position as a teaching assistant with the university. My responsibility was to teach some of the language improvement courses in the intensive English program that students were required to take before being formally accepted into the English Department. While in this position, my interest in language education intensified and fueled my desire to pursue graduate degrees at the master's and doctoral levels. I believed that unless I enhanced my understanding of the basic linguaphonic structure of English, I would not be able to understand which methods hindered or fostered effective teaching of English to speakers of other languages. Enrolling in a graduate program would provide the opportunity to investigate the cognitive, linguistic, and social processes involved in second-language acquisition from both a theoretical and an applied point of view.

In 1993, I came to the United States to enter the master's program in English at the University of Indiana, Bloomington. After taking some theory and methodology courses, I once again had the chance to become an English teacher, but this time with students from different cultural backgrounds. I taught in the evening English program for the spouses of international students or visiting professors and researchers in the spring semester of 1997. I initially thought that this would be a terrifying experience, especially because I was not a native speaker, my teaching experience was insufficient in such areas as lesson planning, class management, and daily organizational tasks, and my class consisted of advanced students, some of whom were professors or experts in their native countries.

To overcome my apprehension, I put my anxieties aside and prepared well. As a result, I was fully confident, well-prepared, and knew what to do and when to do it. My efforts were appreciated and recognized by the students, and, in spite of all my fears, the positive aspects far outnumbered the negative. I did make some errors as a result of my inexperience, and students also occasionally questioned my credibility. They doubted my authenticity as an authority on English because I was not a native speaker; this happened most frequently when presenting an expression or an idiom. Students often asked, "Are you certain this is the way natives say it?" or "Are you positive this is the exact meaning of this phrase?" Despite these bumps, I continued to successfully use the same strategies I had outlined before I began my first semester of teaching.

In September 1997 I enrolled in the Instruction and Learning Department at the University of Pittsburgh to pursue a doctoral degree in applied linguistics. This stage did not involve teaching experience; rather, it focused on academic advancement and research training. Throughout my 4 years of study, I learned about factors that optimize the teaching and learning of a second language, I became informed about issues currently confronting the profession, and I was exposed to available research methodologies. I also was introduced to scholars to whom I could relate, and learned how to present and define a scholarly argument by involving myself in the activities of my academic community.

After gaining some research training, I attempted to make my voice heard, and I sent introspective essays to two Saudi monthly academic magazines, *Al-Mubtaath Magazine* and *Manar Asabeel Magazine.* The first essay, "I Want to Be a Successful Language Learner, But How?" appeared in *Al-Mubtaath Magazine* (Al-Seghayer, 1997) and the second, "Using Arabic as a Medium of Instruction in Teaching English," appeared in *Manar Asabeel Magazine* (Al-Seghayer, 1997). After I had established my identity as a fledgling scholar in the field and built some confidence, I decided to begin submitting articles to academic journals. I was thrilled to have some of these articles and reviews appear in leading journals in the field, such as *TESOL Quarterly, Language Learning and Technology,* and the *Computer Assisted Language Learning Journal.*

Having equipped myself with all of these skills and having acquired a great deal of specialized learning, I feel ready to enter the arena of practice. My hope is to make a difference and to be a productive addition in the field of teaching and learning English.

CONCLUSION

The discussion in this chapter has demonstrated that since its introduction into the Saudi educational system more than 70 years ago, English has continued to be seen as an essential vehicle for personal and national growth. It has also made clear that, despite the well-formed ELT structure and curriculum, the achievement level of learners is unsatisfactory. Although the curriculum has been continually revised over the years, this process has not been fast enough. Ever-changing developments in the field of second-language acquisition require prompt modification of the EFL curriculum.

Overall, the English proficiency level in Saudi Arabia is expected to remain at its current level unless all relevant factors are taken into consideration. School environments must be improved, more emphasis should be placed on teaching methods in teacher preparation programs, there must be timely reform of the EFL curriculum, and student motivation and attitude must be facilitated. Positive results are anticipated in student proficiency levels and the competency of English teachers with the implementation of these measures.

REFERENCES

Abu-Ghararah, A. (1986). *An analysis of the English language curriculum and instruction in the public secondary schools of Medina, Saudi Arabia.* Unpublished doctoral dissertation, University of Southern California, Los Angeles.

Abu-Ghararah, A. (1990). EFL speaking inability: Its causes and remedies. *National Association for Bilingual Education (NABE) Journal, 14,* 63–73.

Al-Abdulkader, A. (1978). *Survey of the contribution of higher education to the development of human resources in the kingdom of Saudi Arabia.* Unpublished doctoral dissertation, University of Denver, Colorado.

Al-Ahaydib, M. (1986). *Teaching English as a foreign language in the schools of Saudi Arabia.* Unpublished doctoral dissertation, University of Kansas, Lawrence.

Alam, M. (1986). *The effects of three experimental interventions on the spoken English proficiency of eighth grade Saudi Arabian students.* Unpublished doctoral dissertation, University of Denver, Colorado.

Al-Hajailan, T. (1999). *Evaluation of English as a foreign language textbook for third grade secondary boy's schools in Saudi Arabia.* Unpublished doctoral dissertation, Mississippi State University.

Allen, S., & Cooke, R. (1961). *Living English for the Arab World.* London: Longman Group Limited.

Almulhim, A. (2001). *An English language needs assessment of Saudi College of Technology students with respect to a number of business sectors in Saudi Arabia.* Unpublished doctoral dissertation, the University of Mississippi, Oxford.

Al-Seghayer, K. (1997a, December). I want to be a successful language learner, but how? *Al-Mubtaath, 177,* 36–38.

Al-Seghayer, K. (1997b, December). Using Arabic as a medium of instruction in teaching English. *Manar Asabeel Magazine,* pp. 6–18.

Al-Shithri, A. (2001, August 29). Tadris al-lugah al-englayzih fi al-marhala al-ebtidaia ba al-am al-qadim [Teaching English at the elementary school after next year]. *Riyadh Newspaper,* 3.

Al-Subahi, A. (1988, August). English in Saudi Arabia: History, approach and problems. *IATEFL Newsletter, 100,* 7.

ARAMCO. (1968). *ARAMCO Handbook: Oil and the Middle East.* Dhahran, Saudi Arabia: Author.

Berns, M. (1990). *Contexts of competence: Social and cultural considerations in communicative language teaching.* New York: Plenum.

Centre for Statistical Data and Educational Documentation (CSDED). (1991). *English for Saudi Arabia: A new English course* (Semiannual Bulletin No. 31-32). Riyadh, Saudi Arabia: Author.

Directorate of Curriculum. (1995). *English for Saudi Arabia: The third grade secondary textbook.* Jeddah, Saudi Arabia: Al-Madina.

Field, J. (1980). *Saudi Arabian Schools English.* London: The Macmillan Press Limited.

General Presidency of Girl's Education. (2001). *The annual statistical report.* Riyadh, Saudi Arabia: Author.

Jan, M. (1984). *An investigation of the problem of the English program in the intermediate boys' schools of Saudi Arabia.* Unpublished doctoral dissertation, Michigan State University, East Lansing.

Kachru, B. (1982). Models for non-native Englishes. In B. Kachru (Ed.), *The other tongue: English for across-cultures* (pp. 31–57). Urbana: University of Illinois Press.

Ministry of Education. (1982). *The current situation of English language instruction in Saudi Arabia.* Riyadh, Saudi Arabia: Ministry Publications.

Ministry of Higher Education. (2000). *Statistical year book.* Riyadh, Saudi Arabia: King Saud University Press.

Ministry of Higher Education. (2001). *Higher education statistics in the Kingdom of Saudi Arabia.* Riyadh, Saudi Arabia: King Saud University Press.

Zaid, M. (1993). *Comprehensive analysis of the current system of teaching English as a foreign language in Saudi Arabian intermediate schools.* Unpublished doctoral dissertation, University of Colorado, Boulder.

13

A SUCCESS STORY: ENGLISH LANGUAGE TEACHING IN SINGAPORE

Antonia Chandrasegaran
Nanyang Technological University, Singapore

Singapore is an island nation situated 137 kilometers north of the equator and separated by the Straits of Johor from the southern tip of the peninsular Malaysia. Singapore's total land area of 647.5 square meters is made up of one main island and a few smaller islands. Peninsular Malaysia, known as Malaya before the formation of Malaysia in 1963, and Singapore were administered by the British until Malaya attained independence in 1957 and Singapore became a self-governing state in 1963.

Singapore's population of 4 million is multiracial, 76.8% of the population being Chinese, 13.9% Malay, 7.9% Indian, and 1.4% Eurasian and others (Singapore Department of Statistics, 2000). There are four official languages: English, Mandarin, Malay, and Tamil. English is widely used in Singapore by virtue of it being the "language of public administration, education, commerce, science and technology, and global communication" (Ministry of Education, Singapore, 2001, p. 2). In education "English has the status of a first language in the national school curriculum" (Ministry of Education, Singapore, 1991, p. 1) and is the medium of instruction in schools, polytechnics, and universities. English is used not only for official purposes but also for informal, social interaction among Singaporeans. In fact, so many Singaporeans have been speaking, reading, and writing in English since English-medium schools began in the late 19th century that a local variety of English, commonly referred to as 'Singlish', has developed.

HISTORY OF ELT IN SINGAPORE

The first English lessons in Singapore were taught in schools set up by Christian missionaries and rich merchants in the years following the founding of modern Singapore in 1819 by Thomas Stamford Raffles. By the end of the 19th century, there were at least 12 English schools in Singapore, many of which have grown to become highly regarded. Although not playing a proactive role in setting up English medium schools, the colonial government of the 19th century supported these schools with grants because English schools met the need for lower-level employees who were literate in English, "young men competent to earn a livelihood in government and mercantile offices" (1870 Woolley Report, cited in Doraisamy, 1969, p. 24).

In the 1870s, elementary schools called "branch English schools" were set up to provide children with "the opportunity of learning elementary English through the medium of their own language" (Doraisamy, 1969, p. 37). The pupils' own language would have been any one from a list that included Hokkien, Cantonese, Teochew, Mandarin, Malay, and Tamil. After 1902 the use of these languages or vernaculars was dropped from Government English primary schools and "English was taught by the use of the direct method from the lowest standard on" (Doraisamy, 1969, p. 37).

The very first teachers of English in Singapore were native English-speaking missionaries from Britain and the United States. Subsequently, nonmissionary teachers came from Britain as senior teachers and headmasters of government English schools. By the 1940s, local teachers, the graduates of the early English schools, had swelled the ranks of English teachers to the extent that Doraisamy (1969) reported, "Before the outbreak of World War II ... the majority of them [teachers] were Singaporeans from all classes of society" (p. 41).

As for instructional materials, up to the 1950s and early 1960s, books for English classes were shipped out from Britain. Needless to say, readers, picture cards, and other materials came packaged with a culture and worldview that was Anglo-European. One of the reasons advanced for the teaching of English in Singapore by the Director of Education in his foreword to the 1958 syllabus for primary English schools was, "it is the language of a rich and living culture", meaning the culture of British native speakers of English.

Young primary school children who had never seen sheep or snow or been into an English home learnt from the Beacon Infant Reading Series (listed in the 1953 syllabus for primary schools) about frolicking lambs, making snowmen, and mother knitting in front of the fireplace. Secondary-school students were further immersed in English culture through literature, the study of which was regarded as synonymous with English language learning. As Howatt (1984) acknowledged in his *History of English Language Teaching,* "assimilation of British culture through the medium of English literature" was the aim of education in colonial schools (p. 212). In the colonial schools of Singapore and the neighboring British-ruled Malayan states, the 1939 English syllabus for Standard Eight recommended "exercises in interpretation and appreciation ... in addition to the exercises based on the set books in Literature" (Suggestive Syllabus for Standard Eight, p. 1). Among the set books were Macaulay's *Lays of Ancient Rome* (1865), *English Narrative Poems* selected by Sir Henry Newbolt (1919), and Lamb's (1906) *Tales from Shakespeare.*

Prior to the 1960s, the packaging of language with British culture was inevitable because there was no local textbook-publishing industry and probably no local authors confident enough to write English-language textbooks. In the late 1960s "when there was evidence of local expertise to write or adapt textbooks" (Ho, 1998, p. 225), practicing teachers were approached by established British publishers to write textbooks or adapt British texts for local use. In the 1970s, local content began to make an appearance in English-language textbooks, and thereafter gradually replaced Anglo-/Euro-centric topics as the English curriculum, in common with all other school subjects, took on the role of shaping the next generation's sense of nationhood.

THE ELT CURRICULUM

English is the medium of instruction in all lessons today except in mother-tongue lessons, for example, Mandarin, Malay, and Tamil, which are officially known as "mother-tongue" languages. Another subject not taught in English in the primary school is moral education, which is taught in Mandarin, Malay, or Tamil, corresponding to the "mother tongue" the child is studying. As English is the language school children hear and read most during the school day, it is the language through which they develop the cognitive skills to handle knowledge in other subjects and to continue learning in adult life. Linguistic facility is, therefore, not the only aim of the English curriculum.

All local schools in Singapore follow the same syllabus prescribed by the Ministry of Education, which also supervises the implementation of the syllabus, and vets and approves textbooks. The current English syllabus, implemented from 2001, conceives language as "a system for making meaning" and "a means of communication and expression" (Ministry of Education, Singapore, 2001, p. 3). The influence of the Hallidayan view of language as a meaning making, social resource (Halliday & Hasan, 1985) is most visible in the aims of the syllabus and its underlying philosophy, which includes the assumption that "language use is determined by purpose, audience, context and culture" (Ministry of Education, Singapore, 2001, p. 3). The social and socializing functions of English highlighted in the syllabus reflect the important role of English in Singapore as the language by means of which young minds are shaped to develop a sense of belonging to a multiracial Singapore.

The aims of the 2001 English Syllabus cluster around two concerns: literacy development and sociocultural awareness. The designers of the syllabus see literacy development as "the heart of an English Language instructional program in school" (Ministry of Education, Singapore, 2001, p. 7). Literacy, in this syllabus, means more than just an ability to read and write. The training of the critical faculties is included, as students are expected to be able to "listen to, read and view with understanding, accuracy and critical appreciation … fiction and nonfiction texts from print, nonprint and electronic sources" (Ministry of Education, Singapore, 2001, p. 3).

The second area of concern, sociocultural skills, is expressed in the aim to equip students with the ability to "speak, write and make presentations in internationally acceptable English that are grammatical, fluent and appropriate for purpose, audience, context and culture … [and] interact effectively with people from their own or different cultures" (Ministry of Education, Singapore, 2001, p. 3). To this end, the syllabus spells out in some detail how the teaching of sociocultural appropriateness will be implemented. In oral communication, for instance, the syllabus directs that "in face-to-face interaction … pupils will be taught to observe social conventions and etiquette in oral communication and to give the appropriate verbal response" (Ministry of Education, Singapore, 2001, p. 8).

The 2001 English Syllabus sets out principles of language learning and teaching, which constitute the spirit in which the syllabus is to be implemented. To ensure the realization of the objectives, the Ministry of Education conducted briefings for teachers, and also textbook publishers who then directed authors to write to the recommended specifications. To prepare new teachers to teach the syllabus, teacher trainers at the National Institute of Education (an Institute of the Nanyang Technological University and Singapore's sole teacher-training body) plan their courses to impart to student teachers an understanding of the philosophy and aims of the syllabus.

Three principles in the syllabus worthy of note, because they reflect the cognitive and social dimensions of language learning, are process orientation, contextualization, and social interaction. A process orientation in language teaching requires teachers to model reading, writing, and oral communication processes. Discrete processes are described in the syllabus as targets to be reached at the end of each level, with levels set at 2-year intervals, that is, at Primary 2, 4, 6, and so on. For example, target outcomes for reading in Primary 6 include the ability to "make predictions about content and development of ideas using title, headings, sub-headings …" and "infer and draw conclusions using contextual clues and knowledge of the topic" (Ministry of Education, Singapore, 2001, p. 30).

The principle of contextualization enjoins upon teachers to teach language skills and grammatical structures "in the context of language use" with the aim of demonstrating "how purpose, audience, context and culture determine the register or appropriateness of speech and writing in both formal and informal situations (Ministry of Education, Singapore, 2001, p. 4). A logical step from teaching grammar in context is to teach grammar in relation to text types (story, informational report, etc.). To influence teachers into linking grammar to its function in texts, the syllabus lists grammatical forms under text types such as adjectives, connectors, and simple present tense listed under the genre of *Expositions* (Ministry of Education, Singapore, 2001, p. 36). Contextualization marks a progressive move from the curriculum's previous focus on correctness of usage at the expense of situational appropriateness.

The principle of "interaction" is to be realized in the classroom as student participation in language-learning activities and interaction among students with the aim of "fostering social relationships among pupils from different cultural backgrounds and religions" and nurturing in them "a sense of their common Singaporean identity" (Ministry of Education, Singapore, 2001, p. 4). Like the contextualization principle, the interaction principle reflects the influence, on the syllabus writers, of Halliday's view of language use as "a social exchange of meanings" (Halliday & Hasan, 1985, p. 11).

Textbooks, published locally, are written expressly to implement the aims of the syllabus, including the sociopolitical aim of building national cohesion. Reading passages, exercises, and other learning activities featured in textbooks must promote national policies like "National Education", a policy to inculcate in young Singaporeans a patriotic awareness of Singapore's history. To attain the goal of turning out students who will be "independent lifelong learners, creative thinkers and problem solvers" (Ministry of Education, Singapore, 2001, p. 2), teachers are expected to set project work that engage students in an information search on their own (such as interviewing senior citizens on their experience during the World War II) and the consequent production of a text (such as a biography or a play using the information obtained from the interview). In addition, because "independent lifelong learners" in the near future will increasingly rely on electronic sources to keep abreast of advances in knowledge, teachers are encouraged to use information technology (IT) in their lessons.

Although it has been noted that English in Singapore is "more of a first language rather than a second language and certainly not a foreign language" (Foley, 2001, p. 16), the level of mastery of the English language among school students varies from proficiency in a standard variety that can be described as "internationally acceptable English" (Ministry of Education, Singapore, 2001, p. 3) to proficiency only in "Singlish" or Singapore colloquial English (or SCE; following Gupta, 1994). Home environment, over which the school has little control, is partly responsible for this variation.

English is spoken in the home of a sizeable proportion of Singapore students. Among the Chinese, who form 77% of the population, English is the language "most frequently spoken at home" for 36% of children aged 5 to 14 years (see Table 13.1). The figure is higher (44%) for Indian children (Indians form 8% of the population).

It will be noted from Table 13.1 that the use of English as a home language rose in the 10 years between 1990 and 2000, a trend that has continued since. The variety of English children learn at home from infancy is likely to be SCE rather than Standard English as speaking English at home is no longer confined to an elite upper- and upper-middle-class minority. Comparing the position of English in the late 1990s with its position 20 years earlier, Gupta (1998) observed, "English as a domestic language has since then begun to spread out of the upper-class population" (p. 132). As for children from homes where no English is spoken, they do not enter

TABLE 13.1
Use of English as Most Frequent Home Language

Ethnic group	Percent Reporting English as "Most Frequently Spoken at Home"	
	In 2000	In 1990
Chinese	35.8	23.3
Indian	43.6	39.6
Malay	9.4	8.3

Note. Singapore Department of Statistics, (2000).

school at primary 1 with no knowledge of English, as they will have learnt at least some SCE from their teachers at a government-sponsored preschool center. Nearly all children attend preschool, either at a privately-run kindergarten or a government-sponsored preschool center. In addition to fluency in SCE, children from upper-class, English-speaking homes who have attended private kindergartens are likely to have the ability to switch from SCE to standard English when the occasion calls for it (Gupta, 1998).

BECOMING AN ENGLISH TEACHER

The story begins in Malaysia, the country of my birth, where I was schooled up to bachelor's degree level. As my parents spoke no English, I grew up speaking two Chinese languages (dialects) and hearing a great deal of a third language, Malay. I spoke Cantonese to my mother and Hokkien to my father, and heard them speak Malay to non-Chinese neighbors and acquaintances. My first contact with the English language was at the primary school my parents enrolled me in when I was 6 years old. At the time, the 1950s, children who came into primary 1 speaking English were a minority, comprising Eurasian children and the children of English-educated parents who spoke English at home. I do not remember feeling alienated by the inability to speak English in the first few months at school, probably because the majority of my classmates and I shared the same sense of bewilderment at being thrown suddenly into the strange new environment of school.

The English-medium school where I received 11 years of primary and secondary education was known as the Convent of the Holy Infant Jesus and it was run by Catholic nuns, although my China-born parents were neither English educated nor Catholic. I gathered from the adult talk at home that the English school was the path to a lucrative job in the civil service or a private-sector institution like a bank or a British trading company. Chinese schools, on the other hand, were regarded as hotbeds of communist activity directed at the overthrow of the British colonial government. The gossip of my parents and their friends often dwelt on young people hauled off in the dead of night by the Special Branch to be locked away or deported to China for being members of communist cells and allegedly participating in subversive activity.

It took a whole school year or two before I understood everything that was said to me in English. I remember getting all my multiplication sums wrong in a primary 2 arithmetic class because the teacher's explanation made no sense to me. But I do not recall feeling miserable probably because the culture of academic success and failure was still alien to me. Besides, I had no previous school experience in a home language with which to compare the English-medium school. On the contrary, I was fascinated by the fairy tales the teacher told with big pictures (*Cinderella, Red Riding Hood*), the nursery rhymes (*Humpty Dumpty, Little Miss Muffet*) we recited with movement, the games we played to English ditties ("Oranges and Lemons," "Ring-a-Ring-a-Roses"), and the imported readers with their white glossy pages covered with colorful pictures of scenes of English life. It soon became natural to speak English in the classroom and on the playground, there being no other common language in the polyglot community of an English-medium school. After a few years of immersion in an English language environment every school day from 7.30 a.m. to 1:00 p.m., children like me came to associate English with sophistication and knowledge of other exciting worlds as opposed to the humdrum, domestic domain of the home language.

Once I learnt to read, a life-long fascination with the written word began. I would read everything I could lay my hands on, including discarded newspapers and magazines, which were very welcome in a home that had no English newspapers. Among the prized reading material were beautifully illustrated storybooks borrowed from more fortunate classmates, whose English-educated parents had the means to indulge their children. It must have been the copious reading that generated the effortless flow of words during writing, whether it was the writing of compositions in the English class or the writing of essay answers in literature, history, and other subjects. I must have unconsciously acquired ways of using language and making meaning that accorded with my teachers' expectations, for I remember getting the highest mark in the class for a literature test without understanding how I did it.

With my affinity for English, I gravitated towards the study of English literature at the university after the Higher School Certificate (HSC) Examination, an examination prepared and marked in Britain by the Cambridge Examinations Syndicate for students completing Sixth Form, which was what the 2-year preuniversity level of school was called. The decision to be an English teacher was made for me when a teaching scholarship provided the means to a university education, which would otherwise not have materialized because of my family's straitened circumstances.

When I was an undergraduate at the University of Malaya in Kuala Lumpur in the late 1960s, the language of instruction across faculties was English. About half the English department's teaching staff was local and the other half hailed from Britain and the United States. To be awarded a bachelor's degree with honors, majoring in English, we dutifully studied and wrote essays on the classics such as Chaucer's *Canterbury Tales,* the plays of Marlowe and Shakespeare, the poetry of John Donne, Edmund Spenser, John Milton, and the Romantic poets, and the novels of Jane Austen, Henry Fielding, and Charles Dickens. To ensure that we did not graduate equating literature with British authors, there were courses in American literature (Ralph Waldo Emerson, William Faulkner, John Dos Passos, to name a few) and European literature translated into English (Dante, Moliere, Gustave Flaubert, Henrik Ibsen, L. N. Tolstoy), as well as the works of notable Commonwealth authors such as V. S. Naipaul, Doris Lessing, and Patrick White. The fare was wholly literary. The only course on language I remember being offered was one on the history of the English language. Nevertheless, on graduation I was considered equipped to teach English language and English literature. All I needed was a Diploma in Education (now called the Postgraduate Diploma in Education). I chose to study for the diploma in the Teachers' Training College (now known as the National Institute of Education) in Singapore because I was living in the Malaysian town of Johor Bahru, which is only three quarters of a mile from Singapore across the Straits of Johor.

The main objective of the Diploma in Education curriculum was to orient trainees to the culture of education as a discipline and a profession through courses in educational psychology, the philosophy of education, and the like. Language teaching methodology did not figure prominently, the assumption being that if you had an honors degree in English literature you were qualified to teach English. One English language-related course that made an impression on me was speech training, which introduced me to the notion of RP (Received Pronunciation). RP was held up to us, future English-medium schoolteachers, as the model of speech we should project to our students. I had not previously paid any attention to the sounds of English speech, having learnt to speak English through an osmosis process from my teachers—Irish nuns and English-educated women at the convent school. After the speech-training course, to be able to read phonetic script and check the pronunciation of words in a dictionary was empowering.

In my first year of teaching, I taught literature (*Julius Caesar, To Kill a Mockingbird*) and English in a boys' school. In addition to the upper-secondary classes of English medium students, whom I was preparing for the Cambridge school certificate examinations, I had a class of students from Chinese medium-primary schools who were making the switch to English-medium-secondary school. It was their first year in an English-medium school and it was my first encounter with non-English speaking students. I spoke no Mandarin, knew nothing of guided composition or pattern drills, and was not evenly remotely knowledgeable about the problems of second-language acquisition. Both students and teacher suffered from my ignorance and the gulf between two cultures—that of the English educated and the Chinese educated.

After 2 year's of teaching, I was awarded a scholarship to study for the Diploma in TESL at RELC (the Regional Language Centre), a center set up by

SEAMEO (Southeast Asian Ministers of Education Organization) to provide expertise and other assistance for developing the skills of language teachers (especially English language teachers) in member nations. The RELC opened a whole new world to me, that of structural linguistics, sociolinguistics, and psycholinguistics, and their application to language teaching. Classes in these disciplines and the reading available in RELC's excellent library began for me an engagement with the issues associated with the theory and practice of language learning and teaching. I gained a more sympathetic understanding of the difficulties my Chinese-medium students grappled with as they struggled to master the mysteries of the English verb and tense system.

My newly acquired knowledge of applied linguistics and more learner-centered attitudes to second-language teaching were put to use when, on obtaining the Diploma in TESL, I found myself in a Malaysian teachers' college, training English teachers for the country's primary and lower-secondary schools. The medium of instruction in Malaysia's mainstream schools was changing from English to Bahasa Malaysia (Malay), thus relegating English to the position of a school subject taught from grade 1. I developed an interest in the attitudinal and social factors that motivated Malaysian students in the study of English, the topic I chose to research for my masters thesis at RELC.

My interest had moved to the development of academic writing skills by the time I decided to embark on a Ph.D. by research in the latter half of the 1980s. I was teaching at the National University of Singapore at its English Language Proficiency Unit (now called the Centre for English Language Communication). Most of my students were from Chinese-medium Singapore schools before these schools were phased out in 1987. Their pressing need was to learn how to write essays in English that would satisfy the expectations of examiners in an English-medium university. Faced with the challenge of helping them develop more effective essay-writing skills, I began to read the literature on composition research, which in the 1980s was dominated by the cognitive view of writing (notably Flower & Hayes, 1981). Influenced by Flower and Hayes' cognitive model of writing, I did a study of student writers' decision-making processes during lengthy pauses in expository writing. The results were reported in my Ph.D. thesis (Chandrasegaran, 1991) that was accepted by the external examiners without revision required.

Since completing the Ph.D. research study, my understanding of what is involved in academic discourse production and the development of academic writing skills has continued to grow through teaching writing-related courses at the National University of Singapore, then at Murdoch University in Perth, and now back in Singapore at the National Institute of Education (NIE). My response to student writing, which was grammar focused and error hunting in approach in the early part of my career in the 1970s, moved to a cognitive-rhetorical perspective in the 1980s and has since evolved to embrace the sociocultural dimension of writing. The growth has been fueled by my own reading as well as by interaction with my students in undergraduate and postgraduate courses, including English language teachers from China who come to NIE to study for the Postgraduate Diploma in English Language Teaching.

CONCLUSION

The English language in Singapore, first taught here soon after Raffles' founding of Singapore in 1819 as a trading post, has seen a dramatic role change since those early days. From being the language used by locals to communicate with their colonial masters on mundane matters like administration and trade, it has become a language that the locals have colonized and made their own to serve the more august functions of shaping national consciousness and creative expression. English is today the medium through which schools nurture in young Singaporeans of diverse ethnicity a common sense of history and destiny. Generations of Singaporeans have graduated from English-medium schools who speak, read, write, think and dream in English. Among them are internationally-acknowledged Singaporean writers and poets like Catherine Lim and Lee Tzu Peng. Testifying to the success of English language teaching/learning in Singapore are the thousands of home-grown English teachers with nativelike proficiency in the language, whose students now include students from other Southeast Asian countries such as Malaysia and Indonesia, and, from further afield, China. Parents from these countries are sending their children to school and university in Singapore in the hope of reaping the benefits of an English-medium education. In a sense, English is being taught to the world *from* Singapore.

REFERENCES

Chandrasegaran, A. (1991). *The composing processes of university student writers.* Unpublished doctoral thesis, National University of Singapore, Singapore.

Doraisamy, T.R. (Ed.). (1969). *150 years of education in Singapore.* Singapore: TTC Publications Board.

Flower, L. S., & Hayes, J. R (1981). A cognitive process theory of writing. *College Composition and Communication, 32,* 365–387.

Foley, J. (2001). Is English a first or second language in Singapore? In V.B.Y. Ooi (Ed.), *Evolving identities. The English language in Singapore and Malaysia* (pp. 12–32). Singapore: Times Academic Press.

Gupta, A. F. (1994). *The step-tongue: Children's English in Singapore.* Clevedon, England: Multilingual Matters.

Gupta, A. F. (1998). A framework for the analysis of Singapore English. In S. Gopinathan, A. Pakir, W. K. Ho, & V. Saravanan (Eds.), *Language, society and education in Singapore* (2nd ed., pp. 119–132). Singapore: Times Academic Press.

Halliday, M. A. K. & Hasan, R. (1985). *Language, context, and text: Aspects of language in a social-semiotic perspective.* Victoria, Australia: Deakin University.

Ho, W. K. (1998). The English language curriculum in perspective: Exogenous influences and indigenization. In S. Gopinathan, A. Pakir, W. K. Ho, & V. Saravanan (Eds.), *Lan-*

guage, society and education in Singapore. Issues and trends (2nd ed., pp. 221–244). Singapore: Times Academic Press.

Howatt, A. P. R. (1984). *A history of English language teaching.* Oxford: Oxford University Press.

Lamb, C., & Lamb, M. (1906). *Tales from Shakespeare.* Everyman's Library. London: Dent.

Macaulay, T.B. (1865). *Lays of ancient Rome.* London: Longman.

Ministry of Education, Singapore. (1991). *English Language Syllabus (Secondary).* Singapore: Curriculum Planning Division, Ministry of Education.

Ministry of Education, Singapore. (2001). *English Language Syllabus 2001 for primary and secondary schools.* Singapore: Curriculum Planning and Development Division, Ministry of Education.

Newbolt, H. (Ed.). (1919). *English narrative poems.* London: Edward Arnold.

Singapore Department of Statistics. (2000). *Advance data release. No. 3, literacy and language. Singapore Census of Population 2000.* [Electronic version] Retrieved on October 17, 2001, from http://www.singstat.gov.sg/c2000/adr-literacy.pdf

Suggestive Syllabus for Standard Eight in English Schools in the Straits Settlements and Federated Malay States. (1939). Singapore: Government Printing Office.

Syllabus for the Teaching of English in Primary English Schools in Singapore. (1958). Singapore: Government Printing Office.

The Primary Syllabus Committee. (1953). *English in the primary School.* Singapore: Ministry of Education.

The Beacon Infant Series. (1938). London: Ginn & Co.

14

TEACHING ENGLISH IN SRI LANKA: FROM COLONIAL ROOTS TO LANKAN ENGLISH

Minoli Samarakkody
Van West College, Canada

George Braine
The Chinese University of Hong Kong, Hong Kong

Sri Lanka (formerly known as Ceylon) is an island situated to the south of India with an area of 25,000 square miles (65,600 square kilometers). The population, which is around 18 million, consists of Sinhalese, Tamils, Muslims, and the descendants of Portuguese, Dutch, and British colonizers. The three main languages are Sinhala, Tamil, and English, and the literacy rate is about 92%. Most Sri Lankans are Buddhist. Hinduism, Christianity, and Islam are also practiced.

Over the centuries, Sri Lanka has been subjected to waves of invasion from India. European colonizers have been the Portuguese, the Dutch, and the British. The Indian as well as the European rulers have left their mark on the culture, the languages, the agriculture, and the architecture of Sri Lanka. But nowhere is this colonial past seen more clearly than in the widespread use of the English language, which today is part-and-parcel of Sri Lankan life.

HISTORY OF ELT IN SRI LANKA

In 1796, as a result of the imposition of British rule on the island, English began to be used as the medium of communication in higher-level domains such as administration, education, the legal system, and commerce. As a result, the indigenous languages, Sinhala and Tamil, were placed in the position of second-class languages. One of the earliest British governors, Sir Frederick North, set up the first English school, the academy at Wolvendhal, in 1800 (Musa, 1981). Although the first English school provided instruction in both English and the indigenous languages, beginning in 1834, the administration adopted a policy of using English as the sole medium of instruction in schools. However, the Morgan Report (1868) gave a definite shape to education and language policy in Ceylon, maintaining that vernacular education should be provided for the people at large and English education for future administrators and the social elite (Jayaweera, 1971, cited in Musa, 1981). As a result, the demand for English education grew tremendously. Table 14.1 shows the increasing number of students enrolled in English schools from 1880 to 1945.

Musa (1981) stated that, as a result of subsequent colonial policy, the social cleavage between English school students and vernacular school students widened, and the mediating category of *bilingual school students* decreased. Thus, the rise of a Western-educated elite was largely the result of a colonial educational policy that was geared to the creation of a Westernized segment among the indigenous population in the country. As time went by, this privileged middle class gradually developed, particularly in speech, a distinctive variety called Lankan English. Kandiah (1981) defined Lankan English as "an independent and viable native linguistic organism which has its own distinctive format and organization and which its habitual users acquired in that form as a first language" (p. 92).

The teaching of English in English schools during the colonial era was quite successful. English was the medium of instruction in all subjects and students developed fluency in every skill area of the language. The language of communication during school hours was English and the use of the indigenous languages was strongly discouraged. As de Souza (1969) pointed out, English was taught as it was in contemporary British schools with identical readers, poetry anthologies, and plays. The grammar and composition books were also identical, as were the exercises such as essays, paraphrases, and summaries. As a result of this rich

TABLE 14.1
Demand for English Education 1880–1945

Year	Number of Students in English Schools
1880	7,000
1900	21,000
1914	37,500
1920	37,000
1931	84,000
1945	100,000
1948	180,000

Note. De Souza, 1969; Musa, 1981.

learning environment, students who attended English schools gained a high level of proficiency in the language. Furthermore, all the teachers in the English schools were required to have a high level of competence in English, irrespective of the subjects they taught.

Because of the growing disparity in terms of the quality of education between the English schools and the vernacular schools, the Special Committee on Education (1943) recommended that English be taught in the vernacular schools as a compulsory subject from grade 3 onwards. Although the number of learners of English increased tremendously as a result of these changes, the number of qualified teachers in English did not increase in the same manner. Further, the English language teaching program in the vernacular schools lacked clear objectives, and was regarded as a sort of a charitable gesture (de Souza, 1969). Because there was a dearth of qualified teachers, English "assistants" who did not have much competence or training in English were recruited to teach English. As a result of this unsatisfactory situation, English was not made a compulsory subject at any school examination taken by vernacular school pupils (de Souza, 1969). Thus, the English program in the vernacular schools, which catered to over 80% of the students, was regarded as a total failure (de Souza, 1969; Kandiah, 1984).

Because English continued in a position of power and dominance even at the time of independence in 1948, the vast majority of the country's population, not proficient in English, was not able to move up the structure of economic, social, and political power. Therefore, with postindependence nationalism, Sinhala replaced English as the official language. In spite of this change, Chitra Fernando (1976) pointed out that there was never a simple takeover by Sinhala, because English continued to be the dominant language in several very important spheres of life. In order to change this situation, the government eliminated English-medium instruction from the school system. This, along with the provision of university education in the Sinhala and Tamil languages, was supposed to pave the way for the vast majority of the rural monolingual intelligentsia to gain social mobility, and free them from the cultural and social constraints that had marginalized them for centuries. However, while the reforms gave those educated in Sinhala and Tamil access to certain levels of the educational and professional world, the raised aspirations, especially among the Sinhala-speaking youth, were not realized due to a stagnating economy and increasing unemployment.

During the late 1970s, therefore, the government opted for an open economic system, which gave a further boost to the position of English and resulted in a far wider spread of English in the country. This was in response to the numerous employment opportunities the private sector was now opening to the rural segments of the population. The new employment opportunities that were created at the professional and administration level attracted many individuals such as university graduates. Educational institutes, as well as officials in both the private and state sectors, began to stress the importance of English at the higher ranks of employment, especially in the private sector and in obtaining tertiary-level educational qualifications. Hence, there was an unprecedented demand for English throughout the country during this time.

The demand for English in the 1990s was such that, every year, large numbers of students attended steadily increasing fee-levying private schools, which provide courses in English that fell far short of expectations. Institutions such as the British Council that offer quality courses for high fees have large numbers registering for their courses annually. Further, there have been a tremendous number of applications for both nonfee-levying and fee-levying courses offered by such institutions as the English Speakers' Association and the English Teachers' Association. Also, the more affluent segments of the population spend exorbitant sums of money to obtain an English education for their children in the mushrooming, so-called international schools around the country.

However, owing to the tremendous sociohistorical, linguistic, political, and ideological changes that have taken place in relation to English in Sri Lanka, particularly since 1956, the vast majority of learners have been provided with varying conditions for learning English. Although they are exposed to the formal rules of English in schools, they have been denied adequate exposure to the language, owing to the unavailability of suitable teachers and adequate resources. Also, these learners use English for highly restricted purposes. Therefore, they are a hugely heterogeneous group in terms of proficiency in English and, in spite of the number of years spent on learning English, many of them are unable to conform to the norms implicitly set down by the small minority who have a high level of competence in the language (Raheem & Ratwatte, 2001).

THE ELT CURRICULUM

The curriculum for teaching English in the primary and secondary government schools is developed by the National Institute of Education (NIE). Although activity-based oral English is taught in grades 1 and 2, formal English is introduced in grade 3 and continues through junior secondary (Grades 6 through 9) and senior secondary (Grades 10 and 11) levels. The only English subject that was available before 1999 for grades 12 and 13 was English literature catering to a minority of students who were proficient in English. Of the students who have tested in this subject on the general certificate of education (GCE) advanced level (A level) examination, which is given at the end of 13th year of education and serves as a university entrance exam, only 25% have been successful in the past 10 years; the most competent of these gain admission to the few universities that offer degree courses in English literature and linguistics. In order to address this situation, in 1999, a group of academics from the universities and the NIE created an additional compulsory course, the General English Course, for advanced-level students. The aim of this course is to give the majority of students, who have varying levels of proficiency, continued access to an English language-proficiency course (Ratnayake, 2000).

Non-English majors who gain admission to the universities take the general English language teaching course conducted by the University Grants Commission. Unless exempted by their scores on a placement test in English, many of them also take short intensive courses in English prior to the commencement of their respective academic programs. The faculties of medicine, science, and engineering in the national university system conduct undergraduate courses only in English. However, in some of the faculties that provide courses in three languages (Sinhala, Tamil, or English), and even in the arts faculties (which do not provide English-medium instruction), proficiency courses in English are available to students throughout the academic year. Many universities also run extension courses in English for learners who are not undergraduates but who wish to learn English for professional and administrative purposes.

Based on the Education Reforms of 1997, the National Education Commission, the Ministry of Education and Higher Education, and the NIE recommend that the time allocated for the teaching of English in the primary grades be 3 hours per week for grades 3 and 4, and 3½ hours for grade 5. The time allocated for junior secondary grades is 5 periods per week, with each period lasting 40 minutes. The number of periods for grades 10 and 11 is 5 periods per week (Curriculum Process Plan, 2000).

As part of the current education reforms, the textbook gradually being introduced at the primary levels is the new *Let's Learn English Series.* The text, which has been produced by a team of writers involved in the Primary English Language Project (PELP), is used in all grade 3 classes across the country. Apart from the student's textbook, this series has a workbook and a teacher's guide accompanying it. The textbook introduced in 1999 at the junior and senior secondary levels is *The World Through English Series,* which is being used in all state schools on the island. The learning package consists of course syllabi, six workbooks, teacher's guides, and student texts. The first volume of the general English course for grades 12 and 13 was compiled by the NIE, the universities of Colombo and Kelaniya, and the Open University of Sri Lanka. This volume is accompanied by an audiocassette, and the textbook is made as self-accessible as possible (Ratnayake, 2000).

Students are assessed on their performance in reading, writing, grammar, and vocabulary on the GCE ordinary level (O level) examination at the end of the 11th year of education. Listening and speaking are two skills that are not tested on the final examination but assessed in the classroom through the school-based assessment program (Guidelines, 2001). Although English is taught as a compulsory subject throughout the school system, it has not been made compulsory on the GCE O level examination due to the dearth of qualified English teachers who are competent in the language, particularly in the rural schools. At the GCE A level, however, examination in English is compulsory for all students. The examination, consisting of General English I and General English II, assesses students on grammar, reading, summarizing skills, expository writing, vocabulary, and speech.

To overcome the variability of English language competence across regions, the inadequacy of the methods of teaching English in government schools, and the general decline of standards, the NEC plans to introduce English gradually as a medium of instruction within the school system. Further, the Ministry of Education is of the view that "IT [information technology] and spoken or conversational English are among the key requirements of the private sector today when employing individuals" (Samath, 2001, p. 4). Thus, recent educational reforms have placed a great deal of emphasis on the skills of speaking and listening through activity-based oral English at the primary levels, and also through the general English subject at the GCE A level. In terms of which variety of English should be used as the model in the English language teaching classroom, the integration of audiocassettes based on standard Sri Lankan English pronunciation into the curriculum is evidence of the growing awareness and acceptance of this variety as the norm. As a first step towards a definition of standard Sri Lankan English, a group of academics have commenced work on establishing a corpus of Sri Lankan English, which will form the Sri Lankan component of the international corpus of English (Raheem & Ratwatte, 2001).

In the case of teacher training, personnel from the NIE, the Ministry of Education, and the universities in Sri Lanka form a core group of trainer trainers to train in-service advisors, who in turn train the English language teachers in the regions across the country. The core group of trainers consists of those who hold either a diploma in teaching English as a second language or a master's degree in applied linguistics, and have experience in the field of English language teaching. Although the NIE provides only an orientation program with a view to familiarizing teachers with textbooks, there are other teacher-training institutes such as the National Colleges of Education and Teacher Training Colleges that provide in-service education and training (INSET) programs for the 190,000 or so English teachers. The preservice teacher education (PPTE) course of the National Colleges of Education prepares primary-school teachers to teach all the subjects of the primary curriculum. The English language component is designed to develop English language proficiency and English language teaching methodology. The INSET and the PPTE are 2-year courses with a 1-year of internship in a school.

The prescribed qualifications for teachers of English are a bachelor of arts degree or a bachelor of education degree with English as a subject, or the national diploma in teaching English conferred by the Colleges of Education. However, although recruitment to government schools is based on a teacher recruitment exam, the minimum qualification that is required is a pass in English on the GCE O-level examination. Therefore, the standard of English among the English language teachers themselves, especially in government schools, falls far short of acceptable levels. Accordingly,

> the major concern with the teaching of English in Sri Lanka remains the lack of competent teachers throughout the island .... What would inevitably result is the further skewing of resource allocation, where better qualified English teachers are concentrated in the major cities, and particularly within the Western Province. (Safstrom, Balasooriya, Masilamani, & Parakrama, 2001, p. 23)

In recent years, 30 Regional English Support Centres (RESC) have been established by the Ministry of Education and Higher Education in cooperation with provincial educational department and the NIE, with support from the British Council. Among the many services provided are in-service training courses for teachers, advice for teachers at primary and secondary levels, and providing ELT resources. The RESCs play a significant role in the PELP project by providing regular teacher-training sessions for primary school teachers across the country. The goal of PELP is to increase the proportion of students in primary schools with good foundation skills in English.

The British Council has long been involved in English language projects throughout Sri Lanka. Apart from two teaching centers in Colombo and Kandy, the British Council administers a wide range of English language examinations, including the International English Language Test System, the University of Cambridge Local Examinations Syndicates main suite exams, and the Cambridge Young Learner Tests. The British Council also supports the teaching and learning of English in local schools through its involvement in the PELP project and the Sri Lanka English Language Teachers' Association (SLELTA). It also works with SLELTA to give English language teachers in Sri Lanka opportunities for professional exchange and development through local and regional seminars, conferences, and workshops.

BECOMING AN ENGLISH TEACHER

In the late 1960s, at a time when the unemployment situation in Sri Lanka was at its worst, George Braine passed a government test to enter the premier teacher's college in the country. In preparation for the teacher's college, he was required to teach English at a government school not far from where he lived. The students were the sons and daughters of peasant farmers or laborers from nearby coconut plantations. They, in keeping with rural Sinhalese–Buddhist tradition, were extremely respectful of the teachers. A quick glance at the textbook was all the preparation George needed to go into class. He would not admit that he bluffed his way through, but he barely managed to pull off what passed for English lessons. At the end of the 3-month period, when his fellow teachers and the students held an emotional meeting to bid him farewell, he attended with a feeling of guilt.

The entrance to the Maharagama Teachers College was not particularly impressive. It was a narrow, tree lined, pot-holed road leading off a highway, a few miles from Sri Lanka's capital, Colombo. About a hundred yards beyond the entrance, the road opened up to the college premises. The sight, in the early 1970s, was more akin to that of an internment camp than of the premier teacher's college in the country. World War II vintage army barracks, made of carelessly white-washed, rough-hewn stones, rusty wire mesh, and grimy asbestos roofs were scattered among overgrown lawns and gravel pathways. To George and his classmates who had gathered there on a January morning in 1970, their first day as teacher trainees, the uninspiring environment did not matter. They had just been admitted to the best teacher's college in the country, chosen to be elite, trained teachers of English.

During their 2 years of training, the students followed lectures in principles and practice of education, educational psychology, and physical and health education. As English teacher trainees, they also had coursework in the English language, literature, speech, and methods of teaching English. All of the courses had been designed with the Sri Lankan context in mind, and the trainees found the courses pragmatic and applicable later in their teaching careers. In the second year of training, they were sent out to schools for teaching practice and to be observed and evaluated weekly by their supervisors. Almost all their lecturers had been trained in Britain and excelled at their tasks. George remembers that the only U.S.-trained lecturer was fondly nicknamed "Chicago" for her ample girth as well as for the place of her graduate studies. Another lecturer staged a Shakespearean drama every year with the English trainees, no mean feat in Sri Lanka. Sometimes eccentric but always inspiring, these lecturers imbibed the trainees with a sense of empowerment, the feeling that they could, if only they tried, change the world through the minds of their young students.

To many of the younger teacher trainees, the training period actually became a time of leisure, a paid holiday. Only the older trainees, with responsibilities of parenthood and accountability to their families, appeared to take the work seriously. The easygoing curriculum, with plenty of free time between lectures, gave the younger trainees time to socialize and to plan extracurricular activities. They acted in the annual Shakespeare production, planned sports events and outings, and campaigned vigorously for election to the Student Council. Some found time for romance.

Fresh from a 2-year stint at teacher's college, full of enthusiasm for his career, George took a job in a remote village more than a day's journey from Colombo. Although the village was set amid lush tea plantations in the central hills of the country, poverty and neglect were everywhere. The local population consisted of subsistence farmers or laborers. Despite the cold and the 5-mile daily walk that some students had, none could afford shoes. George was the first trained teacher of English in the school's 40-year history.

As the only English teacher, he taught grade 4 through grade 10, at least six 50-minute classes per day. The smallest class had 35 students. All had textbooks provided free by the government, but George had no visual aids or English newspapers or magazines. Few students had access to radios, which most households could not afford. Many students attended school without a proper breakfast, most only with a cup of tea.

English had little relevance to the lives of these students. The language was as remote from their lives as Britain or the United States. The remoteness and the limited teaching resources made it a challenge to motivate the students to learn English. In retrospect, George believes it was his youthful enthusiasm that helped him through those 2 years. His additional duties as the teacher in charge of sports also helped, along with weekend visits to the nearest city for a decent meal and meetings with friends.

In 1972, George passed a highly competitive test (of the 200 who applied, only 3 were selected) to become an English instructor at one of the four universities in Sri Lanka. He thought that obtaining a coveted job as a university English instructor would be an escape from the neglect and isolation of a village schoolteacher, but he soon realized that university English teachers were equally low in the social and economic ladder. Like himself, most English instructors did not have college degrees. Because of their low-academic qualifications, and the noncredit service courses they taught, they were at the bottom of the academic ladder, tolerated at the senior common room and academic gatherings more to swell numbers than for their intellectual contributions.

For these instructors, scholarship and intellectual advancement were at a standstill. No ELT journals were published locally, and seminars and workshops were few and often unaffordable; during George's 8 years at the university, he attended just one in-service course. On a monthly salary that was a pittance by Western standards, no instructor could afford to subscribe to international ELT journals. Even university libraries, restricted to a budget less than that of a rural public library in the United States, would spend their meager allocations on journals in science, medicine, and engineering, areas that were considered more important than ELT. The British Council and the U.S. Information Agency, located in two cities, did carry the more popular reference books, but journals publishing current research were unavailable. As for technology, computers, overhead projectors, and video equipment were nonexistent; an unscarred blackboard was a privilege.

Although he had entered teachers college as a teenager, it took George 10 more years to become a student at the university; the obligatory period of service as an English teacher after teacher's college, and the responsibilities of raising a family contributed to the delay. A degree in English meant a degree in English literature; the course work included the study of drama from the Middle Ages to the 17th century, literary criticism, poetry from Geoffrey Chaucer to John Keats, fiction from Daniel Defoe to George Eliot, and modern literature, some of it in translation from the Spanish, Italian, and French. In a course titled "The English Language," he studied the history and structure of the language. During 4 years of course work, the writing consisted almost entirely of literary criticism.

In 1984, George was awarded a scholarship in the United States to obtain a master's degree in TESOL, and entered the American University in Washington, DC. The wide access to sophisticated academic libraries transformed his reading habits. Instead of reading fiction, he was now under pressure to complete the required readings in applied linguistics. Instead of reading popular newsmagazines, he began to read the *ESP Journal* and *TESOL Quarterly*. In a course titled "Curriculum Design in English for Specific Purposes", one assignment was a review of an ESP text. Professor Grace Burkhart, the course instructor, gave the students detailed instructions on how a book review could be written, and also analyzed and discussed sample book reviews from the *ESP Journal.* George remembers that this was the first time he had received explicit advice on writing.

His transition from an ESL generalist to a writing specialist began through necessity. In order to continue his doctoral studies at the University of Texas, he accepted a teaching assistantship in the English department. Somewhat hesitant because he is a nonnative speaker of English, he was startled to learn that he would have to teach a first-year writing course to native speakers. Teach writing? To native speakers? Unaware of current writing pedagogy, and even of the process approach, he walked into each class meeting embarrassed and insecure, doubtful if he was even one step ahead of his students. But during that traumatic first semester, he began to apply to his writing the techniques he taught: invention strategies, audience analysis, peer reviews, and conferencing. As a result, he discovered writing as a shared, creative, and joyous activity.

CONCLUSION

Over the past 200 years, the English language in Sri Lanka has evolved from the language of a colonial power to Lankan English, a distinct variety that finds pride of place in the local curriculum. At the national level, it is the link language between the Sinhala and Tamil speaking ethnic groups, and above all, it is the key to economic and social advancement.

Nevertheless, English in Sri Lanka, as in many other ex-colonial countries, has paid the penalty for being an imported language. With the rise of nationalism in the years following independence, it was no longer the medium of instruction in government schools and universities. Although the rationale—the empowerment of rural masses who spoke only Sinhala or Tamil—was commendable, the result was to withhold English from those who needed it most for economic advancement, and to consolidate the power of the segments of society that could afford to educate their children in expensive, privately run, English-medium schools, and then send them abroad for higher education. In the long run, this emphasis on Sinhala and Tamil also deprived the country of a whole generation of competent English teachers.

In the end, it was the masses themselves who wrested English back from the elite. Aware of the opportunities associated with the language, people made the best use of whatever English instruction was available. What the government schools failed to provide was supplied by privately run (and often dubious) English "tutories" that mainly taught English speech. The wheel has turned full circle now, with the government itself advocating the use of the English medium to teach all subjects in the schools. How far these plans will succeed is yet to be seen.

REFERENCES

Curriculum Process Plan. (June, 2000). Maharagama, Sri Lanka: National Institute of Education.

De Souza, D. (1969, April 18). The teaching of English. *The Ceylon Observer, 18,* 4.

Fernando, C. (1976). English and Sinhala bilingualism in Sri Lanka. *Language in Society, 6,* 341–360.

Guidelines for GCE O/L Examination 2001 and after: English Language. Maharagama, Sri Lanka: National Institute of Education.

Kandiah, T. (1981). Disinherited Englishes: The case of Lankan English. *Navasilu, 4,* 92–113.

Kandiah, T. (1984). Kaduva: Power and the English language weapon in Sri Lanka. In P. Colin-Thome & A. Halpe (Eds.), *Honouring E. F. C. Ludowyk* (pp. 117–154). Colombo, Sri Lanka: Tisara Prakasakayo.

Musa, M. (1981). *Language Planning in Sri Lanka.* Dacca: Bhuiyan Muhammed Imran.

Raheem, R., & Ratwatte, H. (2001). Teaching English: Possibilities and opportunities. In D. Hayes (Ed.), *Selected papers from the 1st International Conference of the Sri Lanka English Language Teachers' Association* (pp. 23–36). Colombo, Sri Lanka: The British Council.

Ratnayake, M. (2000, September 12). English language: Breaking the elitist barrier. *The Sunday Times Plus,* 6.

Safstrom, C. A., Balasooriya, A. S., Masilamani, S., & Parakrama, A. (2001). *Education and intercultural democracy: Report on current efforts to facilitate democratic and pluralistic values through primary and secondary education in Sri Lanka.* Colombo, Sri Lanka: SIDA.

Samath, F. (2001, June 10). English, IT and a hot meal. The Sunday *Times Plus,* 3.

15

ENGLISH LANGUAGE TEACHING IN TURKEY: CHALLENGES FOR THE 21ST CENTURY

Yasemin Kirkgöz
Çukurova University, Turkey

In Turkey, English plays a crucial role in all aspects of life, from politics and economics to education. With a population of approximately 65 million people and a total area of 780,580 square kilometers, 97% in Asia and 3% in Europe, the nation acts as a physical and cultural bridge between the two continents. Its location as a geographical crossroad has meant that throughout history, Turkey has been the cradle of many great civilizations. Bordering eight nations and surrounded by three seas, Turkey has a strategic and geopolitical status that makes the learning of English particularly important. "A member of NATO since 1952, Turkey has engaged in extensive collaboration with Europe from the 1960's on economics, education, politics and cultural affairs."

Turkish is the official language in Turkey; it is the language of instruction and the mother tongue. In this non-English speaking environment, English has the status of a foreign language that is taught as part of the school curriculum and used mainly in the government and business sectors, particularly in written communication. Since the establishment of the Turkish Republic in 1923, Turkey has desired to strengthen her relations with the outside world in order to pursue rapid economic development. English plays a crucial role in this respect.

This chapter highlights the current state of the art in English language education in Turkey. The historical development of English language teaching (ELT) is presented, followed by an outline of the English language curriculum. The chapter concludes following a short profile of an English teacher.

160 KIRKGÖZ

HISTORY OF ELT IN TURKEY

The introduction of ELT in Turkey dates back to the second half of the 18th century, the Tanzimat Period of Turkish history, which marks the beginning of the Westernization of the educational system. The first institution teaching through the medium of English was Robert College, an Anglo-American secondary school, which was founded in Istanbul in 1863 by an American missionary (Council of Higher Education, 2001a). The collapse of the Ottoman Empire and the establishment of the Republic of Turkey in 1923 accelerated the spread of the ELT in the country.

In 1955, the first state-funded English-medium secondary school, called an Anadolu (Anatolian) school, was opened. In response to growing pressure from parents, the state began to increase the number of these schools. In 1974, there were only 12 *Anadolu* schools; by the 2000–2001 school year, 1,457 of these English-medium secondary schools were in operation (see Ministry of National Education, 2001). Nevertheless, at the level of primary education, it was only in 1997 that the English language was included in the curriculum of primary schools at grades 4 and 5.

At the level of higher education, Turkey's efforts to modernize led to the establishment of many English-medium universities, the first one being Middle Eastern Technical University, established in 1956 and based on the American model. In 1981, discussions about English-Medium Education (EME) in the universities began at the national level. The purpose of EME is to enable students to have access to scientific and technological information published in English in their disciplines. In 1990, The Higher Education Law made it possible for private universities offering EME to be established (Council of Higher Education, 2001b). With the establishment of 19 private universities between 1983 and 1999, the country's provision of English-medium higher education has been expanded (YOK: "Yuksek Ogretim Kurumu" [The Council of Higher Education], 2001b). It has been found that students' attitudes toward EME are guided predominantly by career or academic purposes (Akünal, 1992).

The government's current policy is to increase the educational opportunities for a large number of students. Despite the increase in quantity, the quality and efficiency of the current EME has been criticized on the grounds that large numbers of students remain unable to cope with demands imposed by their academic community. Although many studies have been conducted to solve this problem, the English language still constitutes an obstacle to the acquisition of the professional knowledge that universities are expected to provide. Recently, an innovative model, the Enculturation Model, initiated and implemented at Çukurova University, Adana (see Kirkgöz 1999, for details) enabled prospective students of the Department of Economics to function more efficiently in their English-medium academic community. Currently, further research is exploring ways to extend this model to other universities.

At the level of primary education, despite the current popularity of early foreign-language teaching, there is insufficient empirical research to reveal to what

extent children develop proficiency in English. One major problem is the shortage of the English language teachers. Due to the teacher shortage, non-ELT
teachers, having received short training on pedagogy and English language, teach
English (Bada, 1999).

THE ELT CURRICULUM

In Turkey, English is compulsory in the 8 years of primary and 3 years of secondary
school curriculum as well as in higher education. Prior to 1997, students began
learning English in secondary school, in grade 6. In 1997, with the increase in the
duration of primary education from 5 to 8 years, English started to be taught in primary education in grades 4 and 5.

In secondary education, schools are classified into state schools (general, vocational, etc.), *Anadolu* schools, and private schools, or colleges. Unlike private
schools, for which parents have to pay tuition, *Anadolu* schools are state-funded.
Anadolu and private schools are able to attract the nation's brightest students
through a very competitive entrance examination, and provide a 1-year intensive
English language program prior to the 3-year curriculum. Until 1992, English was
used as the language of instruction in certain subjects such as science. However,
many schools have given up teaching content courses in English due to the shortage
of teachers. In universities where the medium of instruction is in the native
language, English is a compulsory subject.

The English language curriculum and the syllabuses of primary and secondary
schools are centrally administered by the Ministry of National Education (MNE).
In order to achieve a coherent national ELT curriculum, the MNE provides comprehensive guidelines to teachers and administrators. The curriculum is divided
into two stages that cover the primary (grades 4 through 8), which lays the foundation of English, and the secondary (grades 9 through 11). According to the MNE,
the general objectives of the curriculum for the secondary education is "to encourage learners to develop skills and knowledge needed to comprehend and use English" and the learning of English is justified on the grounds that "the learning of a
foreign language widens students' cultural horizons" (Ministry of National
Education, 2001, p. 4).

The head of the ELT unit coordinates the English language program in private
schools. Teachers of English at state schools are tied to a relatively fixed syllabus
imposed by the MNE, whereas private schools have the liberty to expand the prescribed course syllabus.

In state primary and secondary schools, the timetable is the responsibility of the
school director. The MNE recommends that two lessons per week (each lesson lasting 40 minutes) be allocated to the teaching of English for primary grades 4 and 5,
and five to six lessons are recommended to primary grades 6 through 8. For secondary grades 1 through 3, the number of lessons recommended ranges from 8 to 14.
Private schools can increase the number of lessons allocated to English. In many

private schools, English starts at kindergarten, with 3 hours weekly, and is included in all grades to enable students to make a faster progress compared to their counterparts in state schools.

Teachers at state schools are required to choose English language course books locally prepared and approved by the MNE. *Anadolu* and private schools adopt commercially available course books. Unlike state schools, which function under quite limited resources, the textbook being the main teaching resource, private schools are more fortunate and can utilize technological facilities in ELT.

The Council of Higher Education (CHE), established in 1973, is a 22-member supreme authority that is responsible for the planning, coordination and governance of higher education within the provisions set forth in the Higher Education Law (Tosun, 2001). Both public and private universities operate under the supervision of the CHE.

Currently, there are 72 universities in Turkey, 22 of which offer full English-medium instruction. Of these, only two are state universities. Six state universities are partly English-medium, with 30% to 40% of the subject courses taught in English (ÖSYM: Ogrenci Secme ve Yerlestirme Merkezi [Student Selection and Placement Center], 2001). Admission to higher education is centralized through a nationwide examination administered by the Student Selection and Placement Center (ÖSYM, 2001) every year. The purpose of English in universities where the medium of instruction is the native language is to equip learners with the language skills they need to read texts published in their fields of specialty. The CHE (Council of Higher Education, 1996) recommends 60 hours of English, and this is generally allocated to first year undergraduates.

Universities that provide instruction in English have their own English language teaching centers that offer 1-year preparatory courses to students. Each center is run by a director and supervised by a team of coordinators, each responsible for a particular aspect of the program: curriculum design, materials development, and teacher training. The language centers generally adopt commercially produced textbooks, and some locally produced textbooks are also available (Kirkgöz, 1990). On the whole, the language centers are well equipped with self-access, multimedia and library facilities.

Assessment is an important part of the curriculum. Primary and secondary schools are subject to the MEB (Milli Egitim Bakanligi) criteria for grading and passing. Those wishing to major in ELT need to take a separate university-entrance examination that assesses knowledge of grammar, translation, vocabulary, and reading.

A national test called the Language Proficiency Examination for The State Personnel (KPDS), which serves to assess English language proficiency of civil employees and those in the academic community, was introduced in 1990. For example, to be promoted to associate professorship, one must score at least 70% on this exam, and to start a doctorate, one must score at least 50% or have an equivalent score on the TOEFL. In response to nationwide protests that the test was too difficult and thus formed an obstacle to academic promotion, a new test called Language Proficiency Examination for Academic Personnel (ÜDS), tailored mainly for those in the academic community, was introduced in 2000. Both tests assess ability in grammar, vocabulary, reading, and both are administered centrally by the Student Selection and Placement Center (see Student Selection and Placement Center, 2000).

Traditionally, the teaching of English in Turkey was based on a teacher-centered transmission model. The predominant method employed was grammar translation with a focus on grammar and vocabulary at the expense of communication. In the 1990s, major attempts were made to revise the ELT syllabi to incorporate communicative language teaching into the curriculum. However, despite the fact that the use of the language is advocated by the MEB, many teachers of English, particularly at state schools, where the teacher–student ratio is high (40 to 50 students per class) found it difficult to be communicative in their classroom practices.

The response to the shift of emphasis from the traditional teacher-centered approach to communicative language teaching has been more promising in private schools. Due to parental pressure and enthusiasm for having their children use the language, these schools generally claim that their major focus is on promoting students' communication skills. Statistics published by the British Council on The Young Learners Test given in Turkey in 1999 supported this claim (Annual Review 1999 Young Learners Test, 2000).

In 1995, the concept of *total quality management* (TQM) in ELT was introduced to the Turkish educational system (Hergüner, 1995). The philosophy and implications of TQM disseminated through various national seminars to create quality awareness among educators, which would eventually lead to quality education.

In 1997, a major project called the Ministry of Education Development Project was initiated by the collaboration of MEB and CHE and financed by the World Bank (Council of Higher Education, 1998). The project aimed to restructure the teacher-training departments of the faculties of education to enhance the quality of teacher training to meet the needs of the nation in the 21st century (Günçer, 2001). With this project and the updated preservice teacher training project described now, Turkey is heading for a major reform in English language education in the new century.

It is mainly during teacher education that the seeds for professionalism in teaching are planted and nourished. Therefore, teacher-training departments were redesigned to increase the number of methodology courses and extend the duration of trainees' teaching practice time in secondary education. To support these developments, a close partnership between the English language teaching departments and the primary and secondary schools was established in 1998 to give trainees systematic school-based teaching practice before they enter their professional community.

This project eventually led to the standardization and the establishment of the Turkish system of accreditation for teacher education based on the British model (Tosun, 2001). The revised teacher-training program was piloted in the 1998–1999 academic year in six faculties. The evaluation of the pilot project by Billing and

Thomas (2000) showed that the intended learning outcomes were largely achieved. Currently, efforts are being made to extend the program to the remaining faculties of education nationwide (Günçer, 2001).

The reform of ELT in Turkey has had far-reaching implications, not only at the level of higher education, but in primary and secondary education as well. ELT has been reconceptualized to encourage (a) students' active participation in the learning process, (b) students' use of the target language in communication, and (c) students' application of knowledge through projects. The new curriculum promotes student-centered learning and emphasizes the philosophy of total quality in ELT. Teachers are encouraged to promote students' communication skills, address students' different learning styles, and minimize the use of the mother tongue. Overall, these curriculum innovations reflect a radical reform of ELT in Turkey.

In Turkey, teaching is a graduate profession; in order to teach English, one is required to have a degree in English. A postgraduate qualification, although preferred by private universities, is not a requirement. All new teachers at state and private universities are required to complete a 1-year probation period.

After English began to be taught in primary grades 4 and 5, the demand for qualified English language teachers far outweighed the supply. To overcome this shortage, the MNE and *Anadolu* University initiated an English-language teacher education project in 2000 (see Ministry of National Education, 2001). In addition, courses were introduced to train non-ELT teachers so that they could teach English, particularly at primary level.

Although the challenges facing teachers have increased, so too have the opportunities for teachers' professional development with the concept of *lifelong learning gaining importance.* Many ELT departments have established in-service (INSET) teacher training and development programs. INSET courses generally have two levels of teacher preparation: for novice teachers, an induction program is offered that addresses certain immediate needs of teachers, enhancing their knowledge and skills of ELT. Some internationally recognized qualifications, such as the Certificate for Overseas Teachers of English (COTE) are also offered. More experienced teachers are encouraged to explore new avenues through such collaborative work as action research and team teaching.

Teacher development has become a central priority of the MNE, and substantial resources of time and money have been allocated to development schemes. To ensure that teachers in all parts of Turkey are kept abreast of new developments in ELT, the INSET office of the MNE regularly organizes local seminars for state primary and secondary school teachers in collaboration with the English Language Researchers' Association in Turkey. Teacher Training facilities are also provided jointly with the support of the British Council and the United States Information Agency.

In line with the government's reform policy in teacher education, the MNE and the CHE collaborated in 1997 to apply a single set of standards in preservice teacher-training programs throughout the country to enhance the quality of English teachers. The Teacher Training National Committee, established by CHE, set the competencies expected of an English language teacher's subject knowledge and pedagogical skills (e.g., mastery and application of subject knowledge and management of the teaching-learning process). The development of standards articulates national expectations for the quality of English language teacher education. It is expected that all new teachers will be required to meet those standards which began in the 2001–2002 academic year.

The recruitment of native English teachers is too expensive for state schools and universities. However, private schools and universities, which are engaged in fierce competition to make English language learning more attractive to students, employ some native-English teachers. Each private primary and secondary school has one or two native-English teachers, who mainly focus on teaching communication skills. In private universities, native-English teachers are recruited to collaborate with local teachers in teaching, and to contribute to teacher training programs.

In Turkey, the British Council and the United States Information Agency also play significant roles in promoting ELT. The British Council with its three centers in Turkey has been providing cultural and educational services to students, teachers, and teacher trainers, and has made a major contribution in training experienced English teachers so that they can function as *formateurs* (Turkish teacher trainers) to carry out local seminars for less experienced teachers (British Council, 2001).

BECOMING AN ENGLISH TEACHER

In this section, I provide a short biography of an English language teacher, Bahtişen Yavuz. She has experienced many of the changes in the Turkish educational system described earlier in this chapter, yet she has made the utmost use of the opportunities to enhance her professional development.

Bahtişen's teaching career has followed an interesting line of development. She majored in ELT at Çukurova University in Adana, graduating from that 4-year degree program in 1985. After graduation, she had a nonteaching job as a computer operator at first, working for an international company that was involved in an urban development and transportation project financed by the World Bank. The project involved building two major infrastructures in Bahtişen's hometown of Adana. Although the job had nothing to do with her major, it was challenging as there were many native-English people in the company, which meant that she was able to practice her English and gain fluency. After a couple of months, the company sent her to work in its headquarters in London, where she stayed for 7 months. This visit provided her with a wonderful opportunity to get to know the British culture closely.

In 1987, Bahtişen obtained her first teaching job, teaching general English in a private English school in her hometown that provided a variety of courses for the general public. Although her university training was based on the grammar-translation method, her own teaching approach was communicative, which she owed to the fluency she acquired in her previous job. She encouraged her students to communicate using the target language. Her teaching load was very heavy, about 11 hours a day, but, being ambitious and having a great love for students, she said to herself, "I must do it".

After some time, she got married and with family responsibilities she thought she could not keep up with such a heavy teaching load. After working at the school for 5 years, she decided it was time for a change, and applied to the MNE for a job in the secondary schools.

From 1992 to 1995, Bahtişen taught English in a vocational secondary school. In this school, most students were from low-income families, they had little interest in learning English, and they all lacked self-esteem. Before teaching the students the language, she had to motivate them. Only then could she start teaching them fundamental language items in the curriculum. The most rewarding aspect of this was to see students becoming interested in English.

She realized that working in such a school would not contribute much toward her professional development. Only 3 hours of English was allocated to each class, which made it highly difficult to make any progress. After working for 4 years in this school and having gained more experience, she applied to the MNE again for placement in an *Anadolu* School where she thought she could have the opportunity to upgrade her professional knowledge. This time, she wanted to have a more long-term teaching job.

Her transition to the *Anadolu* school marked a turning point in her teaching career because in *Anadolu* schools, the English language curriculum is much more intensive. Working in this school was really demanding. The students were advanced learners who had been selected by an entrance examination. Being conscious of the importance of English, they were extremely ambitious and hard working.

While teaching in the *Anadolu* school, Bahtişen also became interested in her own professional development. In October 1997, she attended her first in-service teacher-training seminar, which aimed to train experienced teachers to become teacher trainers. By this time, she had 10 years of teaching experience, and had already scored 82% on the Language Proficiency Examination for State Personnel. This training seminar was organized by the MNE, and presented by experienced trainers from the British Council and ,ngilizce Egitimi Dernegi (the English Language Education Association). It was a 2-week intensive course, with morning sessions devoted to receiving theoretical input on various aspects of pedagogy, and the afternoon sessions to workshops where Bahtişen worked on several projects with other future trainers. She was becoming more and more aware of the gaps in her theoretical knowledge and practical experience. She had to read a lot of books and articles to become acquainted with the professional literature. She completed the seminar with an honors degree and was awarded a certificate. She felt privileged for being qualified as a teacher trainer or, as it is frequently called in Turkey, a *formateur.* From then on, she was eligible to work as a trainer.

Teaching very young learners was a new concept in Turkish education and there was an urgent need for teacher training in this area. In July 1998, she attended two

"Training Trainer" seminars on Teaching Young Learners conducted by the British Council to expand her knowledge in this very popular area. She read Piaget and other psychologists and even talked to psychiatrists to fully familiarize herself with the physical and mental developments of children.

Bahtişen gave her first seminar and training in connection with young learners on February 1998 in two neighboring cities. She was extremely proud of receiving a certificate of appreciation for her presentation. In 1999, she organized a 7-month seminar in her hometown, which involved training Turkish teachers of English and teachers from other subject areas so that they could teach young learners. All her hard work was recognized by the MNE, which awarded her another certificate of appreciation on this occasion.

Believing that a teacher and a teacher educator should be involved in ongoing professional development, she attended a series of national conferences in 1999. She felt honored to have been nominated by the MNE as one of the 10 teachers to lecture to undergraduate students of ELT receiving courses through the Faculty of Education a the Open University in the 2001–2002 academic year. This marked another turning point in her teaching profession. She satisfactorily completed the university's induction course in the summer of 2001, and began teaching there.

Bahtişen firmly believes that all these seminars and workshops have made a significant contribution to her professional development. They have enlarged her vision and helped her reach a level of professional maturity. Comparing her work today with the first years of her teaching, she can see a dramatic change in her theoretical knowledge and teaching practice. She now feels much more confident about her work. Choosing a textbook was a nightmare for her 6 years ago, whereas now she knows what criteria to use in textbook selection. Even the preparation of examination questions has changed. Whereas she was unable to handle the complexity of various classroom situations earlier, she can now easily handle large classes using pair work or group work. She is well aware of the existence of the communicative method, task-based learning, and other teaching methods.

Finally, Bahtişen's concept of an *effective teacher* is that a good teacher should be enthusiastic about teaching and should be able to transmit this enthusiasm to her students. Moreover, she should show evidence of ongoing personal development. The teacher should be involved in life-long learning and keep up-to-date on the latest advances in the teaching profession and transmit these to her students. She is fully committed to being an effective teacher and teacher trainer.

CONCLUSION

English language education in Turkey has been a widely discussed issue at the national level. The discussion has generally focused on increasing the opportunities for learning English and raising the quality of English language education. Yet, there has always existed a big gap between the ideal language policy and actual classroom practices. With the recent reform, which aims to restructure the language programs in order to offer a quality education for the young generation, Turkey is facing new challenges in its English language education.

In this chapter, I have illustrated ELT teaching in Turkey by describing the history of ELT teaching and the structure of the English curriculum, and by providing a history of the professional development of an English teacher. ELT teaching in Turkey has increasingly been a real challenge. I have shown throughout this chapter that the pressing demand for high quality ELT, an increase in the number of students from primary school through higher education, and reforms calling for restructuring of the curriculum have meant that ELT is becoming more and more demanding. Given the importance of English for the nation, Turkey cannot afford to ignore these demands on its English language education. Through its recent education policy, the nation has made a firm commitment to empowering the ELT profession in Turkey so that English language educators can cope more effectively with many of the challenges awaiting them.

REFERENCES

Akünal, Z. (1992). Immersion programmes in Turkey: An evaluation by students and teachers. *System 20*(4), 8–12.

Annual Review 1999 Young Learners Tests. (2000). Ankara, Turkey: The British Council.

Bada, E. (1999). In-service teacher training in ELT: Capturing efficiency. *Language Journal, 75,* 24–33.

Billing, D., & Thomas, H. (2000). Evaluating a transnational university quality assessment project in Turkey. *Higher Education Policy, 4,* 2.

British Council. (2001, May). Teaching the teachers. *Newsletter, 15,* 11–12.

Council of Higher Education. (1996, April 1). Yuksekogretim kurumlarinda yabanci dil egitim-ogretimi ve yabanci dille egitim-ogretim yapilmasinda uyulacak esaslara iliskin yonetmelik [Regulations for foreign language teaching in higher education]. *Official Gazette, 22598,* 4–7.

Council of Higher Education. (1998). Egitim fakulteleri ogretmen yetistirme programlarinin yeniden duzenlenmesi [Restructuring of teacher education programs in departments of education]. Ankara, Turkey: Author.

Council of Higher Education. (2001a). *History of Turkish education.* Retrieved November 20, 2001, from http://www.yok.gov.tr/webeng/history.html

Council of Higher Education. (2001b). *Outline of the Turkish higher education system.* Retrieved November 20, 2001, from http://www.yok.gov.tr/webeng/outline.html

Günçer, B. (2001). *Öwretmen Ewitiminde Akreditasyon: ,ngiltere ve A.B.D Örnekleri* [Accreditation in teacher training: Examples from the U.K. and the U.S.A.]. Retrieved on November 21, 2001, from http://www.yok.gov.tr/egfak/Akredit.html

HergÜner, G. (1995). *Total Quality Management in English language teaching: A case study in Turkish higher education.* Unpublished doctoral dissertation, Aston University, Birmingham, England.

Kirkgöz, Y. (1990). *English for economics in agriculture.* Adana: Çukurova University.

Kirkgöz, Y. (1999). *Knowledge acquisition from L2 specialist texts.* Unpublished doctoral dissertation, Aston University, Birmingham, England.

Ministry of National Education (2001). *2001 Yili Ba_inda Milli E_itim* [Ministry of National Education in 2001]. Web site. Retrieved November 16, 2002, from http://www.meb. gove.tr/index.htm

Student Selection and Placement Center (ÖSYM) (2001). Web site. Retrieved November 9, 2004 from http://www.osym.gov.tr/BelgeGoster.aspx?DIL=1&BELGEBAGLANTIANAH=169

Tosun, I. (2001). *Feasibility study on the establishment of an academic assessment mechanism and structure for higher education in Turkey.* Retrieved on November 21, 2001, from http://www.worldbank.org

AUTHOR BIOGRAPHIES

Brazil

Cristina Rajagopalan has been involved in ELT in Brazil and is currently Examinations Officer at the *Sociedade Brasileira de Cultura Inglesa-São Paulo*, a leading English language school in Brazil which offers courses in EFL at all levels, and administers Cambridge University examinations. She is a holder of RAS certificate in English teaching and also a post-graduate Diploma in Applied Linguistics from the University of Edinburgh, UK.

Kanavillil Rajagopalan, Ph.D., is Professor of Linguistics at the State University at Campinas, Brazil. He was born in India and has studied in India, Britain, Brazil and the USA. His research interests include philosophy of language, linguistic pragmatics, applied linguistics and English language and literature.

China

He An E is a lecturer in the Department of English, The Hong Kong Institute of Education. She obtained her B.A. from LanZhou University, China, and her Master's of Educational Studies and Ph.D. from Monash University, Australia. Her research interests include classroom discourse analysis and task-based learning.

Germany

Claus Gnutzmann is professor of English language and applied linguistics in the English Department of the Technical University of Braunschweig. His main research interests include linguistic and pedagogical grammar, contrastive linguistics, error analysis, the contribution of the new media to language learning as well as the globalisation of English and its classroom implications.

Hong Kong

Icy Lee is an assistant professor in the Department of Education Studies at Hong Kong Baptist University of Hong Kong. She has taught ESL in Hong Kong and Canada. She is a member of the NNEST Caucus of TESOL and winner of 1999 TESOL Award for Excellence in the Development of Pedagogical Materials. Her research interests are in the areas of ESL/EFL writing, learner autonomy, and teacher development. She has published in a number of international journals, such as *ELT Journal, Journal of Second Language Writing,* and TESL Canada Journal.

Hungary

Before he was appointed deputy state secretary at the Hungarian Ministry of Education in 2002, Péter Medgyes was professor and director of the Centre for English Teacher Training at the Eötvös Loránd University, Budapest. He has written numerous professional books and articles, including *The Non-native Teacher* (Macmillan 1994; winner of the Duke of Edinburgh English Language Book Competition), *Changing Perspectives in Teacher Education* (Heinemann 1996; coedited with A. Malderez), *The Language Teacher* (Corvina 1997), and *Laughing Matters* (Cambridge University Press 2002).

India

Premakumari Dheram is an Associate Professor of English in the Osmania University College for Women in Hyderabad, India.

Note: This paper is dedicated to her mentor Kate Mulvey.

Indonesia

Junaidi Mistar is a lecturer at the English Department of the University of Malang (UNISMA), East Java, Indonesia. His articles mainly focussing on psychological aspects of foreign/second language learning have been published in a number of local journals, *TEFLIN Journal, Melbourne Papers in Linguistics and Applied Linguistics,* and the *Asian Journal of English Language Teaching.*

Israel

Dr. Ofra Inbar-Lourie is a senior lecturer on English language education at Beit Berl College and chair of the English Department. Her research interests include language policy and language assessment and curricula. She has recently been involved in the writing and implementation of a new national curriculum for English teaching in Israel.

Japan

Masaki Oda is an associate professor of EFL and Linguistics at Tamagawa University. He was previously a lecturer of Japanese at Georgetown University in Washington, DC where he also received his Ph.D. in Applied Linguistics. His interests are socio-political aspects of language teaching, media discourse, and language of aviation.

Tomoko Takada is a teacher at Gakushuin Girls' Junior and Senior High School and lecturer at Gakushuin University and Gakushuin Women's College in Tokyo. Her research interests include teaching writing, error analysis, and learner characteristics. She has published in *TESOL Matters, JALT Journal, The Language Teacher,* and *Annual Review of English Language Education in Japan.*

Lebanon

Kassim Shaaban is a professor of Applied Linguistics and the chair of the English Department at the American University of Beirut. His research interests are language-in-education, sociolinguistics, and assessment. He has published articles in *Foreign Language Annals, TESL Reporter, Language Problems and Language Planning, Journal of Sociolinguistics,* and *Language, Culture and Curriculum.*

Poland

Joanna Radwanska-Williams is a Professor in the School of Business at the Macao Polytechnic Institute. She received her Ph.D. in 1989 from the University of North Carolina. Before coming to Macao, she taught applied linguistics at Nanjing University in China and at the Chinese University of Hong Kong. Her research interests include language teaching methodology, discourse analysis, and the history of linguistics.

Liliana Piasecka is a teacher and researcher in the Department of English at the University of Opole. She received her Ph.D. in 1996 from Opole University. As indicated in her biographical sketch, she has taught English at both the secondary and tertiary level, and is now a teacher-trainer and lecturer in applied linguistics. Her research interests include ELT methodology, psycholinguistics, and second language acquisition.

Saudi Arabia

Khalid Al-Seghayer earned his Ph.D. in Foreign Language Education/Applied Linguistics from the University of Pittsburgh. His research interests include Computer-Assisted Language Learning and second language reading. He has published in *TESOL Quarterly, Language Learning and Technology, CALL Journal, Internet TESL Journal, CALICO Journal,* and the *APA News.* He has served as the chair-elect (2002-2003) of the EFL Interest Section in TESOL. Currently, he is the editor of the *NNEST Newsletter* in TESOL.

Singapore

Antonia Chandrasegaran is an Associate Professor at the National Institute of Education, an Institute of the Nanyang Technological University in Singapore. She teaches undergraduate and M.A. courses in academic writing, composition research. Her most recent publication in the area of academic writing is *Think Your Way to Effective Writing* (2004), co-authored with Kirsten Schaetzel.

Sri Lanka

Minoli Samarakkody taught ESL and linguistics courses in the Department of English at the University of Colombo, Sri Lanka, where she also obtained an M.Phil. degree in English language and English language teaching. She has also been teaching ESL in Vancouver, where she now resides.

George Braine was born and raised in Sri Lanka, and teaches at The Chinese University of Hong Kong. He edited *Non-native Educators in English Language Teaching* (Lawrence Erlbaum) in 1999. He has been the co-editor of the *Asian Journal of English Language Teaching* since 1996.

Turkey

Yasemin Kirkgöz is a senior instructor at the Center for Foreign Languages of Çukurova University, Adana, Turkey, and the Assistant Director of the Foreign Languages Department. She completed her M.A. and Ph.D. at Aston University, Birmingham in England. Dr. Kirkgöz's research interests include corpus linguistics, constructivist learning, teacher education and knowledge acquisition.

AUTHOR INDEX

A

Abi Najm, T., 105, *112*
Abou, S., 106, *112*
Abu-Ghararah, A., 129, *133*
Adamson, R., 38, *45*
Ad-Daoud, N., 111, *113*
Aggarwal, J. C., 60, 61, *68*
Akrawi, M., 104, *112*
Akunal, Z., 160, *168*
Al-Abdulkader, A., 126, *133*
Al-Ahaydib, M., 129, *133*
Alam, M., 126, *133*
Al-Hajailan, T., 127, *133*
Allen, S., & Cook, R., 128, *133*
Almulhim, A., 129, *133*
Al-Seghayer, K., 132, *133*
Al-Shithri, A., 127, *133*
Al-Subahi, A., 128, *133*
Altbach, P., xii, xviii, *xix*
Alwasilah, A. C., 76, *79*
Amara, M., 84, *90*
Amey, J., xvii, *xx*
Ammon, U., xvi, *xix*
ARAMCO, Saudi Arabia, 126, *133*
Arakawa, S., 95, *101*
Arif, Z., 72, 73, *79*

B

Bada, E., 161, *168*
Bachtiar, S., 72, 73, *79*
Balasooriya, A. S., 152, *157*
Bashshur, M., 103, 105, *112*

Baugh, A., xiii, *xix*
Baydoun, A., 105, *112*
Bazzi, M., 105, *112*
Berns, M., 125, *133*
Bikar, E., 104, *112*
Billing, D., 163–164, *168*
Bodoczky, C., 52, *56*
Boyle, J., 11, 12,16, *21*
Braine, G., *viii*
Bryson, B., xiii, *xix*
Burd, A. S., xiv, *xx*

C

Cable, T., xiii, *xix*
Carless, D., 41, *44*
Celani, M. A. A., 5, 6, *9*
Center for Statistical Data and
   Educational Documentation, Saudi Arabia,
   128, *133*
Central Bureau of Statistics, Israel, 81, *90*
Chan, K. K., 38, *45*
Chandrasegaran, A., 143, *144*
Cheung, Y. S., 35, *44*
Cheung, D., 40, 41, *44*
Christ, H., 26, *33*
Coniam, D., 37, *44*
Cortazzi, M., 16, *21*
Council of Higher Education, Turkey, 160,
   162, 163, 164, *168*
Cran, W., xiii, xiv, *xx*
Crystal, D., xiv, xv, *xix,* 103, *112*
Curriculum Development Centre in Eng-
   lish, India, 64, 65, *69*

179

SUBJECT INDEX